Taste*of*Home.

- MORE -

EASY
EVERYDAY
COOKING

Taste*of*Home

RDA ENTHUSIAST BRANDS, LLC • MILWAUKEE, WI

© 2023 RDA Enthusiast Brands, LLC.
1610 N. 2nd St., Suite 102, Milwaukee WI
53212-3906
All rights reserved. *Taste of Home* is a
registered trademark of RDA Enthusiast
Brands, LLC.
Visit *tasteofhome.com* for other
Taste of Home books and products.

International Standard Book Number:
978-1-62145-963-7
Component Number:
117800113H

INSTANT POT® is a trademark of Double
Insight Inc. This publication has not been
authorized, sponsored or otherwise
approved by Double Insight, Inc.

Chief Content Officer, Home & Garden:
Jeanne Sidner
Content Director: Mark Hagen
Creative Director: Raeann Thompson
Senior Editor: Christine Rukavena
Editor: Amy Glander
Senior Art Director: Courtney Lovetere
Art Director: Maggie Conners
Deputy Editor, Copy Desk: Dulcie Shoener
Copy Editor: Elizabeth Pollock Bruch
Contributing Designer: Jennifer Ruetz
Cover Photography: *Taste of Home*
Photo Studio

Pictured on front cover:
So-Easy Gazpacho (p. 64)
Air-Fryer Raspberry Crumble Coffee Cake
(p. 119)
Chicken-Fried Steaks (p. 147)
Baked Ham & Colby Sandwiches (p. 59)
Steak Fajitas (p. 137)
Layered Strawberry Pound Cake Dessert
(p. 292)
Shrimp Pasta Primavera (p. 154)
Sausage & Kale Soup (p. 65)

Pictured on back cover:
Lemon Blackberry Tortilla French Toast
(p. 44)
Easy Taco Cups (p. 25)
Sausage & Swiss Chard Lasagna (p. 220)
Blackberry Daiquiri Sherbet (p. 258)
Asparagus Ham Dinner (p. 145)
Mini Muffuletta (p. 25)
Peachy Buttermilk Shakes (p. 19)

Printed in China
1 3 5 7 9 10 8 6 4 2

Pictured on opposite page:
Meatballs with Marinara Sauce (p. 11)
Air-Fryer Cheesy Breakfast Egg Rolls (p. 37)
Sweet Potato Bean Soup (p. 59)
Sweet Onion Spoon Bread (p. 92)
Cinnamon Rolls with Cookie Butter Filling
(p. 117)
Saucy Mac & Cheese (p. 140)
Baked Hamburgers (p. 163)
15-Minute Marinated Chicken (p. 184)
Make-Ahead Eggs Benedict Toast Cups
(p. 217)

MORE WAYS TO CONNECT WITH US

SHOP.TASTEOFHOME.COM

EASY
EVERYDAY
COOKING

SAY HELLO TO QUICK & EASY HOMEMADE COMFORT!

It's never been easier to create mouthwatering dishes that don't eat up time in the kitchen. Turn to the all-new *More Easy Everyday Cooking* for fast mealtime solutions your family will love.

There are those days when time is tight, schedules are packed and getting dinner on the table seems like an impossible dream. Shake off that stress because now it's easier than ever to make that dream a dinnertime reality!

Turn the page to find 365 fast, flavorful dishes that taste as if they took hours to prepare. Discover recipes ideal for every type of meal and menu—rich, comforting casseroles, satisfying breakfast and brunch ideas, swift side dishes, sweet desserts and other quick-to-fix favorites. Special chapters make the most of a streamlined cooking approach—with five-ingredient recipes, make-ahead options, recipes sized just right for one or two, and slow-cooked dishes with minimal prep time. Plus, a 30-day meal planner on pages 6-7 helps you budget your time and leverage your leftovers.

Every recipe includes full nutritional information, and easy-to-spot icons identify those that are healthy, ideal for freezing, table-ready in 30 minutes or less, use only five ingredients or fewer, or take advantage of favorite kitchen appliances—the slow cooker, air fryer and Instant Pot. A special icon index makes it easy to find just the type of dish you're looking for—so you won't waste time shuffling through pages.

Shared by talented home cooks and approved by the experts in the *Taste of Home* Test Kitchen, the recipes in this collection prove that some of the best meals come together in a snap. So the next time you want to serve something satisfying and delicious without all the hassle, turn to the 365 wonders inside this collection and feel good knowing you're serving the very best!

Watermelon Fruit Pizza (p. 259)

Pressure-Cooker Tuscan Chicken Pasta (p. 224)

ICONS IN THIS BOOK

- These **fast-fix recipes** are table-ready in just 30 minutes or less.

- Dishes that use **five or fewer ingredients** (they may also call for water, salt, pepper, canola or olive oil, and optional items).

- Our **healthiest recipes**, these dietitian-approved dishes are lower in calories, fat and sodium.

- **Freezer-friendly** items that include directions for freezing and reheating.

- Recipes that use a **slow cooker**—one of the most convenient kitchen tools.

- Recipes made in a handy **Instant Pot®** electric pressure cooker.

- For the flavor and crispness of fried but without added fat, try these **Air Fryer** recipes.

- With prep done the night before, these **overnight** dishes are easy to fit into your schedule.

Cauliflower Parmesan Casserole (p. 276)

Layered Veggie Tortellini Salad (p. 95)

No-Bake Cookie Butter Blossoms (p. 253)

CREATE FAMILY-FAVORITE DISHES WITH
450+ RECIPES & TIPS

IN THIS EDITION:

MAKE-AHEAD MARVELS
Freezer-friendly recipes, slow-cooker meals, overnight breakfasts and more—these are dishes you can prepare in advance and have on the table in minutes. Come home to slow-cooked Hungarian Goulash (p. 206) all ready to serve, while Triple Berry No-Bake Cheesecake (p. 208) waits in the fridge for dessert!

ONE-DISH RECIPES
Stovetop skillet meals, sheet-pan dinners, savory delights that simmer away in a Dutch oven and more ... these recipes all save time in the kitchen and make cleanup a snap! Try Sheet-Pan Chipotle-Lime Shrimp Bake (p. 239) or Potluck Chicken Vegetable Soup (p. 276).

GIVE ME 5 OR FEWER
Every recipe in this chapter calls for just a handful of items, saving you both time and money on your grocery trips. Dishes like Cherry Balsamic Pork Loin (p. 188) and Weekday Beef Stew (p. 191) are budget friendly and easy to whip up on short notice.

30-MINUTE MAINS
These main courses hit the table in just half an hour or less, so they make dinner a breeze, even on busy nights. Check out Speedy Chicken Marsala (p. 138), Pork Veggie Stir-Fry (p. 148) or Saucy Skillet Fish (p. 133) when you need to get dinner on the table fast.

INSTANT POT® & AIR FRYER
These recipes use the newest, most popular kitchen gadgets to create soups, mains, desserts and more. Make Chicken Piccata Pockets (p. 229) or Cheesy Breakfast Egg Rolls (p. 37) in the air fryer, or try Wine-Braised Beef Shanks (p. 242) or BBQ Baked Beans (p. 96) in the Instant Pot.

DELECTABLE DESSERTS
Whether you're in the mood for Simple Lemon Mousse (p. 250), Banana Cream Pie with Cake Mix Crust (p. 257) or Quick & Easy Tiramisu (p. 255), you never have to skimp on sweets because of time!

30-DAY MEAL PLANNER

When making a meal plan, look to both new recipes as well as cherished standbys. To shake things up, consider incorporating meatless Mondays, taco Tuesdays, or fish on Fridays. Leverage leftovers from more elaborate meals to be used in other dishes. Orange-Glazed Ham (Day 7) leaves enough for lunchtime sandwiches and Asparagus Ham Dinner (Day 9). Air-Fryer Rotisserie Chicken (Day 28) makes a great meal on its own or can provide the basis for Chicken Biscuit Skillet (Day 30). Or freeze leftover shredded chicken to toss in future tacos, casseroles or soups. The possibilities are endless!

DAY 1	DAY 2	DAY 3	DAY 4	DAY 5
Fresh Corn & Tomato Fettuccine, p. 141	**Zesty Chicken Soft Tacos, p. 151**	**Sheet-Pan Pork Supper, p. 240**	**Weekday Beef Stew, p. 191**	**Crispy Fish & Chips, p. 142**
SERVE WITH	**SERVE WITH**	**SERVE WITH**	**SERVE WITH**	**SERVE WITH**
• Summertime Tea, p. 22 • Strawberry Crunch Ice Cream Cake, p. 265	• Green Tomato Salsa, p. 14 • Easy Key Lime Pie, p. 267	Frozen Fruit Whip, p. 269	• Quick & Easy Bread Bowls, p. 106 • Pecan Brownies, p. 255	• Pickled Cabbage, p. 98 • Simple Lemon Mousse, p. 250

DAY 11	DAY 12	DAY 13	DAY 14	DAY 15
Pizza Tater Tot Casserole, p. 238	**Sicilian Pizza (Sfincione), p. 241**	**Pressure-Cooked Mesquite Ribs, p. 183**	**Grampa's German-Style Pot Roast, p. 229**	**Salmon Grilled in Foil, p. 132**
SERVE WITH	**SERVE WITH**	**SERVE WITH**	**SERVE WITH**	**SERVE WITH**
Cranberry-Apple Nut Crunch, p. 250	Great Garlic Bread, p. 127	• Pressure-Cooker BBQ Baked Beans, p. 96 • Strawberry Cooler, p. 13	• Special Radicchio-Spinach Salad, p. 99	Quick Corn Salad, p. 89

DAY 21	DAY 22	DAY 23	DAY 24	DAY 25
Chicken-Fried Steaks, p. 147	**Artichoke Spinach Casserole, p. 273**	**Baked Ham & Colby Sandwiches, p. 59**	**Quick Chicken Minestrone, p. 63**	**Coconut Curry Chicken, p. 239**
SERVE WITH	**SERVE WITH**	**SERVE WITH**	**SERVE WITH**	**SERVE WITH**
Spectacular Fingerling Potatoes, p. 83	Easy Apple Crisp, p. 257	Simple Waldorf Salad, p. 102	Herbed Parmesan Bread, p. 120	Bread Machine Naan, p. 121

DAY 6
**Big-Batch Jambalaya,
p. 286**

SERVE WITH
Cheddar Skillet
Cornbread, p. 120

DAY 7
**Orange-Glazed Ham,
p. 179**

SERVE WITH
• Simple Au Gratin
  Potatoes, p. 84
• Triple Berry No-Bake
  Cheesecake, p. 208

DAY 8
**Saucy Mac & Cheese,
p. 140**

SERVE WITH
Malted Chocolate
Cheesecake, p. 210

DAY 9
**Asparagus Ham
Dinner, p. 145**

SERVE WITH
Pots de Creme, p. 266

DAY 10
**Pork Chops with
Rhubarb, p. 140**

SERVE WITH
Fresh Thai Asparagus,
Kale & Garlicky
Mushrooms, p. 91

DAY 16
**Easy Arroz Con Pollo,
p. 241**

SERVE WITH
Creamy Pina Colada
Pies, p. 252

DAY 17
**Sausage Potato Skillet,
p. 148**

SERVE WITH
Air-Fryer Mocha
Pudding Cakes, p. 253

DAY 18
**Quick Almond Chicken
Stir-Fry, p. 134**

SERVE WITH
Cantaloupe a la Mode,
p. 265

DAY 19
**Baked Lemon
Haddock, p. 144**

SERVE WITH
Garlic-Buttered Green
Beans, p. 88

DAY 20
**French Onion Meatloaf,
p. 185**

SERVE WITH
Pressure-Cooker
Rosemary Beets, p. 91

DAY 26
**BLT Turkey Salad,
p. 293**

SERVE WITH
Rosemary-Garlic
Focaccia Bread, p. 122

DAY 27
**Jalapeno Sloppy Joes,
p. 70**

SERVE WITH
Cool Strawberry Cream,
p. 248

DAY 28
**Air-Fryer Rotisserie
Chicken, p. 225**

SERVE WITH
• Sweet Onion Spoon
  Bread, p. 92
• Cherry Grunt, p. 268

DAY 29
**Pizza Potato Toppers,
p. 135**

SERVE WITH
Herbed Bread Twists,
p. 112

DAY 30
**Chicken Biscuit Skillet,
p. 142**

SERVE WITH
Sonoran Sunset
Watermelon Ice, p. 267

- 1 -

APPETIZERS
& BEVERAGES

If you need some quick-to-fix bites and beverages, you've come to the right place.
It's a cinch to impress guests with this mouthwatering lineup of nibbles, sips and
noshes that come together in a flash. Let's get this party started!

Strawberry Cooler (p. 13) **Easy Pickle Dip** (p. 28) **Summertime Tea** (p. 22)
Easy Coconut Shrimp (p. 31) **Green Tomato Salsa** (p. 14) **Mini Muffuletta** (p. 25)
Blueberry Mojitos (p. 29) **Five Cheese Baked Fonduta** (p. 17) **Peachy Buttermilk Shakes** (p. 19)

TACO JOE DIP

My daughter was the first to try this recipe. She thought it was so good that she passed it on to me. My husband and I both think it's terrific. Because it's made in a slow cooker, it's perfect for parties or busy days.
—*Lang Secrest, Sierra Vista, AZ*

PREP: 5 min. • **COOK:** 5 hours
MAKES: about 7 cups

- 1 **can (16 oz.) kidney beans, rinsed and drained**
- 1 **can (15¼ oz.) whole kernel corn, drained**
- 1 **can (15 oz.) black beans, rinsed and drained**
- 1 **can (14½ oz.) stewed tomatoes, undrained**
- 1 **can (8 oz.) tomato sauce**
- 1 **can (4 oz.) chopped green chiles, drained**
- 1 **envelope taco seasoning**
- ½ **cup chopped onion**
  Thinly sliced green onions, optional
  Tortilla chips and fresh mini bell peppers

In a 5-qt. slow cooker, combine the first 8 ingredients. Cover and cook on low for 5-6 hours. If desired, sprinkle with green onions. Serve the dip with tortilla chips and mini peppers.

¼ CUP: 49 cal., 0 fat (0 sat. fat), 0 chol., 291mg sod., 9g carb. (2g sugars, 2g fiber), 2g pro.

TACO JOE SOUP: Add a 29-oz. can of tomato sauce to the slow cooker for a soup that will serve 6-8.

MEATBALLS WITH MARINARA SAUCE

It's easy to pack on the flavor with just a few ingredients! Use your favorite homemade marinara sauce or a store-bought jar for extra convenience.
—*Lauren McAnelly, Des Moines, IA*

TAKES: 30 min. • **MAKES:** 20 servings

- 1 **pkg. (22 oz.) frozen fully cooked Angus beef meatballs**
- 1½ **cups marinara sauce**
- ⅓ **cup chopped ripe olives**
- ½ **cup fresh basil leaves, torn**

1. Prepare meatballs according to package directions.

2. Meanwhile, in a saucepan, combine marinara sauce and olives; heat through. Add meatballs and basil; heat through.

1 MEATBALL: 93 cal., 7g fat (3g sat. fat), 17mg chol., 301mg sod., 3g carb. (1g sugars, 1g fiber), 4g pro.

STRAWBERRY COOLER

This refreshing beverage is easy to double. Just make two batches of the base mixture ahead of time, then add the ginger ale and ice when you're ready to serve!
—*Judy Robertson, Southington, CT*

TAKES: 10 min. • MAKES: 8 servings

- 3 cups water
- 5 cups sliced fresh strawberries
- ¾ to 1 cup sugar
- ¼ cup lemon juice
- 2 tsp. grated lemon zest
- 1 cup ginger ale
  Crushed ice
  Additional strawberries, optional

In a blender, process the water, sliced strawberries, sugar, and lemon juice and zest in batches until smooth. Strain the berry seeds if desired. Pour mixture into a pitcher; stir in the ginger ale. Serve in chilled glasses over ice. If desired, garnish with strawberries.

1 CUP: 116 cal., 0 fat (0 sat. fat), 0 chol., 3mg sod., 29g carb. (26g sugars, 2g fiber), 1g pro.

PEPPER MANGO SALSA

Whenever I make this, the bowl is always left empty! The idea for a homemade mango salsa hit me after I saw a chef on television make something similar. It sounded so good, and it wasn't something I could find in a store at the time. The salsa is especially tasty served with artisan chips—the black bean and roasted garlic ones are my favorite. When strawberries are in season, I add them into the mix, too.
—*Wendy Rusch, Cameron, WI*

PREP: 15 min. + chilling • MAKES: 6 cups

- 3 Tbsp. lime juice
- 3 Tbsp. honey
- 1 tsp. olive oil
  Dash salt
  Dash coarsely ground pepper
- 3 medium mangoes, peeled and finely chopped
- 2 cups finely chopped fresh pineapple
- 1 large sweet red pepper, finely chopped
- 1 Anaheim or poblano pepper, seeded and finely chopped
- ½ cup finely chopped red onion
- ¼ cup chopped fresh cilantro
  Tortilla chips

1. Whisk together first 5 ingredients. In a large bowl, combine fruit, peppers, onion and cilantro; toss with lime juice mixture.
2. Refrigerate, covered, 1 hour to allow flavors to blend. Stir before serving. Serve with chips.

¼ CUP SALSA: 47 cal., 0 fat (0 sat. fat), 0 chol., 63mg sod., 11g carb. (10g sugars, 1g fiber), 1g pro. **DIABETIC EXCHANGES:** ½ starch.

QUICK TORTILLA PINWHEELS

Prepare these easy pinwheels several days in advance if you're crunched for time. Serve with your choice of mild or hot salsa or picante sauce.
—*Barbara Keith, Faucett, MO*

PREP: 15 min. + chilling
MAKES: about 5 dozen

- 1   cup sour cream
- 1   pkg. (8 oz.) cream cheese, softened
- ¾   cup sliced green onions
- ½   cup finely shredded cheddar cheese
- 1   Tbsp. lime juice
- 1   Tbsp. minced seeded jalapeno pepper
- 8   to 10 flour tortillas (8 in.), room temperature
       Salsa or picante sauce

Combine the first 6 ingredients in a bowl; spread on 1 side of each tortilla and roll up tightly. Cover and refrigerate for at least 1 hour. Slice into 1-in. pieces. Serve with salsa or picante sauce.
NOTE: Wear disposable gloves when cutting hot peppers; the oils can burn skin. Avoid touching your face.
1 PINWHEEL: 47 cal., 3g fat (2g sat. fat), 6mg chol., 51mg sod., 4g carb. (0 sugars, 0 fiber), 1g pro.

GREEN TOMATO SALSA

I came up with this fresh salsa to use up all the green tomatoes in my garden. It's a fun variation on red tomato salsa.
—*Vanessa Moon, Tucson, AZ*

PREP: 20 min. + standing • **COOK:** 10 min.
MAKES: 6 cups

- 1   medium green pepper
- 1   serrano pepper
- 5   medium green tomatoes or 5 large tomatillos, husked
- 1   medium onion, chopped
- 2   garlic cloves, minced
- ⅓   cup lime juice
- 2   Tbsp. olive oil
- 4   tsp. agave nectar
- 1   tsp. coarsely ground pepper
- ½   tsp. salt
- 3   Tbsp. fresh cilantro leaves
- 1   medium ripe avocado, peeled, pitted and quartered
       Tortilla chips

1. Preheat broiler. Place peppers on a foil-lined baking sheet. Broil 3-4 in. from heat until skins blister, about 5 minutes. With tongs, rotate peppers a quarter turn. Broil and rotate until all sides are blistered and blackened. Immediately place in a bowl; let stand, covered, 20 minutes.

2. Using tongs, place tomatoes, a few at a time, in a pot of boiling water for 5 minutes. Remove tomatoes; cool slightly. Peel and finely chop tomatoes; place in a large bowl.

3. Remove skin, stems and seeds from charred peppers. Finely chop peppers; add to tomatoes. Stir in onion and garlic.

4. Place all remaining ingredients except chips in a blender; cover and process until smooth. Add to tomato mixture, stirring to combine. Serve with chips.
NOTE: Wear disposable gloves when cutting hot peppers; the oils can burn skin. Avoid touching your face.
¼ CUP SALSA: 27 cal., 2g fat (0 sat. fat), 0 chol., 50mg sod., 2g carb. (1g sugars, 1g fiber), 0 pro. **DIABETIC EXCHANGES:** 1 free food.

TIP

HOW LONG DOES GREEN TOMATO SALSA LAST?
We recommend enjoying this salsa immediately since there's avocado in it. However, you can make it a few hours ahead of time and store it in the refrigerator until you're ready to serve.

CALICO CLAMS CASINO

A few years ago, I came across this recipe in the back of my files when I was looking for a special appetizer. Everyone raved about it. Now it's an often-requested dish.
—Paula Sullivan, Barker, NY

TAKES: 20 min. • **MAKES:** 8 servings

- 3 cans (6½ oz. each) minced clams
- 1 cup shredded part-skim mozzarella cheese
- 1 cup shredded cheddar cheese
- 4 bacon strips, cooked and crumbled
- 3 Tbsp. seasoned bread crumbs
- 3 Tbsp. butter, melted
- 2 Tbsp. each finely chopped onion, celery and sweet red, yellow and green peppers
- 1 garlic clove, minced
   Dash dried parsley flakes

1. Preheat oven to 350°. Drain clams, reserving 2 Tbsp. juice. In a large bowl, combine the clams and remaining ingredients; stir in reserved clam juice. Spoon mixture into 8 greased 6-oz. custard cups or clamshell dishes; place on a baking sheet.

2. Bake until heated through and lightly browned, 10-15 minutes.

1 SERVING: 165 cal., 12g fat (8g sat. fat), 41mg chol., 383mg sod., 4g carb. (1g sugars, 0 fiber), 9g pro.

CAN YOU USE FRESH CLAMS INSTEAD OF CANNED CLAMS?

If you prefer, you can use fresh clams—just try to buy as close to the day you're cooking as possible. At a reputable fishmonger, look for clams with a fresh briny odor. Any open clams should close quickly when tapped. With fresh clams, you may want to bake this recipe in the shells. Increase the oven temperature to 400°F, then stuff the cleaned shells with filling and bake until heated through and lightly browned, 6-8 minutes.

TIP

EASY CITRUS SLUSH

Our church's hostess committee has relied on this refreshing drink for bridal and baby showers and other events. We use different gelatin flavors and colors to match the decor of the occasion.
—*Joy Bruce, Welch, OK*

- -

PREP: 15 min. + freezing • **MAKES:** about 25 servings (about 6 qt.)

2½ cups sugar
1 pkg. (3 oz.) lemon gelatin
1 pkg. (3 oz.) pineapple gelatin
4 cups boiling water
1 can (12 oz.) frozen pineapple juice concentrate, thawed
1 cup lemon juice
1 envelope (0.23 oz.) unsweetened lemonade Kool-Aid mix
10 cups cold water
2 liters ginger ale, chilled
Lime slices, optional

1. In a large container, dissolve sugar and gelatins in the boiling water. Stir in the pineapple juice concentrate, lemon juice, drink mix and cold water. If desired, divide among smaller containers. Cover and freeze, stirring several times.
2. Remove from freezer at least 1 hour before serving. Stir until mixture becomes slushy. Just before serving, place 9 cups slush mixture in a punch bowl; stir in 1 liter ginger ale. Repeat with remaining slush and ginger ale. If desired, garnish individual servings with lime slices.
1 CUP: 157 cal., 0 fat (0 sat. fat), 0 chol., 25mg sod., 40g carb. (39g sugars, 0 fiber), 1g pro.

FIVE CHEESE BAKED FONDUTA

If melted cheese isn't one of the most mouthwatering foods of all time, I don't know what is! You can swap out any of the cheeses for your own favorites.
—*Cheri Gilmore, Festus, MO*

- -

TAKES: 30 min. • **MAKES:** 3 cups

3 Tbsp. melted butter, divided
1 pkg. (8 oz.) cream cheese, softened
2 cups shredded part-skim mozzarella cheese
1 cup shredded fontina cheese
1 cup shredded cheddar cheese
½ cup grated Parmesan cheese
4 garlic cloves, thinly sliced
1 tsp. dried rosemary, crushed
1 tsp. dried thyme
½ tsp. pepper
Optional: Toasted French bread baguette slices, baked pita chips or assorted fresh vegetables

Preheat oven to 450°. Brush an 8-in. cast-iron or other ovenproof skillet with 1 Tbsp. butter; set aside. In a large bowl, beat cream cheese and mozzarella, fontina, cheddar and Parmesan cheeses with garlic, rosemary, thyme, pepper and remaining 2 Tbsp. butter until combined. Spread into prepared skillet. Bake until bubbly and golden brown, 15-20 minutes. Serve with baguette slices, pita chips or vegetables.
¼ CUP: 237 cal., 20g fat (12g sat. fat), 61mg chol., 402mg sod., 4g carb. (1g sugars, 0 fiber), 11g pro.

QUICK & EASY SWEDISH MEATBALLS

Rich and creamy, this classic meatball sauce is a must in your recipe box.
—Taste of Home *Test Kitchen*

TAKES: 30 min. • MAKES: 20 servings

- 1 pkg. (22 oz.) frozen fully cooked Angus beef meatballs
- 2 Tbsp. butter
- 2 Tbsp. all-purpose flour
- 1 cup beef broth
- ½ cup heavy whipping cream
- ¼ tsp. dill weed
- ¼ cup minced fresh parsley, optional

1. Prepare meatballs according to the package directions.
2. Meanwhile, in a large saucepan, melt butter. Stir in flour until smooth; gradually add broth. Bring to a boil; cook and stir until thickened, 1-2 minutes. Stir in cream and dill; simmer for 1 minute. Stir in the meatballs; heat through. Garnish with parsley if desired.

1 MEATBALL: 115 cal., 10g fat (5g sat. fat), 26mg chol., 253mg sod., 2g carb. (1g sugars, 0 fiber), 4g pro.

> REVIEW
> *"This was the first time I've ever made Swedish meatballs and they were excellent. I used fresh dill weed and parsley, and that always makes a big difference. My mama loved it too."*
> —KRISTINDENNISON, TASTEOFHOME.COM

PEACHY BUTTERMILK SHAKES

My husband and grandkids sure enjoy the tang of buttermilk blended with sweet peaches in these delightful shakes.
—Anna Mayer, Fort Branch, IN

TAKES: 10 min. • MAKES: 3 servings

- 1 cup buttermilk
- 3 cups fresh or frozen unsweetened sliced peaches, thawed
- 1 cup vanilla ice cream, softened
- ¼ cup sugar
- ¾ tsp. ground cinnamon
  Optional: Whipped cream and additional sliced peaches

Place the first 5 ingredients in a blender; cover and process until smooth. Pour into chilled glasses; serve immediately. If desired, top with whipped cream and additional sliced peaches.

1 CUP: 250 cal., 6g fat (3g sat. fat), 23mg chol., 191mg sod., 46g carb. (42g sugars, 3g fiber), 6g pro.

FRESH CORN & AVOCADO DIP

I altered my sister's recipe by adding finely chopped jalapeno for a little heat. This is a tasty way to feature fresh corn. The dip can be made ahead and refrigerated until it's time to serve.
—*Pat Roberts, Thornton, ON*

TAKES: 20 min. • **MAKES:** 4 cups

- 2 cups fresh or frozen corn, thawed
- 1 medium ripe avocado, peeled and diced
- 1 small peach, peeled and chopped
- 1 small sweet red pepper, chopped
- 1 small red onion, chopped
- 2 Tbsp. olive oil
- 2 Tbsp. white wine vinegar
- 1 Tbsp. lime juice
- 1½ tsp. ground cumin
- 1 tsp. minced fresh oregano
- 1 garlic clove, crushed
  Salt and pepper to taste
- 1 minced and seeded jalapeno pepper, optional
  Baked tortilla chips

Combine first 11 ingredients; add salt and pepper and, if desired, jalapeno. Serve with tortilla chips.
¼ CUP: 52 cal., 3g fat (0 sat. fat), 0 chol., 4mg sod., 6g carb. (2g sugars, 1g fiber), 1g pro.
DIABETIC EXCHANGES: ½ starch, ½ fat.

TIP

Here's an easy and safe way to remove the pit from an avocado. Using a sharp knife, cut the avocado in half. Then place your index and middle finger on either side of the avocado pit. Put your thumb on the back of the avocado half and press like you're pushing an elevator button. The pit should pop right out.

BLOODY MARIA

Tequila, lime and jalapenos give the brunch classic a fresh Mexican twist.
—Taste of Home *Test Kitchen*

TAKES: 10 min. • **MAKES:** 6 servings

- 4 cups tomato juice, chilled
- 8 oz. (1 cup) tequila
- ½ cup lime juice
- 4 to 8 tsp. juice from pickled jalapeno slices
- 1 Tbsp. Worcestershire sauce
- 2 to 4 tsp. hot pepper sauce
- ¼ tsp. celery salt
- ¼ tsp. pepper
- 2 tsp. prepared horseradish, optional
  Pickled jalapeno slices
  Pepper jack cheese, cubed
  Lime wedges

Mix first 8 ingredients in a 2-qt. pitcher; stir in horseradish if desired.
Pour over ice; serve with jalapenos, cheese cubes and lime wedges.
1 CUP: 122 cal., 1g fat (0 sat. fat), 0 chol., 525mg sod., 8g carb. (5g sugars, 1g fiber), 2g pro.

ITALIAN OLIVES

A friend shared this recipe with me more than 25 years ago, and I still get raves when I serve them as part of an antipasto platter.
—*Jean Johnson, Reno, NV*

PREP: 10 min. + chilling • **MAKES:** 4 cups

- 2 cans (6 oz. each) pitted ripe olives, drained
- 1 jar (5¾ oz.) pimiento-stuffed olives, drained
- 2 Tbsp. finely chopped celery
- 2 Tbsp. finely chopped onion
- 2 Tbsp. capers, rinsed and drained
- ¼ cup olive oil
- 2 Tbsp. red wine vinegar
- 2 garlic cloves, minced
- 1 tsp. dried basil
- 1 tsp. dried oregano
- 1 tsp. crushed red pepper flakes
- ¼ tsp. salt

1. In a large bowl, combine the first 5 ingredients. In a small bowl, whisk oil, vinegar, garlic, basil, oregano, pepper flakes and salt; pour over olive mixture. Toss to coat.

2. Cover and refrigerate for at least 3 hours before serving. Store in the refrigerator for up to 3 days.

2 TBSP.: 36 cal., 4g fat (0 sat. fat), 0 chol., 210mg sod., 1g carb. (0 sugars, 0 fiber), 0 pro.

TIP

HOW LONG DO ITALIAN OLIVES KEEP AND WHAT ARE SOME FUN WAYS TO SERVE THEM?

These olives are best enjoyed the week they're made, stored in a well-sealed jar in the refrigerator. Include them in an antipasto platter or charcuterie board. Nosh on them with crackers and your favorite appetizer meat, such as salami or prosciutto. They also make a great topping for fish fillets or an Italian chopped salad.

5i

SUMMERTIME TEA

You can't have a summer gathering around here without this sweet tea to cool you down. It's wonderful for sipping while basking by the pool.
—*Angela Lively, Conroe, TX*

PREP: 15 min. + chilling
MAKES: 18 servings

- 14 cups water, divided
- 6 black tea bags
- 1½ cups sugar
- ¾ cup thawed orange juice concentrate
- ¾ cup thawed lemonade concentrate
- 1 cup tequila, optional
  Optional: Fresh mint leaves and lemon or lime slices

1. In a large saucepan, bring 4 cups water to a boil. Remove from the heat; add tea bags. Cover and steep for 3-5 minutes. Discard tea bags.

2. Stir in the sugar, concentrates and remaining 10 cups water. Add tequila if desired. Refrigerate until chilled. Garnish with mint and lemon or lime if desired.

¾ CUP: 102 cal., 0 fat (0 sat. fat), 0 chol., 1mg sod., 26g carb. (26g sugars, 0 fiber), 0 pro.

EASY TACO CUPS

These zesty little cups rank high on my list of favorites because they combine three things I look for in a recipe—fast, easy and delicious! They make a fantastic finger food for game-day parties, and guests have fun selecting their desired toppings.
—*Ashley Jarvies, Manassa, CO*

- -

PREP: 30 min. • **BAKE:** 15 min. + cooling
MAKES: 12 servings

- 1   **lb. ground beef**
- ½   **cup chopped onion**
- 1   **envelope taco seasoning**
- 1   **can (16 oz.) refried beans**
- 2   **tubes (8 oz. each) refrigerated seamless crescent dough sheet**
- 1½ **cups shredded cheddar cheese**
      Optional toppings: Chopped tomatoes, sliced ripe olives, shredded lettuce, sour cream, guacamole and salsa

1. Preheat oven to 375°. In a large skillet, cook beef and onion over medium heat 6-8 minutes or until beef is no longer pink, breaking meat into crumbles; drain. Stir in the taco seasoning and refried beans; heat through.

2. Unroll each tube of crescent dough into a long rectangle. Cut each rectangle into 12 pieces; press lightly onto bottoms and up sides of 24 ungreased muffin cups.

3. Fill each muffin cup with a rounded Tbsp. of beef mixture; sprinkle each with 1 Tbsp. cheese. Bake 14-16 minutes or until dough is golden brown. Cool taco cups in pans 10 minutes before removing. Serve with toppings as desired.

2 TACO CUPS: 291 cal., 15g fat (7g sat. fat), 37mg chol., 819mg sod., 25g carb. (4g sugars, 2g fiber), 15g pro.

🅟🅜 MINI MUFFULETTA

Mediterranean meets comfort food when French rolls are slathered with a savory olive spread and stuffed with layers of salami and cheese. You can make these bites the night before and cut them into appetizer-sized slices just before serving.
—*Gareth Craner, Minden, NV*

- -

PREP: 25 min. + chilling • **MAKES:** 3 dozen

- 1   **cup pimiento-stuffed olives, drained and chopped**
- 1   **can (4¼ oz.) chopped ripe olives**
- 1   **Tbsp. balsamic vinegar**
- 1½ **tsp. red wine vinegar**
- 1½ **tsp. olive oil**
- 1   **garlic clove, minced**
- ½   **tsp. dried basil**
- ½   **tsp. dried oregano**
- 6   **French rolls, split**
- ½   **lb. thinly sliced hard salami**
- ¼   **lb. sliced provolone cheese**
- ½   **lb. thinly sliced cotto salami**
- ¼   **lb. sliced part-skim mozzarella cheese**

1. In a large bowl, combine the first 8 ingredients; set aside. Hollow out tops and bottoms of rolls, leaving ¾-in. shells (discard removed bread or save for another use).

2. Spread olive mixture over tops and bottoms of rolls. On roll bottoms, layer with hard salami, provolone cheese, cotto salami and mozzarella cheese. Replace the tops.

3. Wrap each roll tightly. Refrigerate overnight. Cut each into 6 wedges; secure with toothpicks.

1 SERVING: 119 cal., 8g fat (3g sat. fat), 16mg chol., 537mg sod., 7g carb. (0 sugars, 0 fiber), 6g pro.

5

FROSTY CARAMEL CAPPUCCINO

This frothy, frosty beverage is positively delicious for breakfast, a mid-afternoon snack or even an after-dinner dessert. Also, it's a great quick treat to serve with a plate of cookies when friends come to call.
—*Carol Mann, Summerfield, FL*

TAKES: 10 min. • **MAKES:** 2 servings

- 1 cup half-and-half cream
- 1 cup 2% milk
- 3 Tbsp. plus 2 tsp. caramel ice cream topping, divided
- 2 tsp. instant coffee granules
- 8 to 10 ice cubes
- 4 Tbsp. whipped cream in a can

1. In a blender, combine the half-and-half, milk, 3 Tbsp. caramel topping, coffee and ice cubes; cover and process until smooth.
2. Pour the mixture into 2 chilled glasses. Top the beverage with whipped cream and drizzle with the remaining caramel topping. Serve immediately.
1 SERVING: 324 cal., 16g fat (11g sat. fat), 75mg chol., 246mg sod., 33g carb. (32g sugars, 0 fiber), 9g pro.

TIP

Feel free to add espresso powder in place or or in addition to the coffee granules. For a spicy twist, sprinkle ground cinnamon on top. To make this drink even more rich and indulgent, whip your own homemade whipped cream in place of store-bought cream.

SAUSAGE DIP

My warm sausage dip is a family-favorite. Anyone with a hearty appetite will love this country-style appetizer.
—*Susie Wingert, Panama, IA*

TAKES: 30 min. • **MAKES:** 6 cups

- 1½ lbs. bulk pork sausage
- 2½ cups chopped fresh mushrooms
- 2 medium green peppers, chopped
- 1 large tomato, seeded and chopped
- 1 medium red onion, chopped
- 1½ tsp. salt
- 1 tsp. pepper
- 1 tsp. garlic powder
- ½ tsp. onion powder
- 2 pkg. (8 oz. each) cream cheese, cubed
- 1 cup sour cream
  Tortilla chips

In a large skillet over medium heat, cook the sausage until no longer pink; drain. Add the next 8 ingredients; cook until the vegetables are tender. Reduce heat to low; add cream cheese and sour cream. Cook and stir until cheese is melted and well blended (do not boil). Serve warm with tortilla chips.
2 TBSP.: 59 cal., 5g fat (3g sat. fat), 13mg chol., 149mg sod., 1g carb. (1g sugars, 0 fiber), 2g pro.

🟢 CARAMEL FRAPPUCCINO

I love frappuccinos from Starbucks, but they get too expensive. I now make my own, and they are just as good. If you blend the milk with all the other ingredients, it gets too foamy—instead stir it in with a spoon after all the ice is crushed.
—*Heather Egger, Davenport, IA*

PREP: 10 min. + chilling • **MAKES:** 4 cups

- 2 Tbsp. ground dark coffee
- 1 cup water
- 3 Tbsp. sugar
- 2 Tbsp. caramel ice cream topping
- 2 cups ice cubes
- 1 cup fat-free milk
  Whipped cream, optional

Place ground coffee in the coffee filter of a drip coffeemaker. Add water; brew according to manufacturer's directions. Refrigerate until cold. In a blender, combine the cold coffee, sugar, caramel topping and ice cubes; process until smooth. Add milk and pulse to combine. Pour into glasses. If desired, top with whipped cream and additional caramel topping.

2 CUPS: 159 cal., 0 fat (0 sat. fat), 2mg chol., 122mg sod., 37g carb. (37g sugars, 0 fiber), 4g pro.

🕐 🟢 EASY PICKLE DIP

My love for pickles led me to create this dip. It's so easy to whip together. But be warned...it's addicting!
—*April Anderson, Forest Lake, MN*

TAKES: 10 min. • **MAKES:** 3 cups

- 1 pkg. (8 oz.) cream cheese, softened
- 1 cup sour cream
- ¼ cup dill pickle juice
- 1 cup chopped dill pickles
- 1 tsp. garlic pepper blend
  Optional: Ridged potato chips or pretzels

In a small bowl, beat the cream cheese, sour cream and pickle juice until smooth. Stir in the pickles and pepper blend. Serve dip immediately or refrigerate for up to 4 hours. If desired, serve with chips or pretzels.

¼ CUP: 108 cal., 11g fat (6g sat. fat), 24mg chol., 210mg sod., 2g carb. (2g sugars, 0 fiber), 2g pro.

BLUEBERRY MOJITOS

Blueberry and lime are two of my favorite flavors, so I added blueberries to my favorite mixed drink. This recipe can easily be doubled or tripled.
—*Michele Tungett, Rochester, IL*

TAKES: 5 min. • **MAKES:** 1 serving

- 8   fresh blueberries
- 8   fresh mint leaves
- 1   cup ice cubes
- 2   oz. white rum
- 2   Tbsp. fresh lime juice
- 1   Tbsp. simple syrup
- 4   oz. club soda, chilled
      Lime slice, mint sprig and additional fresh blueberries, optional

Add blueberries and mint leaves to a tall glass; muddle with the back of a wooden spoon. Fill the glass with ice cubes; add rum, lime juice and simple syrup. Top glass with club soda; mix well. If desired, garnish with a lime slice, mint sprig and fresh blueberries.

1 DRINK: 202 cal., 0 fat (0 sat. fat), 0 chol., 29mg sod., 20g carb. (17g sugars, 0 fiber), 0 pro.

TIP
To make simple syrup, combine ½ cup sugar and ½ cup water and cook over medium heat until the sugar is dissolved. Simple syrup will keep in the fridge for a week.

Combine 1½ oz. **vodka**, 1½ oz. **Kahlua** and 2 Tbsp. **canned pumpkin** in a rocks glass; stir until smooth. Fill glass with ½-¾ cup **ice cubes** and top with 3 oz. **heavy whipping cream** or milk. Sprinkle with **ground cinnamon**; serve cocktail immediately.

- PUMPKIN SPICE WHITE RUSSIAN -
Here's a quick and easy twist on the classic White Russian.
The pumpkin mixes well with vodka and Kahlua.

EASY COCONUT SHRIMP

Guests are always impressed when I serve these restaurant-quality shrimp. A selection of sauces served alongside adds the perfect touch.
—*Tacy Holliday, Germantown, MD*

TAKES: 25 min. • **MAKES:** about 2 dozen

- 1¼ cups all-purpose flour
- ¼ tsp. seafood seasoning
- 1 large egg, beaten
- ¾ cup pineapple juice
- 1 pkg. (14 oz.) sweetened shredded coconut
- 1 lb. large shrimp, peeled and deveined
  Oil for deep-fat frying
  Optional: Apricot preserves, sweet-and-sour sauce, plum sauce or Dijon mustard

1. In a bowl, combine the flour, seasoning, egg and pineapple juice until smooth. Place coconut in a shallow bowl. Dip the shrimp into batter, then coat with coconut.
2. In an electric skillet or deep-fat fryer, heat oil to 375°. Fry the shrimp, a few at a time, until golden brown, about 1½ minutes, turning occasionally. Drain on paper towels. Serve with dipping sauce or mustard if desired.

1 SHRIMP: 171 cal., 11g fat (6g sat. fat), 31mg chol., 76mg sod., 14g carb. (8g sugars, 1g fiber), 5g pro.

TIP

An easy way to tell if breaded shrimp are thoroughly cooked (and safe to eat) is if they are curled into a nice C shape. Overcooked shrimp are curled tightly into an O shape. So simply, C = cooked, O = overcooked.

- 2 -

BREAKFAST & BRUNCH SPECIALTIES

Whether you and your crew are gathering at the table or dashing out the door, these scrumptious breakfast delights, make-ahead marvels, oven-baked sensations and grab-and-go treats will help you beat the morning rush.

AIR-FRYER HASH BROWNS

These hash browns are one of my go-to sides. They come together quickly, and the air fryer gets them nice and crispy in no time. If you'd like, try topping them with a sprinkling of shredded pepper jack cheese.
—*Cindi Boger, Ardmore, AL*

- -

PREP: 20 min. • **COOK:** 15 min./batch • **MAKES:** 12 servings

- 1 pkg. (30 oz.) frozen shredded hash brown potatoes
- 1 large red onion, finely chopped
- 1 small sweet red pepper, finely chopped
- 1 small green pepper, finely chopped
- 4 garlic cloves, minced
- 2 Tbsp. olive oil
- ½ tsp. salt
- ½ tsp. pepper
- 3 drops hot pepper sauce, optional
- 2 tsp. minced fresh parsley

Preheat the air fryer to 375°. In a large bowl, combine the first 8 ingredients; if desired, add hot sauce. In batches, spread the mixture in an even ¾-in.-thick layer on greased tray in air-fryer basket. Cook until golden and crispy, 15-20 minutes. Sprinkle with parsley just before serving.

NOTE: In our testing, we find cook times vary dramatically between brands of air fryers. As a result, we give wider-than-normal ranges on suggested cook times. Begin checking at the first time listed and adjust as needed.

½ CUP: 87 cal., 2g fat (0 sat. fat), 0 chol., 116mg sod., 15g carb. (2g sugars, 2g fiber), 2g pro. **DIABETIC EXCHANGES:** 1 starch, ½ fat.

MUFFIN-TIN SCRAMBLED EGGS

I made these one year at Christmas as a way to save time, and they were a big hit. I have to make a large batch because my husband and boys can polish them off in a short amount of time. These also freeze well, if there are any left!
—*Jill Darin, Geneseo, IL*

- -

PREP: 15 min. • **BAKE:** 20 min. + standing • **MAKES:** 2 dozen

- 24 large eggs
- 1 tsp. salt
- ½ tsp. pepper
- ¼ tsp. garlic powder
- 1 jar (4 oz.) sliced mushrooms, finely chopped
- 1 can (4 oz.) chopped green chiles
- 3 oz. sliced deli ham, finely chopped
- ½ medium onion, finely chopped
- ½ cup shredded cheddar cheese
   Pico de gallo, optional

1. Preheat oven to 350°. In a large bowl, whisk eggs, salt, pepper and garlic powder until blended. Stir in mushrooms, chiles, ham, onion and cheese. Spoon about ¼ cup mixture into each of 24 greased muffin cups.

2. Bake until eggs are set, 18-20 minutes, rotating pans halfway through baking. Let stand 10 minutes before removing from pans. If desired, serve with pico de gallo.

FREEZE OPTION: Freeze cooled, baked egg cups in airtight freezer containers. To use, microwave each serving on high for 1¼-1½ minutes or until heated through.

1 EGG CUP: 88 cal., 6g fat (2g sat. fat), 190mg chol., 257mg sod., 1g carb. (0 sugars, 0 fiber), 8g pro. **DIABETIC EXCHANGES:** 1 medium-fat meat.

🕐🍎
BRAIN FOOD SMOOTHIE

My grandson refuses to eat nearly all fruits and vegetables. After he and our son moved home, I tried everything to improve his diet. This smoothie is one of the only ways I can sneak him something nutritious—and he loves it!
—Sandra Roberts, Dexter, MO

- -

TAKES: 15 min. • **MAKES:** 6 cups

1½ cups fat-free vanilla Greek yogurt
½ cup 2% milk
2 medium ripe avocados, peeled and pitted
2 cups halved fresh strawberries
1 cup sliced ripe banana
1 cup fresh raspberries or frozen unsweetened raspberries, thawed
1 cup fresh baby spinach
1 cup fresh blueberries
½ cup fresh or frozen blackberries, thawed
¼ cup unflavored whey protein powder

Place all ingredients in a blender; cover and process until smooth. Pour into individual glasses.
1 CUP: 215 cal., 8g fat (1g sat. fat), 3mg chol., 65mg sod., 29g carb. (17g sugars, 7g fiber), 10g pro.

🅿Ⓜ
OVERNIGHT BAKED EGGS BRUSCHETTA

I like to spend as much time as I can with my guests when they stay with me for the holidays, so I rely on make-ahead recipes to free up my time in the kitchen. I came up with this unique breakfast bruschetta for a fun and delicious change of pace from typical make-ahead casseroles.
—Judi Berman-Yamada, Portland, OR

- -

PREP: 45 min. + chilling • **BAKE:** 10 min. • **MAKES:** 9 servings

1 tube (13.8 oz.) refrigerated pizza crust
1 Tbsp. cornmeal
3 Tbsp. olive oil, divided
1½ cups shredded part-skim mozzarella cheese, divided
¾ lb. sliced baby portobello mushrooms
¾ tsp. garlic powder
¾ tsp. dried rosemary, crushed
½ tsp. pepper
¼ tsp. salt
2 cups pizza sauce
1 Tbsp. white vinegar
9 large eggs
2 oz. fresh goat cheese, crumbled
½ cup french-fried onions
   Fresh basil leaves

1. Preheat oven to 400°. Unroll pizza crust and press onto bottom of a greased 15x10x1-in. baking pan that's been sprinkled with cornmeal. Brush crust with 1 Tbsp. oil; sprinkle with ¾ cup mozzarella cheese. Bake 8 minutes.
2. Meanwhile, in a large skillet, heat remaining 2 Tbsp. oil over medium-high heat. Add mushrooms; cook and stir until tender. Stir in garlic powder, rosemary, pepper and salt. Stir pizza sauce into mushrooms; spread mushroom mixture over crust.
3. In a large skillet with high sides, bring vinegar and 2-3 in. water to a boil. Reduce heat to maintain a gentle simmer. Break cold eggs, 1 at a time, into a small bowl. Holding bowl close to surface of water, slip eggs into water.
4. Cook the eggs, uncovered, for 3-5 minutes or until whites are completely set and yolks begin to thicken but are not hard. Using a slotted spoon, remove eggs; place over mushroom mixture in baking pan. Sprinkle goat cheese and remaining mozzarella over eggs and mushrooms. Refrigerate, covered, overnight.
5. Remove pan from refrigerator 30 minutes before baking. Preheat oven to 400°. Sprinkle onions over top. Bake, uncovered, until golden brown and heated through, 10-15 minutes. Top with basil just before serving.
1 PIECE: 345 cal., 17g fat (5g sat. fat), 227mg chol., 798mg sod., 29g carb. (6g sugars, 2g fiber), 17g pro.

AIR-FRYER FRENCH TOAST STICKS

Craving French toast sticks? Try this quick and easy recipe. Store some in the freezer for a hearty breakfast in an instant. They're great for buffets and eating on the go.
—Taste of Home *Test Kitchen*

PREP: 20 min. + freezing • **COOK:** 10 min.
MAKES: 1½ dozen

- 6   slices day-old Texas toast
- 4   large eggs
- 1   cup 2% milk
- 2   Tbsp. sugar
- 1   tsp. vanilla extract
- ¼   to ½ tsp. ground cinnamon
- 1   cup crushed cornflakes, optional
     Confectioners' sugar, optional
     Maple syrup

1. Cut each piece of bread into thirds; place in an ungreased 13x9-in. dish. In a large bowl, whisk eggs, milk, sugar, vanilla and cinnamon. Pour over bread; soak for 2 minutes, turning once. If desired, coat bread with cornflake crumbs on all sides.
2. Preheat air fryer to 350°. Place desired number of bread pieces on greased tray in air-fryer basket. Cook for 3 minutes. Turn; cook until golden brown, 2-3 minutes longer. Sprinkle with confectioners' sugar if desired. Serve with syrup.
FREEZE OPTION: Place uncooked French toast sticks on a greased 15x10x1-in. baking pan. Freeze until firm, about 45 minutes. Transfer to an airtight freezer container and store in the freezer.
3 STICKS: 184 cal., 6g fat (2g sat. fat), 128mg chol., 253mg sod., 24g carb. (8g sugars, 1g fiber), 8g pro.

TIP
If you don't have an air fryer, you can make this recipe in an oven.

AIR-FRYER CHEESY BREAKFAST EGG ROLLS

Whether you have to run out the door in the morning or you take a few minutes to relax at the table, these breakfast egg rolls will hit the spot. The egg-and-sausage mixture can be made the night before so in the morning, you can just roll, fry and go!
—Anne Ormond, Dover, NH

PREP: 30 min. • **COOK:** 10 min./batch
MAKES: 12 servings

- ½   lb. bulk pork sausage
- ½   cup shredded sharp cheddar cheese
- ½   cup shredded Monterey Jack cheese
- 1   Tbsp. chopped green onions
- 4   large eggs
- 1   Tbsp. 2% milk
- ¼   tsp. salt
- ⅛   tsp. pepper
- 1   Tbsp. butter
- 12 egg roll wrappers
     Cooking spray
     Optional: Maple syrup or salsa

1. In a small nonstick skillet, cook sausage over medium heat until no longer pink, 4-6 minutes, breaking it into crumbles; drain. Stir in cheeses and green onions; set aside. Wipe skillet clean.

2. In a small bowl, whisk eggs, milk, salt and pepper until blended. In the same skillet, heat butter over medium heat. Pour in egg mixture; cook and stir until eggs are thickened and no liquid egg remains. Stir in sausage mixture.
3. Preheat air fryer to 400°. With 1 corner of an egg roll wrapper facing you, place ¼ cup filling just below center of wrapper. (Cover remaining wrappers with a damp paper towel until ready to use.) Fold the bottom corner over filling; moisten the remaining wrapper edges with water. Fold side corners toward center over filling. Roll egg roll up tightly, pressing at tip to seal. Repeat.
4. In batches, arrange egg rolls in a single layer on greased tray in air-fryer basket; spritz with cooking spray. Cook until lightly browned, 3-4 minutes. Turn; spritz with cooking spray. Cook until golden brown and crisp, 3-4 minutes longer. If desired, serve with maple syrup or salsa.
1 EGG ROLL: 209 cal., 10g fat (4g sat. fat), 87mg chol., 438mg sod., 19g carb. (0 sugars, 1g fiber), 10g pro.

AIR-FRYER CARROT COFFEE CAKE

Air fryers are great for making small, quick treats. This little cake bakes in about 30 minutes. Enjoy it for breakfast or dessert.
—Leigh Rys, Herndon, VA

PREP: 15 min. • **BAKE:** 35 min. • **MAKES:** 6 servings

- 1 large egg, lightly beaten, room temperature
- ½ cup buttermilk
- ⅓ cup sugar plus 2 Tbsp. sugar, divided
- 3 Tbsp. canola oil
- 2 Tbsp. dark brown sugar
- 1 tsp. grated orange zest
- 1 tsp. vanilla extract
- ⅔ cup all-purpose flour
- ⅓ cup white whole wheat flour
- 1 tsp. baking powder
- 2 tsp. pumpkin pie spice, divided
- ¼ tsp. baking soda
- ¼ tsp. salt
- 1 cup shredded carrots
- ¼ cup dried cranberries
- ⅓ cup chopped walnuts, toasted

1. Preheat air fryer to 350°. Grease and flour a 6-in. round baking pan. In a large bowl, whisk egg, buttermilk, ⅓ cup sugar, oil, brown sugar, orange zest and vanilla. In another bowl, whisk flours, baking powder, 1 tsp. pumpkin pie spice, baking soda and salt. Gradually beat into egg mixture. Fold in carrots and dried cranberries. Pour into prepared pan.
2. In a small bowl, combine walnuts, remaining 2 Tbsp. sugar and remaining 1 tsp. pumpkin spice. Sprinkle evenly over batter. Gently place pan in the basket of a large air fryer.
3. Cook until a toothpick inserted in center of cake comes out clean, 35-40 minutes. Cover tightly with foil if top gets too dark. Cool in pan on a wire rack for 10 minutes before removing from pan. Serve warm.
1 PIECE: 316 cal., 13g fat (1g sat. fat), 32mg chol., 297mg sod., 46g carb. (27g sugars, 3g fiber), 6g pro.

CHEESY VEGETABLE FRITTATA

A side of fresh fruit makes a perfect refreshing counterpart to this cheesy, flavorful egg bake packed with veggies. My husband and I enjoy it just as much for late-night suppers as we do for brunch.
—Pauline Howard, Lago Vista, TX

PREP: 15 min. • **BAKE:** 20 min. • **MAKES:** 2 servings

- 4 large eggs, beaten
- 1 cup sliced fresh mushrooms
- ½ cup chopped fresh broccoli
- ¼ cup shredded sharp cheddar cheese
- 2 Tbsp. finely chopped onion
- 2 Tbsp. finely chopped green pepper
- 2 Tbsp. grated Parmesan cheese
- ⅛ tsp. salt
  Dash pepper

1. Preheat oven to 350°. In a large bowl, combine all ingredients. Pour into a greased shallow 3-cup baking dish.
2. Bake, uncovered, until a knife inserted in the center comes out clean, 20-25 minutes.
1 SERVING: 243 cal., 16g fat (7g sat. fat), 390mg chol., 482mg sod., 6g carb. (2g sugars, 1g fiber), 19g pro.

PEACH-STUFFED FRENCH TOAST

With its make-ahead convenience and scrumptious flavor, this recipe is ideal for holiday brunches—and for busy hostesses with a hungry crowd to feed!
—Julie Robinson, Little Chute, WI

PREP: 25 min. + chilling • **BAKE:** 25 min.
MAKES: 10 servings

- 1 loaf (1 lb.) French bread, cut into 20 slices
- 1 can (15 oz.) sliced peaches in juice, drained and chopped
- ¼ cup chopped pecans
- 4 large eggs
- 4 large egg whites
- 1½ cups fat-free milk
- 3 Tbsp. sugar
- 1¼ tsp. ground cinnamon, divided
- 1 tsp. vanilla extract
- ¼ cup all-purpose flour
- 2 Tbsp. brown sugar
- 2 Tbsp. cold butter
- Maple syrup, optional

1. Arrange half of the bread in a 13x9-in. baking dish coated with cooking spray. Top with the peaches, pecans and remaining bread.
2. In a small bowl, whisk the eggs, egg whites, milk, sugar, 1 tsp. cinnamon and vanilla; pour over bread. Cover and refrigerate for 8 hours or overnight.
3. Remove baking dish from the refrigerator 30 minutes before baking. Bake, uncovered, at 400° for 20 minutes.
4. In a small bowl, combine flour, brown sugar and remaining ¼ tsp. cinnamon; cut in butter until crumbly. Sprinkle over French toast. Bake 5-10 minutes longer or until a knife inserted in the center comes out clean. Serve with syrup if desired.

1 PIECE: 267 cal., 8g fat (3g sat. fat), 92mg chol., 368mg sod., 39g carb. (13g sugars, 2g fiber), 10g pro. **DIABETIC EXCHANGES:** 2½ starch, 1½ fat.

BLUEBERRY STREUSEL COFFEE CAKE

Filled with juicy berries and crunchy pecans, this family favorite smells wonderful as it bakes.
—Lori Snedden, Sherman, TX

PREP: 20 min. • BAKE: 35 min. • MAKES: 9 servings

- 2 cups all-purpose flour
- 2 tsp. baking powder
- ¼ tsp. salt
- ¾ cup sugar
- ½ cup butter, softened
- 1 large egg, room temperature
- ½ cup whole milk
- 1 cup fresh or frozen blueberries
- 1 cup chopped pecans

STREUSEL TOPPING
- ½ cup sugar
- ⅓ cup all-purpose flour
- ¼ cup cold butter

1. Preheat oven to 375°. Whisk flour, baking powder and salt. In another bowl, cream sugar and butter until light and fluffy, 5-7 minutes. Add egg and milk; stir into dry ingredients. Fold in blueberries and pecans. Spread into a greased 9-in. square baking pan.
2. For topping, combine sugar and flour; cut in butter until crumbly. Sprinkle over batter. Bake until a toothpick inserted in the center comes out clean, 35-40 minutes. Cool on a wire rack.
NOTE: If using frozen blueberries, use without thawing to avoid discoloring the batter.
1 PIECE: 476 cal., 26g fat (11g sat. fat), 66mg chol., 323mg sod., 57g carb. (30g sugars, 3g fiber), 6g pro
RASPBERRY STREUSEL COFFEE CAKE: Substitute raspberries for the blueberries.

CAST-IRON SCRAMBLED EGGS

I put my trusty cast-iron skillet to good use with these easy scrambled eggs. They make a quick and simple breakfast.
—Bonnie Hawkins, Elkhorn, WI

TAKES: 25 min. • MAKES: 6 servings

- 12 large eggs
- 2 Tbsp. water
- ¼ tsp. salt
- ¼ tsp. pepper
- ⅔ cup finely chopped sweet onion
- 1 jalapeno pepper, seeded and chopped
- 2 Tbsp. butter
- 1 log (4 oz.) fresh goat cheese, crumbled
- 3 Tbsp. minced chives

1. In a large bowl, whisk the eggs, water, salt and pepper; set egg mixture aside.
2. Place a 10-in. cast-iron skillet over medium-high heat. In the skillet, saute onion and jalapeno in butter until tender. Add egg mixture; cook and stir until almost set. Stir in cheese and chives; cook and stir until eggs are completely set.
NOTE: Wear disposable gloves when cutting hot peppers; the oils can burn skin. Avoid touching your face.
⅔ CUP: 217 cal., 16g fat (7g sat. fat), 446mg chol., 342mg sod., 3g carb. (2g sugars, 0 fiber), 15g pro.

CAST-IRON APPLE NUTMEG COFFEE CAKE

I used up the morning's coffee to make a coffee cake. It is super moist and crumbly and tastes like you dunked your cake right into a cup of hot joe. Add pecans to the apples if you want some crunch.
—Darla Andrews, Boerne, TX

- -

PREP: 25 min. + standing • **BAKE:** 20 min. + cooling
MAKES: 8 servings

- 3 Tbsp. butter, cubed
- 2 cups chopped peeled Gala apple
- ½ cup packed brown sugar, divided
- ¼ cup brewed coffee
- ⅔ cup canola oil
- ½ cup sugar
- 1 large egg plus 1 large egg white, room temperature
- 2 tsp. vanilla extract
- 1½ cups all-purpose flour
- 2 tsp. ground cinnamon
- ½ tsp. salt
- ½ tsp. baking soda
- ¼ tsp. ground nutmeg

DRIZZLE
- ⅓ cup brewed coffee
- ¼ cup heavy whipping cream
- 1½ cups confectioners' sugar

1. Preheat oven to 375°. In a 10-in. cast-iron or other ovenproof skillet, melt butter over low heat. Add chopped apples and ¼ cup brown sugar. Cook and stir until apples are crisp-tender, about 5 minutes. Stir in coffee; remove from heat.
2. In a large bowl, beat the oil, sugar, egg, egg white, vanilla and remaining ¼ cup brown sugar until well blended. In another bowl, whisk flour, cinnamon, salt, baking soda and nutmeg; gradually beat into oil mixture. Gently spread over apple mixture.
3. Bake until a toothpick inserted in center comes out clean, 18-22 minutes. Cool on a wire rack 10 minutes.
4. Meanwhile, for drizzle, in a small saucepan, bring coffee and cream to a boil; cook 10-12 minutes or until liquid is reduced to ¼ cup. Remove from heat; stir in confectioners' sugar. Let stand 10 minutes. Drizzle over cake.
1 PIECE: 532 cal., 27g fat (6g sat. fat), 43mg chol., 284mg sod., 71g carb. (51g sugars, 1g fiber), 4g pro.

ⓅⓂ ITALIAN SAUSAGE EGG BAKE

This hearty entree warms up any breakfast or brunch menu with its herb-seasoned flavor.
—Darlene Markham, Rochester, NY

- -

PREP: 20 min. + chilling • **BAKE:** 50 min. • **MAKES:** 12 servings

- 8 slices white bread, cubed
- 1 lb. Italian sausage links, casings removed, sliced
- 2 cups shredded sharp cheddar cheese
- 2 cups shredded part-skim mozzarella cheese
- 9 large eggs, lightly beaten
- 3 cups 2% milk
- 1 tsp. dried basil
- 1 tsp. dried oregano
- 1 tsp. fennel seed, crushed

1. Place bread cubes in a greased 13x9-in. baking dish; set aside. In a large skillet, cook sausage over medium heat until no longer pink; drain. Spoon sausage over bread; sprinkle with cheeses.
2. In a large bowl, whisk the eggs, milk and seasonings; pour over casserole. Cover and refrigerate overnight.
3. Remove from the refrigerator 30 minutes before baking. Bake, uncovered, at 350° until a knife inserted in the center comes out clean, 50-55 minutes. Let stand for 5 minutes before cutting.
1 PIECE: 316 cal., 20g fat (10g sat. fat), 214mg chol., 546mg sod., 13g carb. (5g sugars, 1g fiber), 21g pro.

APPLE-HONEY DUTCH BABY

I make this dish on Sunday mornings for a special treat. It's so impressive when it's served warm right out of the oven, and the honey-and-apple topping is divine.
—*Kathy Fleming, Lisle, IL*

TAKES: 30 min. • **MAKES:** 4 servings

- 3 large eggs, room temperature
- ¾ cup 2% milk
- ¾ cup all-purpose flour
- 1 Tbsp. sugar
- 2 Tbsp. butter

TOPPING
- 1 Tbsp. butter
- 2 large apples, sliced
- ½ cup honey
- 2 to 3 tsp. lemon juice
- ½ tsp. ground cardamom
- 1 tsp. cornstarch
- 2 tsp. cold water

1. Preheat oven to 400°. In a large bowl, whisk together first 4 ingredients until smooth. Place butter in a 10-in. ovenproof skillet; heat in the oven 2-3 minutes or until melted.

2. Tilt pan to coat bottom and sides. Pour batter into hot skillet. Bake until puffed and edges are lightly browned, 16-20 minutes.

3. Meanwhile, for topping, in a large saucepan, heat butter over medium heat; saute apples until lightly browned. Stir in honey, lemon juice and cardamom. Mix cornstarch and water until smooth; stir into apple mixture. Bring to a boil; cook and stir until thickened, 1-2 minutes. Spoon into pancake; serve immediately.

1 SERVING: 429 cal., 14g fat (7g sat. fat), 166mg chol., 146mg sod., 72g carb. (50g sugars, 3g fiber), 9g pro.

CHERRY CHIP WAFFLES WITH CHERRY SYRUP

While on a recent trip to Door County, Wisconsin, for a family reunion, I created this yummy recipe using freshly picked cherries. It was a hit with all ages, and everyone was asking for more.
—*Heather Karow, Burnett, WI*

PREP: 25 min. • **COOK:** 10 min./batch
MAKES: 6 servings

- ½ cup sugar
- ½ cup plus 2 Tbsp. water, divided
- ½ cup fresh or frozen pitted dark sweet cherries, thawed and finely chopped
- 1 Tbsp. cornstarch

WAFFLES
- 1¼ cups all-purpose flour
- 1 tsp. baking powder
- 1 tsp. ground cinnamon
- 1 tsp. baking soda
- 1½ cups buttermilk
- 2 large eggs, room temperature
- ⅓ cup canola oil
- ½ tsp. almond extract
- 1½ cups fresh or frozen pitted dark sweet cherries, thawed and chopped
- ½ cup miniature semisweet chocolate chips
  Additional miniature semisweet chocolate chips, optional

1. Preheat waffle maker. In a small saucepan, cook and stir sugar and ½ cup water over medium heat until sugar is dissolved. Add cherries; cook and stir until cherries are tender, 3-5 minutes. Mix cornstarch and remaining 2 Tbsp. water until smooth; stir into pan. Bring to a boil; cook and stir until thickened, 1-2 minutes. Remove and keep warm.

2. In a large bowl, whisk flour, baking powder, cinnamon and baking soda. In another bowl, whisk buttermilk, eggs, oil and extract until blended. Add to the dry ingredients; stir just until moistened. Stir in cherries and chocolate chips. Bake waffles according to manufacturer's directions until golden brown. Serve waffles with cherry syrup and, if desired, additional chocolate chips.

FREEZE OPTION: Cool waffles on wire racks. Freeze between layers of waxed paper in an airtight container. Freeze cherry syrup in a freezer container. To use, partially thaw cherry syrup in refrigerator overnight. Heat through in a saucepan, stirring occasionally. Reheat waffles in a toaster on medium setting. Or, microwave each waffle on high until heated through, 30-60 seconds.

2 WAFFLES WITH 2 TBSP. CHERRY SYRUP: 428 cal., 19g fat (4g sat. fat), 64mg chol., 432mg sod., 59g carb. (33g sugars, 2g fiber), 8g pro.

LEMON BLACKBERRY TORTILLA FRENCH TOAST

This twist on crepes is tart-sweet with a creamy lemon filling and juicy blackberries. Think of this as a cross between thin French toast, light crepes and crispy quesadillas.
—Arlene Erlbach, Morton Grove, IL

PREP: 25 min. • **COOK:** 5 min./batch • **MAKES:** 6 servings

    1   pkg. (8 oz.) cream cheese, softened
    6   Tbsp. lemon curd, divided
    2   tsp. grated lemon zest
  ⅛   tsp. almond extract
    2   large eggs
    2   Tbsp. heavy whipping cream
    1   Tbsp. poppy seeds
    3   Tbsp. butter
    6   flour tortillas (6 in.)
  1⅓ cups fresh blackberries
  ¼   cup seedless blackberry spreadable fruit
      Additional grated lemon zest, optional

1. In a small bowl, beat cream cheese, 3 Tbsp. lemon curd, lemon zest and extract until fluffy. Set aside.
2. In a shallow bowl, whisk eggs, cream and remaining 3 Tbsp. lemon curd until blended; stir in poppy seeds. In a large cast-iron or other heavy skillet, heat 1 Tbsp. butter over medium heat. Dip both sides of a tortilla in egg mixture, allowing excess to drip off. Place in skillet; toast until golden brown, 2-3 minutes on each side. Remove to a wire rack. Repeat with remaining tortillas, adding butter to grease the skillet as needed.
3. Spread about 3 Tbsp. cream cheese mixture over each tortilla to within ¼ in. of edges. Fold tortillas in half over filling. In a microwave-safe bowl, combine blackberries and spreadable fruit; microwave, covered, at 50% power 2-3 minutes or until warmed, stirring once. Serve with tortillas and, if desired, additional lemon zest.

1 FILLED TORTILLA: 445 cal., 27g fat (15g sat. fat), 134mg chol., 403mg sod., 42g carb. (21g sugars, 3g fiber), 8g pro.

SLOW-COOKER COCONUT GRANOLA

Here's a versatile treat with a taste of the tropics. You can sub dried pineapple, mango or other tropical fruits for the cherries.
—Taste of Home *Test Kitchen*

PREP: 15 min. • **COOK:** 3½ hours + cooling • **MAKES:** 6 cups

    4   cups old-fashioned oats
    1   cup sliced almonds
    1   cup unsweetened coconut flakes
    1   tsp. ground cinnamon
    1   tsp. ground ginger
  ¼   tsp. salt
  ½   cup coconut oil, melted
  ½   cup maple syrup
    1   cup dried cherries

1. Combine oats, almonds, coconut, cinnamon, ginger and salt in a 3-qt. slow cooker. In small bowl, whisk together oil and maple syrup. Pour into slow cooker; stir to combine. Cook, covered, on low, stirring occasionally, 3½-4 hours. Stir in cherries.
2. Transfer mixture to a baking sheet; let stand until cool.

½ CUP: 343 cal., 19g fat (12g sat. fat), 0 chol., 55mg sod., 41g carb. (18g sugars, 5g fiber), 6g pro.

TIP
There are so many delicious ways to serve this easy granola. Enjoy it as cereal with milk and sliced banana or berries. Sprinkle it over yogurt or ice cream. Pack it in resealable bags for a portable treat to snack on throughout the week.

PUMPKIN & OAT PANCAKES

Looking for the perfect fall breakfast? Give these pancakes a try. The pumpkin and cinnamon are excellent together.
—*Nancy Horsburgh, Everett, ON*

- -

TAKES: 25 min. • **MAKES:** 12 pancakes

- 1 cup all-purpose flour
- 1 cup quick-cooking oats
- 2 Tbsp. toasted wheat germ
- 2 tsp. sugar
- 2 tsp. baking powder
- ½ tsp. salt
  Pinch ground cinnamon
- 1⅔ cups 2% milk
- 1 large egg, room temperature, lightly beaten
- ¾ cup canned pumpkin
- 2 Tbsp. canola oil
  Optional: semisweet chocolate chips, raisins, sugared cranberries, pumpkin seeds, whipped cream, butter, maple syrup and additional ground cinnamon

1. In a large bowl, combine flour, oats, wheat germ, sugar, baking powder, salt and cinnamon. In a small bowl, whisk the milk, egg, pumpkin and oil; stir into dry ingredients just until moistened.
2. Pour batter by ¼ cupfuls onto a hot greased griddle; turn when bubbles form on top of pancakes. Cook until second side is golden brown. Top as desired.

2 PANCAKES: 274 cal., 10g fat (2g sat. fat), 49mg chol., 435mg sod., 38g carb. (6g sugars, 4g fiber), 9g pro.

SOUTHERN HASH BROWNS & HAM SHEET-PAN BAKE

Why not take the convenience of sheet-pan cooking and apply it to breakfast? I love how easily this meal comes together.
—*Colleen Delawder, Herndon, VA*

- -

PREP: 15 min. • **BAKE:** 35 min. • **MAKES:** 4 servings

- 1 pkg. (20 oz.) refrigerated shredded hash brown potatoes
- 3 Tbsp. olive oil
- ½ tsp. salt
- ½ tsp. pepper
- ¼ cup apple jelly
- ¼ cup apricot preserves
- 1 Tbsp. horseradish sauce
- 1 tsp. Dijon mustard
- ¼ tsp. garlic powder
- ¼ tsp. onion powder
- 2 cups cubed fully cooked ham
- 4 large eggs
- 2 green onions, finely chopped

1. Preheat oven to 400°. Place potatoes in a greased 15x10x1-in. baking pan. Drizzle with oil; sprinkle with salt and pepper. Toss to coat. Bake until edges are golden brown, 25-30 minutes.
2. In a small bowl, combine jelly, preserves, horseradish sauce, Dijon, garlic powder and onion powder. Pour over potatoes; add ham. Toss to coat.
3. With the back of a spoon, make 4 wells in the potato mixture. Break an egg into each well. Bake until egg whites are completely set and yolks begin to thicken but are not hard, 10-12 minutes. Sprinkle with green onions and additional pepper.

1 SERVING: 483 cal., 19g fat (4g sat. fat), 228mg chol., 1340mg sod., 55g carb. (23g sugars, 3g fiber), 24g pro.

❄️
EASY CHEESY CAULIFLOWER BREAKFAST CASSEROLE

I love finding new ways to add veggies to my meals. This twist on a breakfast favorite swaps in riced cauliflower for the usual hash browns to make it a keto-friendly and crowd-pleasing addition to the brunch rotation.
—Robyn Warren, Lead Hill, AR

PREP: 30 min. • **BAKE:** 40 min. + standing
MAKES: 12 servings

- 1   lb. bacon strips, chopped
- 1   cup chopped sweet onion
- ½   large sweet red pepper, chopped
- ½   large green pepper, chopped
- 9   large eggs, lightly beaten
- 1½ cups whole-milk ricotta cheese
- 4   cups frozen riced cauliflower, thawed
- 2   cups shredded cheddar cheese
- 1   cup shredded Swiss cheese
- ½   tsp. pepper
- ¼   tsp. salt

1. Preheat oven to 350°. In a large skillet, cook bacon over medium heat until crisp, stirring occasionally. Remove with a slotted spoon; drain on paper towels. Discard the drippings, reserving 1 Tbsp. in the pan.

2. Add onion and chopped peppers to drippings; cook and stir over medium-high heat until tender, 6-8 minutes. In a large bowl, whisk eggs and ricotta. Stir in riced cauliflower, shredded cheeses, bacon, onion mixture, pepper and salt. Pour into a greased 13x9-in. baking dish. Bake, uncovered, until a knife inserted near the center comes out clean, 40-45 minutes. Let stand 10 minutes before serving.

FREEZE OPTION: Cool baked casserole completely; cover tightly and freeze. To use, partially thaw in refrigerator overnight. Remove from refrigerator 30 minutes before baking. Preheat oven to 350°. Bake casserole as directed, increasing the time as necessary to heat through and for a thermometer inserted in center to read 165°.

1 PIECE: 307 cal., 22g fat (11g sat. fat), 194mg chol., 534mg sod., 7g carb. (4g sugars, 2g fiber), 21g pro.

THREE-CHEESE QUICHE

Try eggs and cheese at their best. Guests often remark about how tall, light and fluffy this crustless entree is. You'll love it!
—*Judy Reagan, Hannibal, MO*

PREP: 15 min. • **BAKE:** 45 min. + standing • **MAKES:** 6 servings

- 7   large eggs
- 5   large egg yolks
- 1   cup heavy whipping cream
- 1   cup half-and-half cream
- 1   cup shredded part-skim mozzarella cheese
- ¾   cup shredded sharp cheddar cheese, divided
- ½   cup shredded Swiss cheese
- 2   Tbsp. finely chopped oil-packed sun-dried tomatoes
- 1½ tsp. salt-free seasoning blend
- ¼   tsp. dried basil

1. Preheat oven to 350°. In a large bowl, combine the eggs, egg yolks, whipping cream, half-and-half, mozzarella cheese, ½ cup cheddar cheese, Swiss cheese, tomatoes, seasoning blend and basil; pour into a greased 9-in. deep-dish pie plate. Sprinkle with remaining ¼ cup cheddar cheese.

2. Bake 45-50 minutes or until a knife inserted in the center comes out clean. Let stand 10 minutes before cutting.

1 PIECE: 449 cal., 37g fat (21g sat. fat), 524mg chol., 316mg sod., 5g carb. (3g sugars, 0 fiber), 22g pro.

SLOW-COOKER HAM & EGGS

This dish is appreciated any time of the year, but I love serving it on holiday mornings. Once started, it requires little attention. It's a fun meal for the family.
—*Andrea Schaak, Jordan, MN*

PREP: 15 min. • **COOK:** 3 hours • **MAKES:** 6 servings

- 6   large eggs
- 1   cup biscuit/baking mix
- ⅔   cup 2% milk
- ⅓   cup sour cream
- 2   Tbsp. minced fresh parsley
- 2   garlic cloves, minced
- ½   tsp. salt
- ½   tsp. pepper
- 1   cup cubed fully cooked ham
- 1   cup shredded Swiss cheese
- 1   small onion, finely chopped
- ⅓   cup shredded Parmesan cheese

1. In a large bowl, whisk the first 8 ingredients until blended; stir in remaining ingredients. Pour mixture into a greased 3- or 4-qt. slow cooker.

2. Cook, covered, on low 3-4 hours or until the eggs are set. Cut into wedges.

1 SERVING: 315 cal., 18g fat (9g sat. fat), 256mg chol., 942mg sod., 17g carb. (4g sugars, 1g fiber), 21g pro.

REVIEW

"Very delicious! I didn't have ham so I fried up some turkey bacon and the onion. I also added mushrooms."
—**BIG EYES, TASTEOFHOME.COM**

GARDEN VEGETABLE QUICHE

Make your next brunch special with this fluffy deep-dish quiche. Fresh rosemary enhances a delightful egg dish that's chock-full of savory garden ingredients. It cuts nicely, too.
—Kristina Ledford, Indianapolis, IN

- -

PREP: 30 min. + chilling
BAKE: 40 min. + standing
MAKES: 8 servings

    Dough for single-crust pie
1   Tbsp. butter
1   small red onion, halved and
    thinly sliced
½   cup sliced fresh mushrooms
¼   cup finely chopped yellow
    summer squash
½   cup fresh baby spinach
3   garlic cloves, minced
1   cup shredded Swiss cheese
4   large eggs, lightly beaten
1⅔ cups heavy whipping cream
½   tsp. salt
½   tsp. minced fresh rosemary
¼   tsp. pepper

1. On a lightly floured surface, roll dough to a ⅛-in.-thick circle; transfer to a 9-in. pie plate. Trim to ½ in. beyond rim of plate;

flute edge. Refrigerate for 30 minutes. Preheat oven to 425°. Line unpricked crust with a double thickness of foil. Fill with pie weights, dried beans or uncooked rice. Bake on a lower oven rack until edge is light golden brown, 15-20 minutes. Remove foil and weights; bake until bottom is golden brown, 3-6 minutes longer. Cool on a wire rack. Reduce oven setting to 350°.
2. In a large skillet, melt the butter over medium heat. Add onion, mushrooms and squash; cook and stir until tender, 3-5 minutes. Add spinach and garlic; cook 1 minute longer. Spoon into the crust; top with cheese.
3. In a large bowl, whisk eggs, cream, salt, rosemary and pepper until blended; pour over filling. Cover edge of crust loosely with foil. Bake until a knife inserted in the center comes out clean, 40-45 minutes. Let stand 10 minutes before cutting.
NOTE: For crust, combine 1¼ cups all-purpose flour and ¼ tsp. salt; cut in ½ cup cold butter until crumbly. Gradually add 3-5 Tbsp. ice water, tossing with a fork until dough holds together when pressed. Shape into a disk. Wrap; refrigerate 1 hour.
1 PIECE: 451 cal., 38g fat (23g sat. fat), 196mg chol., 390mg sod., 18g carb. (2g sugars, 1g fiber), 11g pro.

POWER BREAKFAST SANDWICH

This morning stack is totally restaurant-worthy. I store my sammies in the freezer, then pop one in the microwave as I head out for the day. There's no speedier—or tastier—breakfast.
—Jolene Martinelli, Fremont, NH

- -

PREP: 20 min. • **BAKE:** 15 min.
MAKES: 6 servings

1   tsp. olive oil
¼   cup chopped onion
¼   cup chopped sweet red
    or orange pepper
¼   cup chopped fresh baby spinach
6   large eggs
¼   tsp. salt
¼   tsp. pepper
6   Italian turkey sausage links,
    casings removed
1   pkg. (12 oz.) multigrain sandwich
    thins, split
6   slices cheddar, Swiss or
    pepper jack cheese

1. Preheat oven to 350°. In a large nonstick skillet, heat oil over medium-high heat. Add onion and sweet pepper; cook and stir until tender, 3-4 minutes. Add spinach; cook 1 minute longer. Remove from heat; let cool 5 minutes. In a large bowl, whisk eggs, salt, pepper and onion mixture. Divide egg mixture among 6 greased 4-in. muffin top tins. Bake until eggs are set, 12-15 minutes.
2. Meanwhile, shape sausage into six 5-in. patties. In the same skillet, cook patties over medium heat until a thermometer reads 160°, 4-5 minutes on each side. Drain if necessary on paper towels. Layer sandwich bottoms with sausage patties, egg rounds and cheese; replace tops.
FREEZE OPTION: Wrap sandwiches in waxed paper and then in foil; freeze in a freezer container. Remove foil. Microwave a waxed paper–wrapped sandwich at 50% power until thawed, 1-2 minutes. Turn sandwich over; microwave at 100% power until hot and a thermometer reads at least 165°, 30-60 seconds. Let stand 2 minutes before serving.
1 SANDWICH: 434 cal., 23g fat (9g sat. fat), 257mg chol., 1026mg sod., 31g carb. (3g sugars, 7g fiber), 30g pro.

GLUTEN-FREE PANCAKES

SEE PHOTO ON PAGE 33

Since being diagnosed with celiac disease, I've made my gluten-free flapjacks dozens of times. My kids like them best with chocolate chips and maple syrup.
—*Kathy Rairigh, Milford, IN*

- -

PREP: 15 min. • **COOK:** 10 min./batch
MAKES: 12 pancakes

- 1 cup brown rice flour
- ½ cup potato starch
- ½ cup ground almonds
- 3 tsp. sugar
- 3 tsp. baking powder
- ½ tsp. salt
- 2 large eggs, room temperature
- 1 cup fat-free milk
- 2 Tbsp. butter, melted
- 1 tsp. vanilla extract
- ⅓ cup miniature semisweet chocolate chips, optional

1. In a large bowl, combine rice flour, potato starch, almonds, sugar, baking powder and salt.
2. In another bowl, whisk eggs, milk, butter and vanilla; stir into dry ingredients just until moistened. If desired, stir in chocolate chips.
3. Preheat griddle over medium heat. Lightly grease griddle. Pour batter by ¼ cupfuls onto a hot griddle; cook until bubbles on top start to pop and bottoms are golden brown. Turn; cook until second side is golden brown. If desired, serve with additional mini chocolate chips.

FREEZE OPTION: Arrange cooled pancakes in a single layer on sheet pans. Freeze overnight or until frozen. Transfer to an airtight plastic container and freeze for up to 2 months. To use, place pancake on a microwave-safe plate; microwave on high for 40-50 seconds or until heated through.

NOTE: Read all ingredient labels for possible gluten content prior to use. Ingredient formulas can change, and production facilities vary among brands. If you're concerned that your brand may contain gluten, contact the company.

2 PANCAKES: 233 cal., 10g fat (3g sat. fat), 73mg chol., 508mg sod., 30g carb. (5g sugars, 2g fiber), 7g pro. **DIABETIC EXCHANGES:** 2 starch, 2 fat.

CRUNCHY APPLE SIDE SALAD

With fiber-rich fruit, light dressing and crunchy walnuts, this is a great side salad or snack. Try it with low-fat granola.
—*Kathy Armstrong, Post Falls, ID*

- -

TAKES: 15 min. • **MAKES:** 5 servings

- ⅓ cup fat-free sugar-free vanilla yogurt
- ⅓ cup reduced-fat whipped topping
- ¼ tsp. plus ⅛ tsp. ground cinnamon, divided
- 2 medium red apples, chopped
- 1 large Granny Smith apple, chopped
- ¼ cup dried cranberries
- 2 Tbsp. chopped walnuts

In a large bowl, combine the yogurt, whipped topping and ¼ tsp. cinnamon. Add apples and cranberries; toss to coat. Refrigerate until serving. Sprinkle with walnuts and remaining ⅛ tsp. cinnamon before serving.

¾ CUP: 109 cal., 3g fat (1g sat. fat), 0 chol., 12mg sod., 22g carb. (16g sugars, 3g fiber), 2g pro. **DIABETIC EXCHANGES:** 1 fruit, ½ starch, ½ fat.

4. Stir egg and vanilla into cornmeal mixture; add to dry ingredients and stir just until blended. Pour batter over sausages.

5. Bake until a toothpick inserted in the center comes out clean, 30-35 minutes. Serve warm with syrup.

FREEZE OPTION: To freeze, wrap baked cake in foil; transfer to a freezer container. Freeze for up to 3 months. To use frozen cake, remove foil and thaw at room temperature. Serve warm with syrup.

1 SLICE: 481 cal., 23g fat (7g sat. fat), 64mg chol., 940mg sod., 53g carb. (13g sugars, 2g fiber), 15g pro.

TURKEY BREAKFAST SAUSAGE

These hearty sausage patties are loaded with flavor but contain a fraction of the sodium and fat found in commercial breakfast links.
—*Judy Culbertson, Dansville, NY*

TAKES: 20 min. • **MAKES:** 8 servings

  1 **lb. lean ground turkey**
  ¾ **tsp. salt**
  ½ **tsp. rubbed sage**
  ½ **tsp. pepper**
  ¼ **tsp. ground ginger**

1. Crumble turkey into a large bowl. Add the salt, sage, pepper and ginger; mix lightly but thoroughly. Shape mixture into eight 2-in. patties.

2. In a greased cast-iron or other heavy skillet, cook patties over medium heat until a thermometer reads 165° and juices run clear, 4-6 minutes on each side.

1 PATTY: 85 cal., 5g fat (1g sat. fat), 45mg chol., 275mg sod., 0 carb. (0 sugars, 0 fiber), 10g pro. **DIABETIC EXCHANGES:** 1 lean meat, ½ fat.

SAUSAGE JOHNNYCAKE

Here's a nice hearty breakfast with plenty of old-fashioned flavor. I serve it to my bed-and-breakfast customers who love the cake's savory middle and maple syrup topping. It's a great way to start the day!
—*Lorraine Guyn, Calgary, AB*

PREP: 20 min. • **BAKE:** 30 min. • **MAKES:** 6 servings

  1 **cup cornmeal**
  2 **cups buttermilk**
 12 **uncooked breakfast sausage links**
1⅓ **cups all-purpose flour**
  ¼ **cup sugar**
1½ **tsp. baking powder**
  ½ **tsp. baking soda**
  ½ **tsp. salt**
 ⅓ **cup shortening**
  1 **large egg, lightly beaten**
  ½ **tsp. vanilla extract**
    Maple syrup

1. Preheat oven to 400°. In a small bowl, combine cornmeal and buttermilk; let stand for 10 minutes.

2. Meanwhile, in a 9-in. cast-iron skillet over medium heat, cook sausage until no longer pink; drain on paper towels. Arrange 8 links in a spokelike pattern in same skillet or in a greased 9-in. deep-dish pie plate. Cut remaining links in half; place between whole sausages.

3. In a large bowl, combine flour, sugar, baking powder, baking soda and salt. Cut in shortening until the mixture resembles coarse crumbs.

THE BEST EVER PANCAKES

I'm not joking when I say I make pancakes every weekend. I love them in any form and variation, and this is one of my favorite pancake recipes.
—*James Schend, Pleasant Prairie, WI*

PREP: 15 min. • **COOK:** 5 min./batch
MAKES: 12 servings

1½ cups all-purpose flour
 2 Tbsp. sugar
 1 tsp. baking powder
 ½ tsp. baking soda
 ½ tsp. salt
 1 cup buttermilk
 2 large eggs, room temperature
 ¼ cup butter, melted
 1 tsp. vanilla extract
    Optional: Mixed fresh berries, whipped cream, maple syrup and butter

1. In a large bowl, whisk together the first 5 ingredients. In another bowl, whisk remaining ingredients; stir into dry ingredients just until moistened.
2. Preheat griddle over medium heat. Lightly grease griddle. Pour batter by ¼ cupfuls onto griddle; cook until bubbles on top begin to pop and the bottoms are golden brown. Turn; cook until second side is golden brown. Serve the pancakes with toppings as desired.
3 PANCAKES: 360 cal., 15g fat (8g sat. fat), 126mg chol., 817mg sod., 45g carb. (10g sugars, 1g fiber), 10g pro.

TIP

To make these pancakes lactose free, replace the buttermilk and butter with lactose-free 2% milk and lactose-free butter or dairy-free margarine. If you want to make them completely dairy free, replace the buttermilk with any plant-based milk, like soy or almond, and use melted shortening in place of the butter.

CINNAMON MUFFINS

My husband grew up enjoying these tender, yummy muffins that his mother made on special weekend mornings. With cinnamon and a dash of nutmeg in the batter, they are seasoned to please.
—*Katherine McVey, Raleigh, NC*

- -

TAKES: 30 min. • **MAKES:** 1 dozen

- ⅓ cup shortening, room temperature
- ½ cup sugar
- 1 large egg, room temperature
- 1½ cups all-purpose flour
- 2 tsp. ground cinnamon
- 1½ tsp. baking powder
- ½ tsp. salt
- ¼ tsp. ground nutmeg
- ½ cup milk

TOPPING
- 3 Tbsp. butter, melted
- ½ cup sugar
- 1½ tsp. ground cinnamon

1. In a large bowl, cream shortening and sugar until light and fluffy, 5-7 minutes. Beat in egg. Combine the flour, cinnamon, baking powder, salt and nutmeg; add to creamed mixture alternately with milk until well combined.
2. Fill greased muffin cups half full. Bake muffins at 350° for 15-20 minutes or until a toothpick comes out clean.
3. For topping, add melted butter to a shallow bowl. In another shallow bowl, combine sugar and cinnamon. Dip muffin tops in butter, then in cinnamon-sugar. Serve warm.
1 MUFFIN: 209 cal., 9g fat (3g sat. fat), 27mg chol., 188mg sod., 29g carb. (17g sugars, 1g fiber), 3g pro.

FREEZER BREAKFAST SANDWICHES

On a busy morning, these freezer breakfast sandwiches save the day. A hearty combo of eggs, Canadian bacon and cheese will keep you fueled through lunchtime and beyond.
—*Christine Rukavena, Milwaukee, WI*

- -

PREP: 25 min. • **BAKE:** 15 min. • **MAKES:** 12 sandwiches

- 12 large eggs
- ⅔ cup 2% milk
- ½ tsp. salt
- ¼ tsp. pepper

SANDWICHES
- 12 English muffins, split
- 4 Tbsp. butter, softened
- 12 slices Colby-Monterey Jack cheese
- 12 slices Canadian bacon

1. Preheat oven to 325°. In a large bowl, whisk eggs, milk, salt and pepper until blended. Pour into a 13x9-in. baking pan coated with cooking spray. Bake until set, 15-18 minutes. Cool on a wire rack.
2. Meanwhile, toast English muffins (or bake at 325° until lightly browned, 12-15 minutes). Spread 1 tsp. butter on each English muffin bottom.
3. Cut eggs into 12 portions. Layer muffin bottoms with an egg portion, a cheese slice (tearing cheese to fit) and Canadian bacon. Replace muffin tops. Wrap sandwiches in waxed paper and then in foil; freeze in a freezer container.
4. To use frozen sandwiches, remove foil. Microwave a waxed paper–wrapped sandwich at 50% power until thawed, 1-2 minutes. Turn sandwich over; microwave at 100% power until hot and a thermometer reads at least 160°, 30-60 seconds. Let stand for 2 minutes before serving.
1 SANDWICH: 334 cal., 17g fat (9g sat. fat), 219mg chol., 759mg sod., 26g carb. (3g sugars, 2g fiber), 19g pro.

CHEDDAR BACON GRITS

In the South, grits can be served plain with a little butter or loaded with extras, as in my recipe with bacon, cheddar and green chiles.
—*Amanda Reed, Nashville, TN*

TAKES: 30 min. • **MAKES:** 12 servings

- 8 cups water
- 2 cups uncooked old-fashioned grits
- 1 tsp. salt
- ¼ tsp. paprika
- 2 cups shredded white cheddar cheese
- 5 bacon strips, cooked and crumbled
- 1 can (4 oz.) chopped green chiles
  Sliced green onions, optional

1. In a 6-qt. stockpot, bring water to a boil. Slowly stir in grits, salt and paprika. Reduce heat; cook, covered, 15-20 minutes or until thickened, stirring occasionally.
2. Reduce heat to low. Stir in cheese, bacon and chiles until cheese is melted. If desired, sprinkle with green onions.

¾ CUP: 199 cal., 8g fat (4g sat. fat), 22mg chol., 418mg sod., 24g carb. (0 sugars, 1g fiber), 7g pro.

LIGHT & FLUFFY WAFFLES

These melt-in-your-mouth waffles are so tender that you can skip butter and syrup, but why would you want to?
—*James Schend, Pleasant Prairie, WI*

PREP: 15 min. + standing • **COOK:** 5 min./batch • **MAKES:** 12 waffles

- 2 large eggs
- 1½ cups all-purpose flour
- ½ cup cornstarch
- 1 tsp. baking powder
- ½ tsp. baking soda
- ½ tsp. salt
- ½ cup 2% milk
- 5 Tbsp. canola oil
- 2 tsp. vanilla extract
- 1 tsp. white vinegar
- 2 Tbsp. sugar
- ½ cup club soda, chilled
  Optional: Butter and maple syrup

1. Separate eggs. Place egg whites in a clean, dry bowl; let stand at room temperature 30 minutes.
2. In another bowl, whisk together next 5 ingredients. In a small bowl, whisk egg yolks, milk, oil, vanilla and vinegar until blended. Beat egg whites until soft peaks form. Gradually add the sugar; continue beating until stiff peaks form.
3. Preheat waffle maker. Stir together flour mixture, egg yolk mixture and club soda just until combined. Fold egg whites into batter. Bake waffles according to manufacturer's directions until golden brown. Serve with butter and maple syrup if desired.

2 WAFFLES: 312 cal., 14g fat (2g sat. fat), 64mg chol., 421mg sod., 39g carb. (5g sugars, 1g fiber), 6g pro.

- TROPICAL BERRY SMOOTHIES -

This fruity, healthy smoothie is a big hit with kids and adults alike because it tastes like a treat and still delivers the vitamins. The recipe is easy to increase based on the number of people you'll be serving.

In a blender, combine 1 cup **pina colada juice blend**, 1 container (6 oz.) **vanilla yogurt**, ⅓ cup **frozen unsweetened strawberries**, ¼ cup **frozen mango chunks** and ¼ cup **frozen unsweetened blueberries**. Cover and process for 30 seconds or until smooth. Pour into chilled glasses; serve immediately.

- 3 -

FAVORITE SOUPS & SANDWICHES

Nothing is more comforting than a bowl of hot soup paired with a hearty sandwich, especially if this ultimate duo is whipped up in a flash. Treat yourself to a cozy lunch or dinner with these impossibly easy recipes you'll turn to time and again.

BAKED HAM & COLBY SANDWICHES

This yummy recipe is a winner with our friends and family. Not only are the warm sandwiches a snap to prepare, but they also smell so good when they are baking that no one has been able to resist them.
—*Sherry Crenshaw, Fort Worth, TX*

TAKES: 30 min. • **MAKES:** 8 sandwiches

- ½ cup butter, melted
- 2 Tbsp. prepared mustard
- 1 Tbsp. dried minced onion
- 1 Tbsp. poppy seeds
- 2 to 3 tsp. sugar
- 8 hamburger buns, split
- 8 slices Colby cheese
- 16 thin slices deli ham (about 1 lb.)
- 1½ cups shredded part-skim mozzarella cheese

1. Preheat oven to 350°. In a small bowl, combine the butter, mustard, onion, poppy seeds and sugar. Place bun bottoms, cut side up, in an ungreased 15x10x1-in. baking pan. Top each with Colby cheese, ham and mozzarella. Brush with half the butter mixture.

2. Replace bun tops. Brush with remaining butter mixture. Bake, uncovered, until cheese is melted, 10-15 minutes.

1 SANDWICH: 504 cal., 32g fat (18g sat. fat), 102mg chol., 1444mg sod., 27g carb. (5g sugars, 1g fiber), 27g pro.

TIP

Turn this classic ham and cheese sandwich into a Reuben. Swap in corned beef or pastrami for the ham, add a layer of sauerkraut and substitute caraway seeds for the poppy seeds.

SWEET POTATO BEAN SOUP

I felt like making some black bean soup, but I had a sweet potato that needed to be used, so I combined the two and created this delicious soup. It combines the creaminess of sweet potato with the crunch of corn and bell pepper.
—*Michelle Sweeny, Bloomington, IN*

TAKES: 30 min. • **MAKES:** 4 servings

- 1 medium sweet potato, peeled and cubed
- 1 small green pepper, chopped
- 1 small onion, chopped
- 2 garlic cloves, minced
- 1 tsp. minced fresh cilantro
- 1 tsp. ground cumin
- 1 can (15 oz.) black beans, rinsed and drained
- 2 cups water
- 1½ cups frozen corn
- 1 can (8 oz.) tomato sauce
- ¼ tsp. pepper
- 2 green onions, thinly sliced
- 1 plum tomato, seeded and chopped

1. Place sweet potato in a small saucepan and cover with water. Bring to a boil. Reduce heat; cover and cook until tender, 13-18 minutes. Drain, reserving ¼ cup liquid. Cool slightly. Place sweet potato and reserved liquid in a blender or food processor; cover and process until smooth. Set aside.

2. In a small saucepan coated with cooking spray, cook the green pepper, onion and garlic until almost tender, 2-3 minutes. Stir in cilantro and cumin; cook and stir until vegetables are tender, 1-2 minutes. Add the beans, water, corn, tomato sauce, pepper and reserved sweet potato puree; heat through. Top with the green onions and chopped tomato.

1½ CUPS: 211 cal., 1g fat (0 sat. fat), 0 chol., 472mg sod., 44g carb. (10g sugars, 9g fiber), 9g pro. **DIABETIC EXCHANGES:** 2½ starch, 1 vegetable, 1 lean meat.

VEGETARIAN SPLIT PEA SOUP

Even the pickiest soup lover will request this version time and again. Well-seasoned and thick, it's a nutritional powerhouse packed with fiber and protein. It's wonderful served with a slice of crusty French bread.

—*Michele Doucette, Stephenville, NL*

PREP: 15 min. • **COOK:** 1½ hours • **MAKES:** 7 servings

- 6 cups vegetable broth
- 2 cups dried green split peas, rinsed
- 1 medium onion, chopped
- 1 cup chopped carrots
- 2 celery ribs with leaves, chopped
- 2 garlic cloves, minced
- ½ tsp. dried marjoram
- ½ tsp. dried basil
- ¼ tsp. ground cumin
- ½ tsp. salt
- ¼ tsp. pepper
- Optional: Shredded carrots and sliced green onions

1. In a large saucepan, combine the first 9 ingredients; bring to a boil. Reduce heat; cover and simmer until peas are tender, about 1 hour, stirring occasionally.

2. Add salt and pepper; simmer 10 minutes longer. Remove soup from heat; cool slightly. Process in batches in a blender or food processor until smooth; return to the pan and heat through. If desired, garnish with carrots and green onions.

1 CUP: 227 cal., 1g fat (0 sat. fat), 0 chol., 771mg sod., 42g carb. (7g sugars, 15g fiber), 14g pro.

BRATS WITH SAUERKRAUT

I've made many variations of this classic summertime sandwich. The bratwurst can be plain, smoked or cheese flavored, served whole or cut in slices, with a bun or without.

—*Darlene Dixon, Hanover, MN*

PREP: 10 min. • **COOK:** 6 hours • **MAKES:** 8 servings

- 8 uncooked bratwurst links
- 1 can (14 oz.) sauerkraut, rinsed and well drained
- 2 medium apples, peeled and finely chopped
- 3 bacon strips, cooked and crumbled
- ¼ cup packed brown sugar
- ¼ cup finely chopped onion
- 1 tsp. ground mustard
- 8 brat buns, split

1. Place the bratwurst in a 5-qt. slow cooker. In a large bowl, combine the sauerkraut, apples, bacon, brown sugar, onion and mustard; spoon over bratwurst.

2. Cover and cook on low until a thermometer inserted in the sausage reads 160°, 6-8 hours.

3. Place the brats in buns. Using a slotted spoon, top with the sauerkraut mixture.

1 BRAT: 534 cal., 28g fat (11g sat. fat), 53mg chol., 1188mg sod., 51g carb. (18g sugars, 4g fiber), 21g pro.

EASY SLOW-COOKER POTATO SOUP

This hearty soup tastes just like a loaded baked potato. Add the ingredients to the slow cooker before leaving in the morning to come home to a fuss-free supper.
—Taste of Home *Test Kitchen*

PREP: 10 min. • **COOK:** 6 hours • **MAKES:** 8 servings (2 qt.)

- 1 carton (32 oz.) chicken broth
- 1 pkg. (30 oz.) frozen shredded hash brown potatoes, thawed
- 1 small onion, finely chopped
- 2 garlic cloves, minced
- ¼ tsp. pepper
- 1 pkg. (8 oz.) cream cheese, softened and cubed
- 1 cup half-and-half cream
- 1 cup shredded cheddar cheese
  Optional: Crumbled cooked bacon and chopped green onions

1. In a 4- or 5-qt. slow cooker, combine broth, potatoes, onion, garlic and pepper. Cook, covered, on low 6-8 hours or until vegetables are tender.

2. Mash potatoes to desired consistency. Whisk in cream cheese until melted. Stir in half-and-half. Cook, covered, until heated through, 5-10 minutes longer. Serve with cheese and, if desired, bacon and green onions.

1 CUP: 294 cal., 18g fat (10g sat. fat), 60mg chol., 711mg sod., 24g carb. (4g sugars, 1g fiber), 9g pro.

> **REVIEW**
>
> *"This was a tasty recipe. I did put bacon and cheese on top. If a recipe says you can add bacon, you can bet I'll be adding it."*
> —QUEENLALISA, TASTEOFHOME.COM

GARLIC BREAD PIZZA SANDWICHES

I love inventing new ways to make grilled cheese sandwiches for my kids. This version tastes like pizza. Using frozen garlic bread is a timesaver.
—Courtney Stultz, Weir, KS

TAKES: 20 min. • **MAKES:** 4 servings

- 1 pkg. (11¼ oz.) frozen garlic Texas toast
- ¼ cup pasta sauce
- 4 slices provolone cheese
- 16 slices pepperoni
- 8 slices thinly sliced hard salami
  Additional pasta sauce, warmed, optional

1. Preheat griddle over medium-low heat. Add garlic toast; cook until lightly browned, 3-4 minutes per side.

2. Spoon 1 Tbsp. sauce over each of 4 pieces of toast. Top with cheese, pepperoni, salami and remaining toast. Cook until crisp and cheese is melted, 3-5 minutes, turning as necessary. If desired, serve with additional sauce.

1 SANDWICH: 456 cal., 28g fat (10g sat. fat), 50mg chol., 1177mg sod., 36g carb. (4g sugars, 2g fiber), 19g pro.

EASY ITALIAN BEEF SANDWICHES

These party-sized sandwiches make the meal! Just add your favorite Italian salad on the side. If you like, top the sandwiches with sliced provolone.
—*Troy Parkos, Verona, WI*

PREP: 20 min. • **COOK:** 5 hours • **MAKES:** 12 servings

- 1 boneless beef chuck roast (3 lbs.)
- 1 tsp. Italian seasoning
- ¼ tsp. cayenne pepper
- ¼ tsp. pepper
- ¼ cup water
- 1 jar (16 oz.) sliced pepperoncini, undrained
- 1 medium sweet red pepper, julienned
- 1 medium green pepper, julienned
- 1 garlic clove, minced
- 1 envelope reduced-sodium onion soup mix
- 2 Tbsp. Worcestershire sauce
- 2 loaves (1 lb. each) Italian bread, split

1. Cut roast in half; place in a 5-qt. slow cooker. Sprinkle with the Italian seasoning, cayenne and pepper. Add the water. Cover and cook on high for 4 hours or until meat is tender.
2. Remove roast; shred meat with 2 forks and return to the slow cooker. In a large bowl, combine the pepperoncini, peppers, garlic, soup mix and Worcestershire sauce; pour over meat. Cover and cook on high for 1 hour or until peppers are tender.
3. Spoon beef mixture over the bottom halves of bread loaves; replace tops. Cut each loaf into 6 sandwiches.
1 SERVING: 428 cal., 14g fat (5g sat. fat), 74mg chol., 661mg sod., 43g carb. (2g sugars, 3g fiber), 29g pro.

CREAMY BACON MUSHROOM SOUP

I've always enjoyed cooking and recently created this rich soup. It's always a hit. You can also garnish it with chopped green onion tops or shredded Swiss cheese. For a creamier, smoother consistency, try pouring the soup through a strainer.
—*Toby Mercer, Inman, SC*

TAKES: 30 min. • **MAKES:** 8 servings (2 qt.)

- 10 bacon strips, diced
- 1 lb. sliced fresh mushrooms
- 1 medium onion, chopped
- 3 garlic cloves, minced
- 1 qt. heavy whipping cream
- 1 can (14½ oz.) chicken broth
- 1¼ cups shredded Swiss cheese
- 3 Tbsp. cornstarch
- ½ tsp. salt
- ½ tsp. pepper
- 3 Tbsp. cold water
  Minced fresh parsley, optional

1. In a large saucepan, cook bacon over medium heat until crisp. Using a slotted spoon, remove to paper towels; drain, reserving 2 Tbsp. drippings. In the drippings, saute mushrooms and onion until tender, 5-7 minutes. Add garlic; cook 1 minute longer. Stir in cream and broth; bring mixture to a simmer. Gradually stir in cheese until melted.
2. In a small bowl, combine cornstarch, salt, pepper and the cold water until smooth. Stir into the soup. Bring to a boil; cook and stir for about 2 minutes or until thickened. Garnish soup with bacon and if desired, parsley.
1 CUP: 592 cal., 56g fat (33g sat. fat), 193mg chol., 649mg sod., 12g carb. (3g sugars, 1g fiber), 13g pro.

QUICK CHICKEN MINESTRONE

You'll love this flavorful soup that comes together with pantry ingredients. Dress it up by serving the dish with garlic bread.
—*Patricia Harmon, Baden, PA*

PREP: 20 min. • **COOK:** 20 min.
MAKES: 8 servings (3 qt.)

- 1 lb. boneless skinless chicken breasts, cubed
- 1 large onion, chopped
- 1 celery rib, chopped
- 1 Tbsp. olive oil
- 1 garlic clove, minced
- 3 cups reduced-sodium chicken broth
- 2½ cups water
- 1 can (15 oz.) white kidney or cannellini beans, rinsed and drained
- 1 can (14½ oz.) diced tomatoes, undrained
- 1 pkg. (5.9 oz.) chicken and garlic-flavored rice and vermicelli mix
- 1½ cups frozen vegetable blend (broccoli, red pepper, onion)
- ½ cup chopped pepperoni
- ½ tsp. dried basil
- ½ tsp. dried oregano
- ⅔ cup shredded Parmesan cheese
  Crushed red pepper flakes, optional

1. In a Dutch oven over medium heat, cook the chicken, onion and celery in oil until chicken is no longer pink. Add garlic; cook 1 minute longer. Add the broth, water, beans, tomatoes, rice and vermicelli mix, vegetables, pepperoni, basil and oregano. Bring to a boil.

2. Reduce heat; simmer, uncovered, until rice is tender, 18-20 minutes. Sprinkle each serving with cheese and, if desired, pepper flakes.

1½ CUPS: 299 cal., 10g fat (3g sat. fat), 44mg chol., 932mg sod., 31g carb. (5g sugars, 5g fiber), 22g pro.

QUICK CRANBERRY CHICKEN SALAD SANDWICHES

This tasty, filling chicken sandwich is a great way to use up leftover cranberry sauce. It will brighten your day.
—Michaela Rosenthal, Indio, CA

TAKES: 20 min. • **MAKES:** 2 servings

- 2 sandwich buns, split
- 2 tsp. butter, softened
- 2 tsp. cream cheese, softened
- 1 cup shredded cooked chicken
- 1/3 cup whole-berry cranberry sauce
- 3 Tbsp. mayonnaise
- 2 green onions, chopped
- 1 tsp. lemon juice
- 2 lettuce leaves

1. Place buns cut side up on an ungreased baking sheet. Spread the butter over bun bottoms. Broil 3-4 in. from the heat for 1-2 minutes or until golden brown. Spread cream cheese on bun tops.
2. In a small bowl, combine the chicken, cranberry sauce, mayonnaise, onions and lemon juice. Spread over bun bottoms. Top each with a lettuce leaf; replace tops.
1 SANDWICH: 520 cal., 20g fat (5g sat. fat), 79mg chol., 697mg sod., 56g carb. (18g sugars, 2g fiber), 29g pro.

> **REVIEW**
> "Great way to use turkey leftovers too! I changed it up a bit—used red onion, added chopped grapes and used homemade cranberry sauce. Allowed to sit in the fridge for a few hours and wow, the taste is spectacular! Served on dry toasted rye with romaine lettuce."
> —CINDY_NEFF, TASTEOFHOME.COM

SO-EASY GAZPACHO

My daughter got this recipe from a friend a few years ago. Now I serve it often as an first course or appetizer. It is the talk of any party!
—Lorna Sirtoli, Cortland, NY

PREP: 15 min. + chilling
MAKES: 5 servings

- 2 cups tomato juice
- 4 medium tomatoes, peeled and finely chopped
- 1/2 cup chopped seeded peeled cucumber
- 1/3 cup finely chopped onion
- 1/4 cup olive oil
- 1/4 cup cider vinegar
- 1 tsp. sugar
- 1 garlic clove, minced
- 1/4 tsp. salt
- 1/4 tsp. pepper

In a large bowl, combine all ingredients. Cover and refrigerate until chilled, at least 4 hours.
1 CUP: 146 cal., 11g fat (2g sat. fat), 0 chol., 387mg sod., 11g carb. (8g sugars, 2g fiber), 2g pro. **DIABETIC EXCHANGES:** 2 vegetable, 2 fat.
BLACK BEAN ZUCCHINI GAZPACHO: Substitute 2 large tomatoes for 4 medium. Add 1 can (15 oz.) drained rinsed black beans, 2 chopped medium zucchini and 1/4 tsp. cayenne.
REFRESHING GAZPACHO: Increase tomato juice to 4 1/2 cups. Add 2 chopped celery ribs, 1 finely chopped red onion, 1 each chopped medium sweet red pepper and green pepper, 1/4 minced fresh cilantro, 2 Tbsp. lime juice, 2 tsp. sugar and 1 tsp. Worcestershire. Serve with cubed avocado if desired.

SAUSAGE & KALE SOUP

This is my family's absolute favorite soup, and I can have it on the table in less than 45 minutes. I usually double the recipe so the flavors can blend, making the soup even better the next day.
—Dawn Rohn, Riverton, WY

PREP: 15 min. • **COOK:** 25 min. • **MAKES:** 14 servings (3½ qt.)

- 1 lb. smoked kielbasa or Polish sausage, cut into ¼-in. slices
- 3 medium Yukon Gold or red potatoes, chopped
- 2 medium onions, chopped
- 2 Tbsp. olive oil
- 1 bunch kale, trimmed and torn
- 4 garlic cloves, minced
- ¼ tsp. pepper
- ¼ tsp. salt
- 2 bay leaves
- 1 can (14½ oz.) diced tomatoes, undrained
- 1 can (15 oz.) garbanzo beans or chickpeas, rinsed and drained
- 1 carton (32 oz.) chicken broth

1. In a Dutch oven over medium-low heat, cook the sausage, potatoes and onions in oil for 5 minutes or until the sausage is heated through, stirring occasionally. Add kale; cover and cook for 2-3 minutes or until the kale is wilted. Add the garlic; cook 1 minute longer.
2. Add the remaining ingredients. Bring to a boil. Reduce heat; cover and simmer for 9-12 minutes or until potatoes are tender. Discard bay leaves.
1 CUP: 187 cal., 11g fat (3g sat. fat), 22mg chol., 706mg sod., 16g carb. (3g sugars, 3g fiber), 7g pro.

SAVORY BEEF SANDWICHES

I get this going in the slow cooker before heading to work in the morning. Then it's all ready to serve—usually with hard rolls and potato salad or another salad—as soon as my husband and I walk in. When my son moved to another state recently, I cut up a beef roast into smaller portions, repackaged it and sent seasonings for a two-person slow cooker as his housewarming present.
—Lynn Williamson, Hayward, WI

PREP: 15 min. • **COOK:** 6 hours • **MAKES:** 10 servings

- 1 Tbsp. dried minced onion
- 2 tsp. salt
- 2 tsp. garlic powder
- 2 tsp. dried oregano
- 1 tsp. dried rosemary, crushed
- 1 tsp. caraway seeds
- 1 tsp. dried marjoram
- 1 tsp. celery seed
- ¼ tsp. cayenne pepper
- 1 boneless beef chuck roast (3 to 4 lbs.), halved
- 10 sandwich rolls, split

Combine seasonings; rub over roast. Place in a 5-qt. slow cooker. Cover and cook on low for 6-8 hours or until meat is tender. Shred with a fork. Serve on rolls.
1 SANDWICH: 404 cal., 17g fat (7g sat. fat), 88mg chol., 805mg sod., 30g carb. (5g sugars, 2g fiber), 33g pro.

PRESSURE-COOKER PORK PICADILLO LETTUCE WRAPS

Warm, savory pork and cool, crisp lettuce are a combination born in culinary heaven. My spin on a lettuce wrap is chock full of scrumptious flavor and spice.
—*Janice Elder, Charlotte, NC*

PREP: 30 min. • **COOK:** 25 min. + releasing
MAKES: 2 dozen

- 3 garlic cloves, minced
- 1 Tbsp. chili powder
- 1 tsp. salt
- ½ tsp. pumpkin pie spice
- ½ tsp. ground cumin
- ½ tsp. pepper
- 2 pork tenderloins (1 lb. each)
- 1 large onion, chopped
- 1 small Granny Smith apple, peeled and chopped
- 1 small sweet red pepper, chopped
- 1 can (10 oz.) diced tomatoes and green chiles, undrained
- 1 cup water
- ½ cup golden raisins
- ½ cup chopped pimiento-stuffed olives
- 24 Bibb or Boston lettuce leaves
- ¼ cup slivered almonds, toasted

1. Mix garlic and seasonings; rub over pork. Transfer to a 6-qt. electric pressure cooker. Add onion, apple, sweet pepper, tomatoes and water. Lock lid; close the pressure-release valve. Adjust to pressure-cook on high for 25 minutes. Allow pressure to release naturally for 10 minutes, then quick-release any remaining pressure.
2. Remove pork; cool slightly. Using 2 forks, shred the meat into bite-size pieces; return to the pressure cooker
3. Select saute setting and adjust for low heat. Stir in raisins and olives; heat through. Serve in lettuce leaves; sprinkle with almonds.
1 LETTUCE WRAP: 75 cal., 3g fat (1g sat. fat), 21mg chol., 232mg sod., 5g carb. (3g sugars, 1g fiber), 8g pro.

CONTEST-WINNING EASY MINESTRONE

This recipe is special to me because it's one of the few dinners my entire family loves. And I can feel good about serving it because it's full of nutrition and low in fat.
—*Lauren Brennan, Hood River, OR*

PREP: 25 min. • **COOK:** 40 min.
MAKES: 11 servings (2¾ qt.)

- 2 large carrots, diced
- 2 celery ribs, chopped
- 1 medium onion, chopped
- 1 Tbsp. olive oil
- 1 Tbsp. butter
- 2 garlic cloves, minced
- 2 cans (14½ oz. each) reduced-sodium chicken broth
- 2 cans (8 oz. each) no-salt-added tomato sauce
- 1 can (16 oz.) kidney beans, rinsed and drained
- 1 can (15 oz.) chickpeas, rinsed and drained
- 1 can (14½ oz.) diced tomatoes, undrained
- 1½ cups shredded cabbage
- 1 Tbsp. dried basil
- 1½ tsp. dried parsley flakes
- 1 tsp. dried oregano
- ½ tsp. pepper
- 1 cup uncooked whole wheat elbow macaroni
- 11 tsp. grated Parmesan cheese

1. In a large saucepan, saute the carrots, celery and onion in oil and butter until tender. Add garlic; cook 1 minute longer.
2. Stir in the broth, tomato sauce, beans, chickpeas, tomatoes, cabbage, basil, parsley, oregano and pepper. Bring to a boil. Reduce heat; cover and simmer for 15 minutes. Add the macaroni; cook, uncovered, 6-8 minutes or until macaroni and vegetables are tender.
3. Ladle the soup into bowls. Sprinkle with Parmesan cheese.
FREEZE OPTION: Before adding cheese, freeze cooled soup in freezer containers. To use, partially thaw in refrigerator overnight. Heat through in a saucepan, stirring occasionally and adding a little broth or water if necessary.
1 CUP: 180 cal., 4g fat (1g sat. fat), 4mg chol., 443mg sod., 29g carb. (7g sugars, 7g fiber), 8g pro. **DIABETIC EXCHANGES:** 2 starch, 1 lean meat.

ITALIAN ZUCCHINI SOUP

This recipe was given to me by my neighbor. Nice and simple, it's a good way to use a lot of your zucchini and other garden vegetables. It freezes well and is great to have on hand on a cold winter day.
—*Clara Mae Chambers, Superior, NE*

- -

PREP: 5 min. • **COOK:** 1 hour 20 min.
MAKES: 8 servings (2 qt.)

1 lb. bulk Italian sausage
1 cup chopped onion
2 cups chopped celery
1 medium green pepper, chopped
2 to 4 Tbsp. sugar
2 tsp. salt
½ tsp. dried basil
½ tsp. dried oregano
½ tsp. pepper
4 cups diced tomatoes, undrained
4 cups diced zucchini
   Grated Parmesan cheese, optional

In a Dutch oven, brown the sausage with the onion; drain excess fat. Add the next 8 ingredients; cover and simmer 1 hour. Stir in zucchini and simmer 10 minutes. Sprinkle with cheese if desired.

1 CUP: 156 cal., 8g fat (3g sat. fat), 23mg chol., 1046mg sod., 15g carb. (10g sugars, 4g fiber), 8g pro.

REVIEW

"I've been making this (or some version of it, depending what ingredients I have on hand) for years. I make a huge pot and freeze portions to pull out whenever I have a taste, or need something quick for dinner or lunch."

—BOBBIEROBERTSON, TASTEOFHOME.COM

EASY SOUTHWESTERN VEGGIE WRAPS

I developed this recipe when corn was at the farmers market and big, red, juicy tomatoes were in my garden. To keep this wrap light and healthy, I use fat-free sour cream, whole grain tortillas and brown rice. If you have a meat-lover in the family, add diced cooked chicken breast.

—Cindy Beberman, Orland Park, IL

- -

TAKES: 30 min. • **MAKES:** 6 servings

1   can (15 oz.) black beans, rinsed and drained
2   large tomatoes, seeded and diced
1   cup fresh or frozen corn, thawed
1   cup cooked brown rice, cooled
⅓   cup fat-free sour cream
¼   cup minced fresh cilantro
2   shallots, chopped
1   jalapeno pepper, seeded and chopped
2   Tbsp. lime juice
½   tsp. ground cumin
½   tsp. chili powder
½   tsp. salt
6   romaine leaves
6   whole wheat tortillas (8 in.), at room temperature

Place all ingredients except romaine and tortillas in a large bowl; toss to combine. To serve, place romaine on tortillas; top with bean mixture and roll up, securing with toothpicks if desired. Cut in half.

NOTE: Wear disposable gloves when cutting hot peppers; the oils can burn skin. Avoid touching your face.

2 HALVES: 295 cal., 4g fat (0 sat. fat), 2mg chol., 525mg sod., 53g carb. (6g sugars, 7g fiber), 11g pro.

GRANDMA'S BAKED HAM SANDWICHES

Here's a tried-and-true recipe from my grandmother. I love seeing her handwriting on faded recipe cards.

—Crystal Jo Bruns, Iliff, CO

- -

TAKES: 30 min. • **MAKES:** 6 servings

2   cups cubed fully cooked ham
½   cup sliced sweet pickles
4   hard-boiled large eggs, finely chopped
¾   cup finely chopped celery
½   cup finely chopped sweet onion
¼   cup mayonnaise
6   onion rolls, split

Preheat oven to 350°. Place ham and pickles in a food processor; pulse until almost smooth. Transfer to a small bowl; stir in eggs, celery, onion and mayonnaise. Spread ½ cup over each roll bottom; replace tops. Wrap each in foil and place on a baking sheet. Bake until heated through, 10-15 minutes.

1 SANDWICH: 338 cal., 15g fat (4g sat. fat), 153mg chol., 971mg sod., 30g carb. (6g sugars, 2g fiber), 21g pro.

CAULIFLOWER BROCCOLI CHEESE SOUP

Even my husband, who's never been a big fan of broccoli, digs in to this creamy soup. It's a perfect way to enjoy the produce from our vegetable garden.
—*Betty Corliss, Stratton, CO*

TAKES: 30 min. • **MAKES:** 2 servings

- ¾ cup small cauliflowerets
- ¾ cup small broccoli florets
- ¼ cup chopped onion
- ¼ cup halved thinly sliced carrot
- 1 to 2 Tbsp. butter
- 1½ cups 2% milk, divided
- ½ tsp. chicken bouillon granules
- ¼ tsp. salt
  Dash pepper
- 2 Tbsp. all-purpose flour
- ⅓ cup cubed Velveeta

1. In a large saucepan, cook cauliflower, broccoli, onion and carrot in butter until the vegetables are crisp-tender, about 5 minutes. Stir in 1¼ cups milk, bouillon, salt and pepper. Bring to a boil. Reduce heat; simmer, uncovered, until vegetables are tender, about 5 minutes, stirring occasionally.

2. Combine flour and remaining ¼ cup milk until smooth; add to the saucepan. Bring to a boil; cook and stir until soup is thickened, 1-2 minutes. Reduce heat; add cheese and stir until melted. Serve immediately.

1 CUP: 267 cal., 15g fat (9g sat. fat), 48mg chol., 909mg sod., 23g carb. (13g sugars, 2g fiber), 12g pro.

JALAPENO SLOPPY JOES

My husband loves jalapenos—and I just love any and all heat. This savory meal with some spice is a perfect make-ahead solution for busy weeknights. Serve on buns or with your favorite chips.
—*Julie Herrera-Lemler, Rochester, MN*

PREP: 20 min. • **COOK:** 15 min.
MAKES: 8 servings

- 1 Tbsp. butter
- 1½ lbs. ground turkey
- 1 small onion, chopped
- 1 jalapeno pepper, seeded and finely chopped
- 4 garlic cloves, minced
- 1 cup ketchup
- ½ cup juice from pickled jalapeno slices
- 2 tsp. minced pickled jalapeno slices
- 2 Tbsp. brown sugar
- 2 Tbsp. Worcestershire sauce
- 1½ tsp. chili powder
- ½ tsp. crushed red pepper flakes
- ¼ tsp. salt
- 8 sesame seed hamburger buns, split

1. Heat butter in a large skillet over medium heat. Add turkey, onion, fresh jalapeno and garlic; cook until turkey is no longer pink and the vegetables are tender, 8-10 minutes, breaking up the turkey into crumbles.

2. Stir in ketchup, jalapeno juice, pickled jalapenos, brown sugar, Worcestershire sauce and seasonings. Bring to a boil. Reduce the heat; simmer, uncovered, 15-20 minutes to allow flavors to blend, stirring occasionally. Serve on buns.

FREEZE OPTION: Freeze cooled meat mixture in freezer containers. To use, partially thaw in refrigerator overnight. Heat through in a saucepan, stirring occasionally and adding a little water if necessary.

NOTE: Wear disposable gloves when cutting hot peppers; the oils can burn skin. Avoid touching your face.

1 SANDWICH: 322 cal., 11g fat (4g sat. fat), 60mg chol., 888mg sod., 37g carb. (15g sugars, 1g fiber), 22g pro.

QUICK & EASY STROMBOLI

Sandwich fixings get rolled into this dinner favorite, thanks to convenient refrigerated pizza dough. Use any combo of cheese, deli meat and veggies that you like or whatever you have on hand.
—*Catherine Cassidy, Milwaukee, WI*

TAKES: 30 min. • **MAKES:** 8 servings

- 1   tube (13.8 oz.) refrigerated pizza crust
- ½   lb. thinly sliced deli turkey
- ½   lb. thinly sliced Muenster cheese
- ¼   cup pickled pepper rings
- 2   tsp. yellow mustard
- 2   tsp. minced fresh herbs or ½ tsp. dried herbs
- 1   large egg
- 1   Tbsp. water

1. Preheat oven to 350°. Unroll pizza dough onto the bottom of a greased 15x10x1-in. baking pan. Layer with the turkey, cheese and peppers. Spread with mustard; sprinkle with herbs.

2. Roll dough into a log; pinch ends to seal. In a small bowl, combine egg and water; brush over dough. Bake until the crust is lightly browned, 20-25 minutes. Slice and serve.

1 PIECE: 271 cal., 11g fat (6g sat. fat), 42mg chol., 965mg sod., 25g carb. (3g sugars, 1g fiber), 19g pro.

> **TIP**
>
> To prevent your stromboli from getting soggy, make sure you don't stuff the dough too full. Follow the recipe directions closely and you should have the perfect texture and consistency. If you're worried about burning your stromboli, bake it on the lower rack of your oven and keep an eye on it.

HONEY PULLED PORK SUBS

Honey and ground ginger are the flavor boosters behind my no-stress sandwiches. A bottle of barbecue sauce quickly ties it all together.
—*Denise Davis, Porter, ME*

PREP: 15 min. • **COOK:** 5 hours
MAKES: 16 servings

- 1   small onion, finely chopped
- 1   boneless pork shoulder butt roast (2½ lbs.)
- 1   bottle (18 oz.) barbecue sauce
- ½   cup water
- ¼   cup honey
- 6   garlic cloves, minced
- 1   tsp. seasoned salt
- 1   tsp. ground ginger
- 8   submarine buns, split

1. Place onion and roast in a 5-qt. slow cooker. In a small bowl, combine the barbecue sauce, water, honey, garlic, seasoned salt and ginger; pour over meat. Cover and cook on high 5-6 hours or until meat is tender.

2. Remove meat; cool slightly. Shred meat with 2 forks and return to the slow cooker; heat through. Serve meat on buns. Cut the sandwiches in half.

FREEZE OPTION: Place individual portions of cooled meat mixture in freezer containers. To use, partially thaw in refrigerator overnight. Microwave, covered, on high in a microwave-safe dish until heated through, gently stirring and adding a little water if necessary. Serve meat on buns.

½ SANDWICH: 417 cal., 13g fat (4g sat. fat), 81mg chol., 867mg sod., 44g carb. (12g sugars, 2g fiber), 29g pro.

ITALIAN PULLED PORK: Omit all ingredients except roast and buns. Combine 1 Tbsp. crushed fennel seed, 1 Tbsp. steak seasoning and ½ tsp. cayenne. Rub mixture over roast. In a skillet, brown roast on all sides in 1 Tbsp. olive oil. Place roast in slow cooker. Add 2 thinly sliced medium green or sweet red peppers, 2 thinly sliced medium onions and 1 can (14½ oz.) diced tomatoes with liquid. Proceed as recipe directs.

SPEEDY CREAM OF WILD RICE SOUP

Add homemade touches to a can of potato soup to get cozy comfort food on the table quickly. The result is a thick and creamy soup textured with wild rice and flavored with smoky bacon.

—Joanne Eickhoff, Pequot Lakes, MN

TAKES: 20 min. • **MAKES:** 2 servings

- ½ cup water
- 4½ tsp. dried minced onion
- ⅔ cup condensed cream of potato soup, undiluted
- ½ cup shredded Swiss cheese
- ½ cup cooked wild rice
- ½ cup half-and-half cream
- 2 bacon strips, cooked and crumbled

In a small saucepan, bring water and onion to a boil. Reduce heat. Stir in the potato soup, cheese, wild rice and half-and-half cream; heat through (do not boil). Garnish with bacon.

1 CUP: 333 cal., 18g fat (11g sat. fat), 68mg chol., 835mg sod., 24g carb. (5g sugars, 2g fiber), 15g pro.

GOLDEN BEET & PEACH SOUP WITH TARRAGON

One summer we had a bumper crop of peaches from our two trees, so I had fun experimenting with different recipes. After seeing a beet soup recipe in a cookbook, I changed it a bit to include our homegrown golden beets and sweet peaches.

—Sue Gronholz, Beaver Dam, WI

PREP: 20 min. • **BAKE:** 40 min. + chilling
MAKES: 6 servings

- 2 lbs. fresh golden beets, peeled and cut into 1-in. cubes
- 1 Tbsp. olive oil
- 2 cups white grape-peach juice
- 2 Tbsp. cider vinegar
- ¼ cup plain Greek yogurt
- ¼ tsp. finely chopped fresh tarragon
- 2 medium fresh peaches, peeled and diced
- Fresh tarragon sprigs

1. Preheat oven to 400°. Place beets in a 15x10x1-in. baking pan. Drizzle with the olive oil; toss to coat. Roast until tender, 40-45 minutes. Cool slightly.

2. Transfer the beets to a blender or food processor. Add juice and vinegar; process until smooth. Refrigerate at least 1 hour. In a small bowl, combine Greek yogurt and chopped tarragon; refrigerate.

3. To serve, divide beet mixture among individual bowls; place a spoonful of yogurt mixture in each bowl. Top with diced peaches and tarragon sprigs.

⅔ CUP: 159 cal., 4g fat (1g sat. fat), 3mg chol., 129mg sod., 31g carb. (26g sugars, 4g fiber), 3g pro. **DIABETIC EXCHANGES:** 2 vegetable, 1 fruit, ½ fat.

> **TIP**
> For a whole different taste sensation, substitute ½ tsp. chopped fresh basil, fresh thyme or fresh chives for the tarragon. If you prefer, you can blend the herb of your choice with the beets rather than mixing it with the yogurt. For a creamier soup, add more plain Greek yogurt.

PINEAPPLE CHICKEN SALAD SANDWICHES

These are always welcome at our house. Sweet pineapple and crunchy pecans are nice additions to ordinary chicken salad.
—*Carol Alexander, Midland, MI*

TAKES: 15 min. • **MAKES:** 6 servings

- 2 cups cubed cooked chicken breast
- ½ cup crushed pineapple, drained
- ¼ cup chopped pecans
- ¼ cup chopped celery
- 2 Tbsp. finely chopped onion
- 2 Tbsp. sweet pickle relish
- ½ cup mayonnaise
- ¼ tsp. onion salt
- ¼ tsp. garlic salt
- ¼ tsp. paprika
- 6 lettuce leaves
- 6 sandwich rolls, split

In a medium bowl, combine the first 6 ingredients. In a small bowl, combine the mayonnaise, onion salt, garlic salt and paprika; add to chicken mixture and mix well. Serve on lettuce-lined rolls.

1 SANDWICH: 433 cal., 22g fat (3g sat. fat), 43mg chol., 637mg sod., 38g carb. (9g sugars, 2g fiber), 20g pro.

REVIEW

"This is a family favorite! Sometimes I add cranberries, chopped apple, almonds and a hint of curry."

—AMYMARGOLIS, TASTEOFHOME.COM

GREEN CHILE GRILLED CHEESE MELT

My daughter created a masterpiece with her ultimate grilled cheese and chiles sandwich. Want more heat? Use a 4-ounce can of diced jalapenos instead of the mild green chiles.
—*Julia Huntington, Cheyenne, WY*

TAKES: 30 min. • **MAKES:** 6 servings

- 4 oz. cream cheese, softened
- 1 cup shredded Colby-Monterey Jack cheese
- 1 cup shredded part-skim mozzarella cheese
- 1 can (4 oz.) chopped green chiles, drained
- 2 Tbsp. mayonnaise
- ¼ tsp. garlic powder
  Dash seasoned salt
- 12 slices white bread
- 6 slices tomato
- ¼ cup butter, melted

1. In a small bowl, mix the first 7 ingredients until blended. Spread over half the bread slices. Top with the tomato and remaining bread.

2. Brush outsides of sandwiches with melted butter. In a large cast-iron or other heavy skillet, toast the sandwiches in batches over medium-low heat until golden brown and heated through, 3-4 minutes on each side.

1 SANDWICH: 431 cal., 29g fat (15g sat. fat), 70mg chol., 730mg sod., 29g carb. (4g sugars, 2g fiber), 15g pro.

MUSTARD BARBECUE SHAVED HAM

This recipe makes enough ham sandwiches to feed a crowd and is so easy to put together. Have your butcher slice the ham very thin. I make this on the stovetop and serve it from my slow cooker.
—*Joyce Moynihan, Lakeville, MN*

TAKES: 30 min. • **MAKES:** 20 servings

- 1 cup cider vinegar
- 1 cup yellow mustard
- 1 cup ketchup
- ⅓ cup packed brown sugar
- ¼ cup butter, cubed
- 1 Tbsp. Worcestershire sauce
- 2 tsp. onion powder
- 1 tsp. garlic powder
- ½ tsp. cayenne pepper
- ½ tsp. pepper
- 5 lbs. shaved deli ham
- 20 sandwich rolls, split

In a Dutch oven, combine the first 10 ingredients. Cook and stir over medium heat until butter is melted. Bring to a boil; reduce heat. Simmer, covered, for 15 minutes. Add ham; heat through. Serve on rolls.

1 SANDWICH: 382 cal., 10g fat (2g sat. fat), 57mg chol., 1761mg sod., 46g carb. (15g sugars, 2g fiber), 29g pro.

In a large saucepan, cook and stir 1 lb. **ground beef**, 1 chopped **medium onion** and 1 chopped **medium green pepper** over medium heat until the meat is no longer pink; drain. Add 2-3 tsp. **chili powder**, 1 tsp. **ground cumin**, 1 can (14½ oz.) **Mexican stewed tomatoes**, 1 can (16 oz.) undrained **chili beans** and 1 cup **frozen corn**. Cover and simmer for 20 minutes. Serve with **shredded cheddar cheese** if desired.

- QUICK & EASY CHILI -

This chili recipe can be made in a flash and easily doubled or tripled to satisfy any famished family. You don't have to wait until the weekend to throw it together.

FAMILY-PLEASING SLOPPY JOE SANDWICHES

My grandchildren love these sandwiches. I like this recipe because it can be made ahead of time and can also be put in the slow cooker. I've found it freezes well, too.
—*Patricia Ringle, Edgar, WI*

- -

PREP: 10 min. • **COOK:** 45 min.
MAKES: 8 servings

- 2 lbs. ground beef
- 1 large onion, chopped
- 1¼ cups ketchup
- ½ cup water
- 1 Tbsp. brown sugar
- 1 Tbsp. white vinegar
- ½ tsp. salt
- ½ tsp. ground mustard
- ½ tsp. chili powder
- ¼ tsp. ground allspice
- 8 sandwich buns, split

1. In a Dutch oven, cook beef and onion over medium heat until meat is no longer pink; drain. Stir in the ketchup, water, brown sugar, vinegar, salt, mustard, chili powder and allspice. Bring to a boil. Reduce heat; simmer, uncovered, until heated through, 35-40 minutes.

2. Spoon about ½ cup meat mixture onto each bun.

1 SANDWICH: 441 cal., 15g fat (7g sat. fat), 56mg chol., 1016mg sod., 49g carb. (12g sugars, 3g fiber), 28g pro.

SALMON SALAD SANDWICHES

We love this combiation of salmon, cream cheese and dill tucked inside a crusty roll. The carrots and celery add a nice crunch. These are perfect to pack in lunchboxes when your kids can't face another boring sandwich.
—*Yvonne Shust, Shoal Lake, MB*

- -

TAKES: 10 min. • **MAKES:** 2 servings

- 3 oz. cream cheese, softened
- 1 Tbsp. mayonnaise
- 1 Tbsp. lemon juice
- 1 tsp. dill weed
- ¼ to ½ tsp. salt
- ⅛ tsp. pepper
- 1 can (6 oz.) pink salmon, drained, bones and skin removed
- ½ cup shredded carrot
- ½ cup chopped celery
  Lettuce leaves
- 2 whole wheat buns, split
  Sliced tomatoes

In a large bowl, beat the cream cheese, mayonnaise, lemon juice, dill, salt and pepper until smooth. Add the salmon, carrot and celery; mix well. Place a lettuce leaf and about ½ cup salmon salad on each bun and top with tomato.

1 SANDWICH: 463 cal., 29g fat (12g sat. fat), 87mg chol., 1158mg sod., 28g carb. (5g sugars, 5g fiber), 25g pro.

– 4 –

FRESH SALADS & SIDES

When you need a dish to round out your meal, look no further than these quick and easy recipes. Find simply delicious ideas for fresh salads, dressed-up veggies, cheesy potatoes, and other bold and flavorful dinnertime sidekicks.

SPECTACULAR FINGERLING POTATOES

My children absolutely love these tender mini potatoes. Fingerling potatoes can be found at the farmers market and specialty grocery stores, though Yukon Gold would work too.
—*Michelle Herren, Las Vegas, NV*

TAKES: 30 min. • **MAKES:** 5 servings

- 1 lb. fingerling potatoes
- 3 Tbsp. grated Parmesan cheese
- 3 Tbsp. minced fresh parsley
- 2 Tbsp. olive oil
- 1 Tbsp. minced fresh rosemary or 1 tsp. dried rosemary, crushed
- 1 Tbsp. butter, melted
- ¼ tsp. salt
- ¼ tsp. pepper

1. Preheat oven to 425°. Place potatoes in a large saucepan and cover with water. Bring to a boil. Reduce heat; cover and cook 10 minutes. Drain. Transfer to a greased 15x10x1-in. baking pan. Combine the remaining ingredients; drizzle over potatoes and toss to coat.

2. Bake, uncovered, 8-10 minutes or until tender, stirring once.

¾ CUP: 141 cal., 9g fat (3g sat. fat), 9mg chol., 184mg sod., 12g carb. (1g sugars, 2g fiber), 3g pro.

WHAT ELSE CAN YOU PUT ON FINGERLING POTATOES?

You can substitute or add any of your favorite fresh herbs to this recipe. Add a tablespoon of minced fresh thyme and oregano, or use a teaspoon of dried herbs. If you're a big garlic fan, add a teaspoon or two of minced garlic to the mixture as well.

TIP

CORN & BLACK BEAN SALAD

This colorful, crunchy black bean and corn salad is chock-full of easy-to-swallow nutrition that all ages will love. Try it with a variety of summer entrees, or as a wholesome salsa!
—*Krista Frank, Rhododendron, OR*

PREP: 15 min. + chilling
MAKES: 8 servings

- 1 can (15½ oz.) black-eyed peas, rinsed and drained
- 1 can (15 oz.) black beans, rinsed and drained
- 2 large tomatoes, finely chopped
- 1½ cups fresh or frozen corn
- ½ cup finely chopped red onion
- ¼ cup minced fresh cilantro
- 2 garlic cloves, minced

DRESSING
- 2 Tbsp. sugar
- 2 Tbsp. white vinegar
- 2 Tbsp. canola oil
- 1½ tsp. lime juice
- ¼ tsp. salt
- ¼ tsp. ground cumin
- ¼ tsp. pepper

In a large bowl, combine the first 7 ingredients. In a small bowl, whisk dressing ingredients; pour over corn mixture and toss to coat. Cover and refrigerate at least 1 hour. Stir before serving. Serve with a slotted spoon.

¾ CUP: 167 cal., 4g fat (0 sat. fat), 0 chol., 244mg sod., 27g carb. (8g sugars, 5g fiber), 7g pro. **DIABETIC EXCHANGES:** 2 starch, 1 fat.

SIMPLE AU GRATIN POTATOES

These cheesy spuds are always welcome at our table, and they're so simple to make. They're a perfect complement to ham, but they also go well with pork, chicken and other entrees.

—Cris O'Brien, Virginia Beach, VA

- -

PREP: 20 min. • **BAKE:** 1½ hours
MAKES: 8 servings

  3 Tbsp. butter
  3 Tbsp. all-purpose flour
1½ tsp. salt
⅛ tsp. pepper
  2 cups 2% milk
  1 cup shredded cheddar cheese
  5 cups thinly sliced peeled potatoes
      (about 6 medium)
½ cup chopped onion
      Additional pepper, optional

1. Preheat oven to 350°. In a large saucepan, melt butter over low heat. Stir in flour, salt and pepper until smooth. Gradually add milk. Bring to a boil; cook and stir 2 minutes or until thickened. Remove from heat; stir in cheese until melted. Add potatoes and onion.
2. Transfer to a greased 2-qt. baking dish. Cover and bake 1 hour. Uncover; bake 30-40 minutes or until the potatoes are tender. If desired, top the potatoes with additional pepper.
¾ CUP: 224 cal., 10g fat (7g sat. fat), 35mg chol., 605mg sod., 26g carb. (4g sugars, 2g fiber), 7g pro.

WHY DID MY POTATOES AU GRATIN CURDLE?

Curdling can occur when high heat affects the fat in dairy. In this recipe, we thicken the milk with flour to prevent curdling. Starch will also help, so make sure to use a high-starch potato like a russet.

TIP

ACINI DI PEPE SALAD

Looking for a quick lunch idea or fun new side dish? Try this blend of veggies, tiny pasta and juicy pineapple bits for a change-of-pace salad that's jam-packed with flavor.
—*June Herke, Watertown, SD*

PREP: 20 min. + chilling • **MAKES:** 2 servings

- ¼ cup uncooked acini di pepe pasta
- ¼ cup mayonnaise
- ¼ cup whipped topping
- 1 Tbsp. finely chopped onion
  Dash celery seed
- ¾ cup chopped fresh cauliflower
- 1 snack-size cup (4 oz.) pineapple tidbits, drained
- ⅓ cup frozen peas, partially thawed
- 1 Tbsp. raisins
  Optional: Lettuce leaves and minced fresh parsley

Cook pasta according to package directions; drain and rinse in cold water. In a small bowl, combine mayonnaise, whipped topping, onion and celery seed. Add cauliflower, pineapple, peas, raisins and pasta; toss to coat. Cover and refrigerate 1 hour. If desired, serve on a lettuce-lined plate and sprinkle with parsley.

¾ CUP: 295 cal., 11g fat (3g sat. fat), 11mg chol., 284mg sod., 42g carb. (14g sugars, 4g fiber), 7g pro.

STIR-FRIED ZUCCHINI

I plant many vegetables to use in my cooking. Zucchini is among our favorites and often grows in abundance. This dish is always a hit at our house.
—*Deborah Elliot, Ridge Spring, SC*

TAKES: 10 min. • **MAKES:** 8 servings

- 2 lbs. sliced zucchini
- 2 garlic cloves, minced
- ¼ cup olive oil
- 1 tsp. salt
- ½ tsp. Italian seasoning
- ¼ tsp. pepper

In a large cast-iron or other heavy skillet, saute the zucchini and garlic in oil until zucchini is crisp-tender, about 5 minutes. Sprinkle with seasonings. Serve immediately.

½ CUP: 77 cal., 7g fat (1g sat. fat), 0 chol., 299mg sod., 4g carb. (2g sugars, 1g fiber), 1g pro.

TIP

WHAT OTHER SEASONINGS CAN YOU ADD TO STIR-FRIED ZUCCHINI?

Try adding red chili pepper flakes for a little extra heat. Or, throw in a dash of an herb like thyme or rosemary. You can also add your favorite homemade spice blend.

BLACK-EYED PEAS & HAM

Every New Year's Day we have these slow-cooked black-eyed peas to bring good luck for the coming year.
—*Dawn Legler, Fort Morgan, CO*

PREP: 20 min. + soaking • **COOK:** 5 hours
MAKES: 12 servings

- 1 pkg. (16 oz.) dried black-eyed peas, rinsed and sorted
- ½ lb. fully cooked boneless ham, finely chopped
- 1 medium onion, finely chopped
- 1 medium sweet red pepper, finely chopped
- 5 bacon strips, cooked and crumbled
- 1 large jalapeno pepper, seeded and finely chopped
- 2 garlic cloves, minced
- 1½ tsp. ground cumin
- 1 tsp. reduced-sodium chicken bouillon granules
- ½ tsp. salt
- ½ tsp. cayenne pepper
- ¼ tsp. pepper
- 6 cups water
  Minced fresh cilantro, optional
  Hot cooked rice

1. Soak black-eyed peas according to the package directions.
2. Transfer peas to a 6-qt. slow cooker; add the next 12 ingredients. Cover and cook on low 5-7 hours, until peas are tender. Sprinkle with cilantro if desired. Serve with rice.
NOTE: Wear disposable gloves when cutting hot peppers; the oils can burn skin. Avoid touching your face.
¾ CUP: 170 cal., 3g fat (1g sat. fat), 13mg chol., 386mg sod., 24g carb. (5g sugars, 7g fiber), 13g pro. **DIABETIC EXCHANGES:** 1½ starch, 1 lean meat.

AIR-FRYER BAKED POTATOES

By rubbing the potatoes with a butter-garlic mixture before cooking them, you end up with a very flavorful potato skin. It's just a little incentive to eat what I think is the best part of the potato.
—*Teresa Emrick, Tipp City, OH*

PREP: 10 min. • **COOK:** 35 min.
MAKES: 4 servings

- 4 medium russet potatoes
- 2 Tbsp. butter, softened
- 2 garlic cloves, minced
- ¼ tsp. salt
- ¼ tsp. pepper
  Optional: Sour cream, butter, crumbled bacon, minced chives, guacamole, shredded cheddar cheese and minced fresh cilantro

1. Preheat air fryer to 400°. Scrub the potatoes; pierce each several times with a fork. In a small bowl, mix butter, garlic, salt and pepper. Rub potatoes with butter mixture. Wrap each potato tightly in a piece of foil.
2. Place potatoes in a single layer on tray in air-fryer basket. Cook until fork tender, 35-45 minutes, rotating halfway through.
NOTE: In our testing, we find cook times vary dramatically between brands of air fryers. As a result, we give wider than normal ranges on suggested cook times. Begin checking at the first time listed and adjust as needed.
1 POTATO: 217 cal., 6g fat (4g sat. fat), 15mg chol., 206mg sod., 38g carb. (2g sugars, 5g fiber), 5g pro.

> TIP
>
> ### CAN YOU USE OTHER KINDS OF POTATOES TO MAKE AIR-FRYER BAKED POTATOES?
>
> Russet potatoes are preferred for baked potatoes—they bake up with a nice crisp skin and fluffy interior. However, if you prefer a different kind of potato, you can certainly make a substitute. Keep in mind that not all potatoes bake the same, so you may need to adjust your cooking time a bit.

SUMMER SQUASH & ZUCCHINI SIDE DISH

I'm trying to cut my risk for cardiac disease by changing the way I eat. My colorful side dish is packed with as much nutrition as fresh-picked flavor.
—*Marlene Agnelly, Ocean Springs, MS*

TAKES: 30 min. • **MAKES:** 6 servings

1 Tbsp. olive oil
1 medium yellow summer squash, quartered and sliced
1 medium zucchini, quartered and sliced
1 medium onion, chopped
1 medium sweet red pepper, cut into 1-in. pieces
2 garlic cloves, minced
½ tsp. salt-free spicy seasoning blend
¼ tsp. salt
⅛ tsp. pepper
1 medium tomato, chopped

In a large skillet, heat oil over medium heat; add yellow squash, zucchini, onion and red pepper. Cook and stir 5 minutes. Add garlic and seasonings; cook until vegetables are crisp-tender, 2-3 minutes. Stir in tomato; heat through.

⅔ CUP: 50 cal., 3g fat (0 sat. fat), 0 chol., 106mg sod., 6g carb. (4g sugars, 2g fiber), 1g pro. **DIABETIC EXCHANGES:** 1 vegetable, ½ fat.

> **TIP**
>
> **HOW DO YOU PICK THE BEST ZUCCHINI AND SUMMER SQUASH?**
> The best squash should be firm and full of vibrant color. And don't just reach for the largest ones—smaller squash can be more tender and flavorful.

GARLIC-BUTTERED GREEN BEANS

These dressed-up beans are simple to make but look and taste special. They're a perfect side dish for nearly any meal.
—*Adeline Piscitelli, Sayreville, NJ*

TAKES: 15 min. • **MAKES:** 6 servings

1 lb. fresh or frozen green beans
½ cup sliced fresh mushrooms
6 Tbsp. butter, cubed
2 to 3 tsp. onion powder
1 to 1½ tsp. garlic powder
Salt and pepper to taste

1. Place green beans in a large saucepan, cover with water. Bring to a boil; cover and cook until crisp-tender, 8-10 minutes.
2. Meanwhile, in a large skillet, saute mushrooms in butter until tender, 2-3 minutes. Add onion powder and garlic powder. Drain beans; add to skillet and toss. Season with salt and pepper.

¾ CUP: 131 cal., 12g fat (7g sat. fat), 31mg chol., 97mg sod., 7g carb. (2g sugars, 3g fiber), 2g pro.

QUICK CORN SALAD

This sensational salad is a delight to serve because you can make it ahead and it's an easy way to put garden bounty to good use. With colorful ingredients like corn, tomato and green pepper, it's also pretty in the bowl and on your plate.

—*Rita Reifenstein, Evans City, PA*

TAKES: 10 min. • **MAKES:** 4 servings

- 2 cups fresh or frozen sweet corn
- ¾ cup chopped tomato
- ½ cup chopped green pepper
- ½ cup chopped celery
- ¼ cup chopped onion
- ¼ cup ranch salad dressing

In a large bowl, combine vegetables; stir in dressing. Cover and refrigerate salad until serving.

¾ CUP: 138 cal., 7g fat (1g sat. fat), 2mg chol., 169mg sod., 18g carb. (7g sugars, 3g fiber), 3g pro. **DIABETIC EXCHANGES:** 1.5 fat, 1 starch.

REVIEW

"This is such a great recipe to use the great bounty of our summer garden. Of course homemade ranch dressing is needed to make the best salad."

—BUTTERMILK MAID, TASTEOFHOME.COM

FRESH THAI ASPARAGUS, KALE & GARLICKY MUSHROOMS

Hit the local farmers market and stock up! This simple side is a perfect complement to any meal. The fish sauce gives it a nice depth of flavor without much effort.
—Julie Peterson, Crofton, MD

- -

TAKES: 30 min. • **MAKES:** 4 servings

- 3 Tbsp. coconut oil
- 10 oz. medium fresh mushrooms, quartered (about 4 cups)
- 1 lb. fresh asparagus, trimmed and cut into 1½-in. pieces
- 2 garlic cloves, thinly sliced
- ½ tsp. dried oregano
- ¼ tsp. salt
- ¼ tsp. pepper
- 2 cups chopped fresh kale
- 2 tsp. fish sauce or soy sauce
- 1 tsp. balsamic vinegar
  Toasted sesame seeds, optional

In a large cast-iron or other heavy skillet, heat oil over medium-high heat. Add the mushrooms; cook, stirring occasionally, until lightly browned, 4-6 minutes. Add the asparagus, garlic, oregano, salt and pepper; cook and stir until asparagus is crisp-tender, 2-4 minutes. Stir in kale; cook and stir until wilted, 2-4 minutes. Remove from heat; stir in fish sauce and vinegar. If desired, top with sesame seeds.
¾ CUP: 129 cal., 11g fat (9g sat. fat), 0 chol., 383mg sod., 7g carb. (1g sugars, 1g fiber), 4g pro.

> **TIP**
> One of the key ingredients to this side dish—besides the tasty mix of herbs and spices—is the fish sauce. This convenient item is a smart and easy way to supply a burst of rich flavor even when you're short on time. Look for it in the condiment aisle or Asian foods section in most grocery stores.

PRESSURE-COOKER ROSEMARY BEETS

We're a family of beet eaters. For a simple side, I use a one-dish cooker and let the beets mellow with rosemary and thyme.
—Nancy Heishman, Las Vegas, NV

- -

PREP: 20 min.
COOK: 20 min. + releasing
MAKES: 8 servings

- 5 large fresh beets (about 3½ lbs.)
- 1 Tbsp. olive oil
- 1 medium red onion, chopped
- 2 garlic cloves, minced
- 1 medium orange, peeled and chopped
- ⅓ cup honey
- ¼ cup white balsamic vinegar
- 1 Tbsp. minced fresh rosemary or 1 tsp. dried rosemary, crushed
- 2 tsp. minced fresh thyme or ¾ tsp. dried thyme
- ¾ tsp. salt
- ½ tsp. Chinese five-spice powder
- ½ tsp. coarsely ground pepper
- 1 cup crumbled feta cheese

1. Place trivet insert and 1 cup water in a 6-qt. electric pressure cooker. Scrub beets, trimming tops to 1 in.; set on trivet. Lock lid; close pressure-release valve. Adjust to pressure-cook on high for 20 minutes. Let pressure release naturally.

2. Remove beets and cool enough to handle. Remove trivet; discard cooking juices. Wipe pot clean. Peel and cut beets into wedges.

3. Select saute setting; adjust for medium heat. Add oil. When oil is hot, cook and stir onion until crisp-tender, 4-5 minutes. Add garlic; cook 1 minute longer. Stir in orange, honey, vinegar, rosemary, thyme, salt, five-spice powder, pepper and beets; heat through. Press cancel. Serve warm, or refrigerate and serve cold. Serve with a slotted spoon; sprinkle with cheese.
¾ CUP: 200 cal., 4g fat (2g sat. fat), 8mg chol., 511mg sod., 37g carb. (31g sugars, 5g fiber), 6g pro. **DIABETIC EXCHANGES:** 2 vegetable, 1 starch, 1 fat.

EASY ITALIAN POTATO SALAD

You'll want to take this simple-to-assemble potato salad to all your picnics and outings. It's always on the menu when my tomato plants yield a bumper crop. Feel free to improvise by adding other fresh vegetables.

—*Jeannette Macera, Utica, NY*

TAKES: 20 min. • **MAKES:** 10 servings

- 6 medium red potatoes, cooked and cut into 1-in. pieces
- 2 garlic cloves, minced
- ½ cup chopped red onion
- 3 to 4 plum tomatoes, quartered
- ⅓ cup olive oil
- 3 to 4 fresh basil leaves, chopped
- 1 jar (5¾ oz.) pimiento-stuffed olives, drained and halved
- 1 tsp. dried oregano
- 1½ tsp. salt
- ¼ tsp. pepper

In a large bowl, combine all ingredients; toss to coat. Cover and refrigerate until serving.

¾ CUP: 170 cal., 10g fat (1g sat. fat), 0 chol., 638mg sod., 19g carb. (2g sugars, 2g fiber), 2g pro. **DIABETIC EXCHANGES:** 2 fat, 1 starch.

TIP

SHOULD YOU PEEL THE POTATOES?

Red potatoes do not need to be peeled for potato salad recipes. The skin is thin and tender enough to eat, but you can peel them before cooking if you like. Just make sure to use the potato peeler the right way: holding the potato in your nondominant hand and peeling away from you.

SWEET ONION SPOON BREAD

This unique recipe has been a family favorite for years. The layers of tangy cheese, sour cream and sweet onions in the moist cornbread taste so amazing together. Add chopped green chiles for extra zip.

—*Heather Thomas, Fredericksburg, VA*

PREP: 15 min. • **BAKE:** 25 min. • **MAKES:** 9 servings

- 1⅓ cups chopped sweet onions
- 1 Tbsp. butter
- 1 can (8¼ oz.) cream-style corn
- 1 pkg. (8½ oz.) cornbread/muffin mix
- 2 large egg whites, lightly beaten
- 2 Tbsp. fat-free milk
- ½ cup reduced-fat sour cream
- ⅓ cup shredded sharp cheddar cheese

1. In a small nonstick skillet, saute onions in butter until tender; set aside.

2. Meanwhile, in a large bowl, combine the corn, muffin mix, egg whites and milk. Pour into a 9-in. square baking dish coated with cooking spray. Combine sour cream and onions; spread over batter. Sprinkle with cheese.

3. Bake, uncovered, at 350° until a toothpick inserted in the center comes out clean, 25-30 minutes.

1 PIECE: 191 cal., 6g fat (3g sat. fat), 18mg chol., 361mg sod., 29g carb. (10g sugars, 1g fiber), 6g pro. **DIABETIC EXCHANGES:** 2 starch, ½ fat.

EASY BROCCOLI SALAD

After sampling this salad at a barbecue, I was given the recipe but without any measurements. I refined the salad at home, and now it's a regular.
—*Sara Sherlock, Port Alice, BC*

- -

PREP: 15 min. + chilling
MAKES: 2 servings

1½ cups fresh broccoli florets
¾ cup shredded cheddar cheese
4 bacon strips, cooked and crumbled
¼ cup finely chopped onion
3 Tbsp. mayonnaise
2 Tbsp. white vinegar
1 Tbsp. sugar

In a bowl, combine broccoli, cheese, bacon and onion. In another bowl, whisk mayonnaise, vinegar and sugar. Pour over broccoli mixture and toss to coat. Cover and refrigerate salad for at least 1 hour before serving.

¾ CUP: 420 cal., 35g fat (13g sat. fat), 63mg chol., 585mg sod., 12g carb. (8g sugars, 2g fiber), 15g pro.

MINTY SUGAR SNAP PEAS

Fresh mint adds a lively touch to cooked sugar snap peas. It's also nice on green beans or carrots.
—*Alice Kaldahl, Ray, ND*

- -

TAKES: 10 min. • **MAKES:** 4 servings

3 cups fresh sugar snap peas, trimmed
¼ tsp. sugar
2 to 3 Tbsp. minced fresh mint
2 Tbsp. butter

Place 1 in. of water in a large skillet. Add peas and sugar; bring to a boil. Reduce heat; simmer, covered, until peas are crisp-tender, 4-5 minutes; drain. Stir in mint and butter.

¾ CUP: 102 cal., 6g fat (4g sat. fat), 15mg chol., 45mg sod., 9g carb. (4g sugars, 3g fiber), 4g pro. **DIABETIC EXCHANGES:** 2 vegetable, 1½ fat.

SANTA FE SALAD

My family loves this colorful salad. The zippy dressing and mix of crunchy veggies with beans is a winning combination.
—*Gail Park, Newport News, VA*

TAKES: 30 min. • **MAKES:** 10 servings

2½ cups cut fresh green beans
1 cup minced fresh cilantro
¼ cup fat-free sour cream
2 Tbsp. lime juice
2 Tbsp. balsamic vinegar
2 garlic cloves, minced
1½ tsp. ground cumin
¼ tsp. salt
    Dash cayenne pepper
2 cups frozen corn, thawed
1 can (15 oz.) pinto beans, rinsed and drained
1 can (15 oz.) black beans, rinsed and drained
1 small sweet red pepper, finely chopped
1 small red onion, chopped
1 can (4 oz.) chopped green chiles
1 can (2¼ oz.) sliced ripe olives, drained
½ cup shredded reduced-fat cheddar cheese

1. Place green beans in a small saucepan and cover with water. Bring to a boil; cover and cook for 3-5 minutes or until crisp-tender. Drain and immediately place beans in ice water. Drain and pat dry.
2. For dressing, in a small bowl, combine the cilantro, sour cream, lime juice, vinegar, garlic, cumin, salt and cayenne.
3. In a large bowl, combine the green beans, corn, pinto beans, black beans, red pepper, onion, chiles and olives. Sprinkle with cheese. Pour dressing over salad; toss gently to coat. Cover and refrigerate until serving.
¾ CUP: 151 cal., 2g fat (1g sat. fat), 5mg chol., 374mg sod., 26g carb. (4g sugars, 6g fiber), 8g pro.

TIP
This salad is best if eaten within 24-48 hours. If you make it a day ahead, the beans will soak up the vinegar and other flavors in the dressing—making it taste even better the next day.

LAYERED VEGGIE TORTELLINI SALAD

Tortellini and a Parmesan dressing give this layered salad an unexpected twist. It's great for a potluck.
—*Dennis Vitale, New Preston, CT*

TAKES: 30 min. • **MAKES:** 10 servings

1 pkg. (16 oz.) frozen cheese tortellini
2 cups fresh broccoli florets
2 cups cherry tomatoes, quartered
2 celery ribs, finely chopped
1 can (2¼ oz.) sliced ripe olives, drained
1 cup shredded cheddar cheese
PARMESAN DRESSING
¾ cup mayonnaise
3 Tbsp. grated Parmesan cheese
2 Tbsp. lemon juice
2 Tbsp. heavy whipping cream
1 tsp. dried thyme

1. Cook tortellini according to package directions; drain and rinse in cold water. In a 2½-qt. glass bowl, layer the tortellini, broccoli, tomatoes, celery, olives and cheddar cheese.
2. In a small bowl, whisk the dressing ingredients; spoon over salad or serve alongside. Cover and refrigerate until ready to serve.
1 CUP: 286 cal., 20g fat (6g sat. fat), 32mg chol., 374mg sod., 18g carb. (2g sugars, 2g fiber), 8g pro.

MISO-BUTTERED SUCCOTASH

The miso paste used in this super simple recipe gives depth and a hint of savoriness to canned or fresh vegetables. To brighten the flavor profile even more, you could add a splash of your favorite white wine.
—*William Milton III, Clemson, SC*

TAKES: 20 min. • **MAKES:** 6 servings

- 2 tsp. canola oil
- 1 small red onion, chopped
- 2 cans (15¼ oz. each) whole kernel corn, drained
- 1½ cups frozen shelled edamame, thawed
- ½ medium sweet red pepper, chopped (about ½ cup)
- 2 Tbsp. unsalted butter, softened
- 1 tsp. white miso paste
- 3 green onions, thinly sliced
  Coarsely ground pepper

1. In a large skillet, heat oil over medium-high heat. Add red onion; cook and stir until crisp-tender, 2-3 minutes. Add corn, edamame and red pepper. Cook until vegetables reach desired tenderness, 4-6 minutes longer.

2. In a small bowl, mix butter and miso paste until combined; stir into pan until melted. Sprinkle with green onions and pepper before serving.

¾ CUP: 193 cal., 9g fat (3g sat. fat), 10mg chol., 464mg sod., 20g carb. (11g sugars, 6g fiber), 8g pro.

TIP

White miso paste has a subtle, salty flavor. You can increase the amount of miso in this recipe for more flavor. If you have any leftover miso paste, try adding it to a homemade soup. Or mix a bit of leftover miso paste into cold spreads—mix it with mayonnaise, cream cheese or sour cream, for example—to boost flavor. It can give salad dressings and marinades a lift too.

PRESSURE-COOKER BBQ BAKED BEANS

I was under doctor's orders to reduce the amount of sodium I was eating, but I just couldn't part with some of my favorite foods. After many experiments I came up with this potluck favorite—now everyone's happy!
—*Sherrel Hendrix, Arkadelphia, AR*

PREP: 10 min. + soaking
COOK: 35 min. + releasing
MAKES: 12 servings

- 1 pkg. (16 oz.) dried great northern beans
- 2 smoked ham hocks (about ½ lb. each)
- 2 cups water
- 1 medium onion, chopped
- 2 tsp. garlic powder, divided
- 2 tsp. onion powder, divided
- 1 cup barbecue sauce
- ¾ cup packed brown sugar
- ½ tsp. ground nutmeg
- ¼ tsp. ground cloves
- 2 tsp. hot pepper sauce, optional

1. Rinse and sort beans. Transfer to a 6-qt. electric pressure cooker. Add ham hocks, water, onion, 1 tsp. garlic powder and 1 tsp. onion powder. Lock lid; close pressure-release valve. Adjust to pressure-cook on high for 30 minutes. Let pressure naturally release for 10 minutes; quick-release any remaining pressure.

2. Remove ham hocks; cool slightly. Cut meat into small cubes, discarding bones; return meat to pressure cooker. Stir in barbecue sauce, brown sugar, nutmeg, cloves, remaining garlic powder, remaining onion powder and, if desired, pepper sauce. Lock lid; close pressure-release valve. Adjust to pressure-cook on high for 3 minutes. Let pressure naturally release for 5 minutes; quick-release any remaining pressure.

½ CUP: 238 cal., 1g fat (0 sat. fat), 4mg chol., 347mg sod., 48g carb. (22g sugars, 8g fiber), 10g pro.

PICKLED CABBAGE

My mother picked up this recipe in Pennsylvania, and as long as I can remember, there was always a bucket of slaw in the refrigerator. Now I have an old stoneware butter crock in my refrigerator filled with the same!

—*Marion Glasgow, Lavallette, NJ*

PREP: 10 min. + chilling • **MAKES:** 4 servings

- 2½ cups shredded cabbage
- ½ medium green pepper, diced
- 1 celery rib, diced
- ¾ cup sugar
- ½ cup vinegar
- ½ tsp. celery seed
- ½ tsp. salt
- ⅛ tsp. pepper

In a large bowl, combine all ingredients. Toss to coat. Cover and refrigerate at least 1 hour before serving.

⅔ CUP: 31 cal., 0 fat (0 sat. fat), 0 chol., 11mg sod., 6g carb. (4g sugars, 1g fiber), 1g pro.

TIP

HOW LONG WILL THIS PICKLED CABBAGE LAST?
Since this recipe is a quick pickled vegetable, not processed and canned, it is not shelf-stable and must be stored in the refrigerator. While this pickled cabbage won't last as long if it were canned, it will safely keep for up to 2 weeks in your refrigerator if stored in an airtight container.

EASY SAUTEED GREEN BEANS

Skip the standard can of green beans and try this recipe that's delicious and simple to whip up on a busy weeknight. For extra heartiness, add cooked crumbled bacon and sprinkle with toasted sesame seeds.

—*Nick Iverson, Denver, CO*

TAKES: 15 min. • **MAKES:** 4 servings

- 1 lb. fresh green beans, trimmed
- ½ cup water
- 2 Tbsp. butter
- ½ tsp. salt
- ¼ tsp. pepper

1. Place beans and water in a large skillet. Bring to a boil; cook covered until beans are crisp tender, 4-6 minutes. Drain.
2. In now-empty skillet, melt butter over medium-high heat. Add beans; cook and stir until beans are tender, 1-2 minutes. Sprinkle with salt and pepper.

1 SERVING: 86 cal., 6g fat (4g sat. fat), 15mg chol., 347mg sod., 8g carb. (3g sugars, 4g fiber), 2g pro. **DIABETIC EXCHANGES:** 1½ fat, 1 vegetable.

SPECIAL RADICCHIO-SPINACH SALAD

When you hear of mint, chipotle pepper and honey blended together, you may wonder how it will taste. Prepare to be amazed—my spicy-sweet salad is simply delicious!
—*Roxanne Chan, Albany, CA*

TAKES: 20 min. • **MAKES:** 12 servings

- 6 cups fresh baby spinach
- 1 head radicchio, torn
- 2 cups fresh raspberries
- ½ cup raisins
- ¼ cup pine nuts, toasted
- ¼ cup thinly sliced red onion
- ¼ cup minced fresh mint
- 3 Tbsp. lime juice
- 2 Tbsp. olive oil
- 2 tsp. honey
- 1½ to 3 tsp. chopped chipotle pepper in adobo sauce
- ¼ tsp. salt
- ½ cup crumbled feta cheese

In a large salad bowl, combine the first 7 ingredients. In a small saucepan over medium heat, combine lime juice, oil, honey, chipotle pepper and salt. Cook and stir until blended and heated through. Immediately pour over salad; toss to coat. Sprinkle with cheese.

NOTE: Also known as pignolia or pinyon, the pine nut is the small seed from one of several pine tree varieties. They are small elongated ivory-colored nuts measuring about ⅜ in. long, with a soft texture and a buttery flavor. Frequently used in Italian dishes and sauces such as pesto, pine nuts are often toasted to enhance their flavor.

¾ CUP: 92 cal., 5g fat (1g sat. fat), 3mg chol., 117mg sod., 11g carb. (6g sugars, 3g fiber), 3g pro. **DIABETIC EXCHANGES:** 1 vegetable, 1 fat, ½ starch.

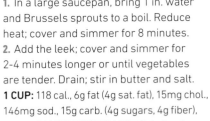

BRUSSELS SPROUTS WITH LEEKS

My husband and I both love Brussels sprouts, so I often experiment with different combinations to enhance the taste. We discovered that leeks give the sprouts a special flavor.
—*Patricia Mickelson, San Jose, CA*

- -

TAKES: 15 min. • **MAKES:** 2 servings

- 10 Brussels sprouts, trimmed and halved
- 1 medium leek (white portion only), thinly sliced
- 1 Tbsp. butter
  Dash salt

1. In a large saucepan, bring 1 in. water and Brussels sprouts to a boil. Reduce heat; cover and simmer for 8 minutes.
2. Add the leek; cover and simmer for 2-4 minutes longer or until vegetables are tender. Drain; stir in butter and salt.
1 CUP: 118 cal., 6g fat (4g sat. fat), 15mg chol., 146mg sod., 15g carb. (4g sugars, 4g fiber), 4g pro. **DIABETIC EXCHANGES:** 1 starch, 1 fat.

SLOW-COOKED SUMMER SQUASH

We love squash, but I got tired of fixing just plain squash and cheese. I decided to jazz it up a bit. This was a huge hit with the family.
—*Joan Hallford, North Richland Hills, TX*

- -

PREP: 15 min. • **COOK:** 2½ hours
MAKES: 8 servings

- 1 lb. medium yellow summer squash
- 1 lb. medium zucchini
- 2 medium tomatoes, chopped
- ¼ cup thinly sliced green onions
- ½ tsp. salt
- ¼ tsp. pepper
- 1 cup vegetable broth
- 1½ cups Caesar salad croutons, coarsely crushed
- ½ cup shredded cheddar cheese
- 4 bacon strips, cooked and crumbled

1. Cut the squash and zucchini into ¼-in.-thick slices. In a 3- or 4-qt. slow cooker, combine squash, zucchini, tomatoes and green onions. Add salt, pepper and broth. Cook, covered, on low until tender, 2½-3½ hours. Remove with a slotted spoon.
2. To serve, top vegetables with croutons, cheese and bacon.
¾ CUP: 111 cal., 6g fat (2g sat. fat), 12mg chol., 442mg sod., 10g carb. (4g sugars, 2g fiber), 6g pro. **DIABETIC EXCHANGES:** 1 vegetable, 1 fat.

TIP
If you prefer, substitute 1½ cups crushed buttery crackers for the croutons. To take this dish to potlucks, place the croutons, cheese and bacon in resealable bags and top once you arrive.

Combine 3 cups unpeeled, chopped **Gala** or **Honeycrisp apples** (about 2 large), 2 cups **celery**, ¼ cup **raisins** and ¼ cup chopped, toasted **walnuts**. Add ⅓ cup **reduced-fat mayonnaise** and ⅓ cup **plain yogurt**; toss to coat. Refrigerate, covered, until serving.

- SIMPLE WALDORF SALAD -
This delicious simple salad couldn't be easier! It's great as a first course for a celebration feast, or as a light side dish any time of year.

CHARD WITH BACON-CITRUS SAUCE
Chard is a leafy veggie often used in Mediterranean cooking. I dress it with orange juice and bacon, and my family gobbles it up.
—Teri Rasey, Cadillac, MI

- -

TAKES: 25 min. • **MAKES:** 6 servings

  ½ lb. thick-sliced peppered bacon strips
  2 lbs. rainbow Swiss chard, chopped
  1 cup orange juice
  2 Tbsp. butter
  4 tsp. grated orange zest
  ⅛ tsp. salt
  ⅛ tsp. pepper

1. In a large cast-iron or other heavy skillet, cook bacon over medium heat until crisp; drain on paper towels. Discard all but 1 Tbsp. drippings. Cut bacon into small pieces.
2. Add the chard to drippings; cook and stir just until wilted, 5-6 minutes. Add remaining ingredients; cook 1-2 minutes, stirring occasionally. Top with bacon.
½ CUP: 162 cal., 11g fat (5g sat. fat), 22mg chol., 655mg sod., 10g carb. (5g sugars, 3g fiber), 7g pro.

QUICK MACARONI SALAD
You can't go wrong with this time-tested winner. Here it is pared down for two.
—Carma Blosser, Livermore, CO

- -

TAKES: 20 min. • **MAKES:** 2 servings

  ¾ cup uncooked elbow macaroni
  ⅓ cup frozen peas
  ⅓ cup cubed cheddar cheese
  ¼ cup mayonnaise
  3 Tbsp. chopped celery
  1 tsp. finely chopped onion
  1 tsp. diced pimientos
  1 tsp. finely chopped green pepper
  ⅛ tsp. salt

1. Cook macaroni according to package directions, adding the peas during the last 2 minutes of cooking. Drain and rinse in cold water.
2. In a small bowl, combine the remaining ingredients. Stir in macaroni and peas. Chill until serving.
1 CUP: 276 cal., 15g fat (4g sat. fat), 24mg chol., 544mg sod., 28g carb. (4g sugars, 2g fiber), 10g pro.

- 5 -

EASY BREADS

Bring the aroma of homemade bread to your kitchen by baking these time-honored beauties, including classic loaves, muffins, biscuits, cornbread, quick breads, garlic bread and other fuss-free favorites. Some are even easier with the help of a bread machine, air fryer or slow cooker!

STRAWBERRY BREAD

My husband and I are strawberry lovers, so each spring we pick about 30 quarts. This recipe makes two delicious loaves. One we eat right away; the other we freeze to serve when company comes.
—*Shirley Durham, Poplar Bluff, MO*

PREP: 15 min. • **BAKE:** 70 min. + cooling
MAKES: 2 loaves (16 pieces each)

    3   cups all-purpose flour
    2   cups sugar
    1   tsp. baking soda
    1   tsp. ground cinnamon
    1   tsp. salt
    1   large egg plus 3 large egg whites,
        room temperature, lightly beaten
 1¼   cups vegetable oil
    2   cups chopped fresh or frozen strawberries
 1½   cups chopped walnuts

1. In a large bowl, combine flour, sugar, baking soda, cinnamon and salt. Add egg, egg whites and oil; stir just until moistened. Fold in strawberries and nuts. Spoon into 2 greased 8x4-in. loaf pans.
2. Bake at 350° for 70 minutes or until bread tests done. Cool in pans 10 minutes before removing to a wire rack.
1 PIECE: 209 cal., 12g fat (1g sat. fat), 7mg chol., 121mg sod., 23g carb. (13g sugars, 1g fiber), 3g pro.

> **TIP**
> Top slices of this fruity bread with spreadable cream cheese, strawberry jam, orange butter or a decadent vanilla-strawberry glaze.

🟥 5ɪ

QUICK & EASY BREAD BOWLS

Impress all of your friends by serving cream soups or dips in bread bowls. It's one of the most popular recipes on my blog, Yammie's Noshery.
—*Rachel Preus, Marshall, MI*

PREP: 35 min. + rising • **BAKE:** 20 min+ cooling
MAKES: 6 servings

    2   Tbsp. active dry yeast
    3   cups warm water (110° to 115°)
    2   Tbsp. sugar
    2   tsp. salt
 6½   to 7½ cups bread flour
        Optional: Cornmeal and sesame seeds

1. In a small bowl, dissolve yeast in warm water. In a large bowl, combine the sugar, salt, yeast mixture and 3 cups flour; beat on medium speed 3 minutes. Stir in enough remaining flour to form a soft dough (dough will be sticky).
2. Turn onto a floured surface; knead until smooth and elastic, 6-8 minutes. Place in a greased bowl, turning once to grease the top. Cover with a kitchen towel and let rise in a warm place until doubled, about 30 minutes.
3. Preheat oven to 500°. Punch dough down. Divide and shape into 6 balls. Place 3 in. apart on 2 baking sheets that have been greased or generously sprinkled with cornmeal. Cover with a kitchen towel; let dough rise in a warm place until doubled, about 15 minutes. Spray the loaves with water; if desired, generously sprinkle with sesame seeds. Using a sharp knife, score each top with 2 shallow cuts in an X pattern. Bake 2 minutes. Reduce the oven setting to 425°. Bake until golden brown and internal temperature reaches 190°-200°. Remove from pans to wire racks to cool completely.
4. Cut a thin slice off the top of each loaf. Hollow out bottom portion of each loaf, leaving a ½-in. shell. Discard removed bread or save for another use, such as croutons.
1 BREAD BOWL: 283 cal., 1g fat (0 sat. fat), 0 chol., 396mg sod., 57g carb. (2g sugars, 2g fiber), 10g pro.

SLOW-COOKER MONKEY BREAD

I often take this monkey bread to church potlucks—children and adults love it! The rum extract is optional.
—*Lisa Leaper, Worthington, OH*

- -

PREP: 20 min. • **COOK:** 2½ hours + standing • **MAKES:** 10 servings

- 1 cup sugar
- ¾ cup packed brown sugar
- 2 tsp. ground cinnamon
- ½ tsp. ground allspice
- 4 tubes (6 oz. each) refrigerated buttermilk biscuits
- ¾ cup butter, melted
- ½ cup apple juice
- 1 tsp. vanilla extract
- 1 tsp. rum extract
  Toasted chopped pecans, optional

1. Line a 5-qt. slow cooker with a piece of aluminum foil, letting ends extend up the sides. Grease foil.
2. Combine the sugars, cinnamon and allspice in a large bowl; sprinkle 3 Tbsp. sugar mixture in the bottom of prepared slow cooker. Cut all biscuits into quarters. Add biscuit pieces to bowl; toss to coat. Transfer coated biscuits to slow cooker; sprinkle any remaining sugar mixture over biscuits.
3. Stir together the butter, apple juice and extracts; pour over the biscuits.
4. Cook, covered, on low 2½-3 hours. Remove lid and let stand for 10 minutes. Carefully invert onto serving platter. If desired, sprinkle with pecans.
8 BISCUIT PIECES: 473 cal., 22g fat (12g sat. fat), 37mg chol., 675mg sod., 68g carb. (41g sugars, 0 fiber), 4g pro.

SAVORY BISCUIT-BREADSTICKS

I love to experiment in the kitchen with simple ingredients like refrigerated biscuits. The results are usually a big hit—these super fast breadsticks are an example.
—*Billy Hensley, Mount Carmel, TN*

- -

TAKES: 20 min. • **MAKES:** 10 breadsticks

- ½ cup grated Parmesan cheese
- 2 tsp. dried minced garlic
- ¼ tsp. crushed red pepper flakes
- 1 tube (12 oz.) refrigerated buttermilk biscuits
- 2 Tbsp. olive oil

Preheat oven to 400°. In a shallow bowl, mix cheese, garlic and pepper flakes. Roll each biscuit into a 6-in. rope. Brush lightly with oil; roll in cheese mixture. Place on a greased baking sheet. Bake until golden brown, 8-10 minutes.
1 BREADSTICK: 142 cal., 8g fat (2g sat. fat), 3mg chol., 353mg sod., 16g carb. (2g sugars, 0 fiber), 3g pro.

> **REVIEW**
>
> *"This is my favorite breadstick recipe I've tried so far! A new favorite for pizza nights at our house. I didn't have dried minced garlic so I used a teaspoon of garlic salt, and it turned out delicious."*
>
> —ANGEL182009, TASTEOFHOME.COM

BEST BRAN MUFFINS

My husband loves pineapple, which is the ingredient that makes these muffins so moist and delicious! They're a healthy way to start off a busy day.
—*Suzanne Smith, Framingham, MA*

TAKES: 30 min. • **MAKES:** 18 muffins

- ½ cup old-fashioned oats
- 1 cup all-purpose flour
- 1 cup whole wheat flour
- ½ cup All-Bran cereal
- ½ tsp. salt
- 1 tsp. baking powder
- 1 tsp. baking soda
- 1 large egg, room temperature, beaten
- ¼ cup vegetable oil
- ½ cup molasses
- ¾ cup buttermilk
- 1 can (8 oz.) crushed pineapple in natural juice, undrained
- ½ cup chopped nuts, dates or raisins

1. In a bowl, combine the first 7 ingredients. Make a well in the center. Combine the egg, oil, molasses, buttermilk and pineapple with juice. Pour into well; mix just until the dry ingredients are moistened. Stir in the nuts, dates or raisins.

2. Fill 18 greased muffin cups two-thirds full. Bake at 400° until golden brown, 12 minutes.

NOTE: To substitute for each cup of buttermilk, use 1 Tbsp. white vinegar or lemon juice plus enough milk to measure 1 cup. Stir, then let stand 5 min. Or, use 1 cup plain yogurt or 1¾ tsp. cream of tartar plus 1 cup milk.

1 MUFFIN: 151 cal., 6g fat (1g sat. fat), 11mg chol., 194mg sod., 22g carb. (9g sugars, 2g fiber), 4g pro. **DIABETIC EXCHANGES:** 1½ starch, 1 fat.

ORANGE-CHIP CRANBERRY BREAD

Tart berries, crunchy nuts and sweet chocolate are simply scrumptious when mixed together in this easy quick bread. Sometimes I'll top it off with an orange-flavored glaze.
—*Donna Smith, Fairport, NY*

PREP: 20 min. • **BAKE:** 50 min. + cooling • **MAKES:** 2 loaves

- 2½ cups all-purpose flour
- 1 cup sugar
- ½ tsp. baking powder
- ½ tsp. baking soda
- ¼ tsp. salt
- 2 large eggs, room temperature
- ¾ cup vegetable oil
- 2 tsp. grated orange zest
- 1 cup buttermilk
- 1½ cups chopped fresh or frozen cranberries, thawed
- 1 cup miniature semisweet chocolate chips
- 1 cup chopped walnuts
- ¾ cup confectioners' sugar, optional
- 2 Tbsp. orange juice, optional

1. In a bowl, combine the first 5 ingredients. In another bowl, combine eggs, oil and orange zest; mix well. Add to the dry ingredients alternately with buttermilk. Fold in cranberries, chocolate chips and walnuts.

2. Pour into 2 greased 8x4-in. loaf pans. Bake at 350° until a toothpick inserted in the center comes out clean, 50-60 minutes. Cool for 10 minutes before removing from pans to wire racks. If glaze is desired, combine confectioners' sugar and orange juice until smooth; drizzle over cooled loaves.

1 PIECE: 220 cal., 13g fat (3g sat. fat), 18mg chol., 76mg sod., 25g carb. (14g sugars, 1g fiber), 4g pro.

NO-KNEAD HONEY OATMEAL BREAD

We especially enjoy this tasty bread because we like using honey as a natural sweetener. We use the bread for both toast and sandwiches. It's great for special occasions too.
—*Janice Dancer, Williamstown, VT*

PREP: 25 min. + rising • **BAKE:** 40 min.
MAKES: 2 loaves (12 pieces each)

2 cups water, divided
1 cup rolled oats
⅓ cup butter, softened
⅓ cup honey
1 Tbsp. salt
2 pkg. (¼ oz. each) active dry yeast
1 large egg, room temperature
4 to 5 cups all-purpose flour
Melted butter, optional

1. In a small saucepan, heat 1 cup water to boiling. Stir in the oats, butter, honey and salt. Let stand until mixture cools to 110°-115°, stirring occasionally. Heat remaining 1 cup water to 110°-115°.
2. In a large bowl, dissolve yeast in warm water. Add the egg, oat mixture and 2 cups flour. Beat until smooth. Stir in enough remaining flour to form a soft dough (dough will be sticky). Do not knead. Place in a greased bowl, turning once to grease the top. Cover and let rise in a warm place until doubled, about 1 hour.
3. Punch down dough; divide evenly between 2 greased 8x4-in. loaf pans. Smooth tops of loaves. Cover and let rise in a warm place until doubled, 35-40 minutes. Using a sharp knife, make a shallow slash down the center of each loaf.
4. Bake at 375° until golden brown, 40-45 minutes. Remove from pans to wire racks to cool. If desired, brush with melted butter.
1 PIECE: 132 cal., 3g fat (2g sat. fat), 16mg chol., 325mg sod., 22g carb. (4g sugars, 1g fiber), 3g pro.

OLD-FASHIONED BLUEBERRY MUFFINS

At the end of the summer years ago, our family often gathered to pick wild blueberries. Mother canned them and saved them for special pie treats during the holidays. If there were any left over she made them into these delicious blueberry muffins.
—*June Morris, Water Mill Long Island, NY*

TAKES: 30 min. • **MAKES:** 6 muffins

1 cup all-purpose flour
⅓ cup sugar
1 tsp. baking powder
¼ tsp. salt
1 large egg, room temperature
¼ cup milk
2 Tbsp. butter, melted
½ tsp. vanilla extract
¾ cup fresh or frozen blueberries

1. Preheat oven to 400°. In a small bowl, combine the flour, sugar, baking powder and salt. In another bowl, whisk the egg, milk, butter and vanilla; stir into dry ingredients just until moistened. Fold in blueberries.
2. Fill greased or paper-lined muffin cups three-fourths full. Bake until a toothpick inserted in the center comes out clean, 18-22 minutes. Cool for 5 minutes before removing from pan to a wire rack. Serve warm.
NOTE: If using frozen blueberries, use without thawing to avoid discoloring the batter.
1 MUFFIN: 192 cal., 5g fat (3g sat. fat), 42mg chol., 226mg sod., 33g carb. (15g sugars, 2g fiber), 4g pro.

LEMON BREAD

I often bake this sunshiny, sweet lemon bread when company stops by. It has a beautiful cakelike texture.
—*Kathy Scott, Lingle, WY*

PREP: 10 min. • **BAKE:** 40 min. + cooling
MAKES: 1 loaf (12 pieces)

- ½ cup butter, softened
- 1 cup sugar
- 2 large eggs, room temperature
- 1 Tbsp. grated lemon zest
- 2 Tbsp. lemon juice
- 1½ cups all-purpose flour
- 1 tsp. baking powder
- ⅛ tsp. salt
- ½ cup 2% milk

GLAZE
- ½ cup confectioners' sugar
- 2 Tbsp. lemon juice

1. Preheat oven to 350°. In a large bowl, cream butter and sugar until light and fluffy, 5-7 minutes. Beat in eggs, lemon zest and juice. Combine flour, baking powder and salt; gradually stir into creamed mixture alternately with milk, beating well after each addition.
2. Pour into a greased 8x4-in. loaf pan. Bake until a toothpick inserted in the center comes out clean, 40-45 minutes. Cool in pan 15 minutes before removing to a wire rack. Combine glaze ingredients; immediately drizzle over bread. Serve bread warm.

1 PIECE: 228 cal., 9g fat (5g sat. fat), 52mg chol., 143mg sod., 35g carb. (22g sugars, 0 fiber), 3g pro.

TIP

IS LEMON EXTRACT THE SAME AS LEMON JUICE?

While you'll get bright, lemony flavor from both, lemon extract and lemon juice are not the same. Lemon extract is traditionally made by extracting essential oils from lemon peels by soaking the peels in alcohol. It has an intense flavor that's much stronger than lemon juice, which is squeezed from fresh lemons.

5i
HOMEMADE FRY BREAD

Crispy, doughy and totally delicious, this fry bread is fantastic with nearly any sweet or savory toppings you can think of. We love it with a little butter, a drizzle of honey and a squeeze of lemon.
—*Thelma Tyler, Dragoon, AZ*

PREP: 20 min. + standing • **COOK:** 15 min.
MAKES: 12 pieces

- 2 cups all-purpose flour
- ½ cup nonfat dry milk powder
- 3 tsp. baking powder
- ½ tsp. salt
- 4½ tsp. shortening
- ⅔ to ¾ cup water
  Oil for deep-fat frying
  Optional: Butter, honey and fresh lemon juice

1. Combine flour, dry milk powder, baking powder and salt; cut in the shortening until crumbly. Add water gradually, mixing to form a firm ball. Divide dough; shape into 12 balls. Let stand, covered, for 10 minutes. Roll each dough ball into a 6-in. circle. With a sharp knife, cut a ½-in.-diameter hole in center of each.
2. In a large cast-iron skillet, heat oil over medium-high heat. Fry dough circles, 1 at a time, until puffed and golden, about 1 minute on each side. Drain on paper towels. Serve warm, with butter, honey and fresh lemon juice if desired.

1 PIECE: 124 cal., 5g fat (1g sat. fat), 1mg chol., 234mg sod., 17g carb. (2g sugars, 1g fiber), 3g pro.

HERBED BREAD TWISTS

A special shape and a blend of herbs dress up ordinary frozen bread dough in this unbelievably easy recipe.
—*Deb Stapert, Comstock Park, MI*

PREP: 30 min. + rising • **BAKE:** 10 min. • **MAKES:** 2 dozen

- ¼ cup butter, softened
- ¼ tsp. garlic powder
- ¼ tsp. each dried basil, marjoram and oregano
- 1 loaf (1 lb.) frozen bread dough, thawed
- ¾ cup shredded part-skim mozzarella cheese
- 1 large egg
- 1 Tbsp. water
- 4 tsp. sesame seeds

1. In a small bowl, combine butter and seasonings. On a lightly floured surface, roll dough into a 12-in. square. Spread with butter mixture to within ½ in. of edges; sprinkle with cheese.
2. Fold dough into thirds. Cut widthwise into 24 strips. Twist each strip twice; pinch ends to seal. Place 2 in. apart on greased baking sheets. Cover and let rise in a warm place until doubled, about 40 minutes.
3. Beat egg and water; brush over dough. Sprinkle with sesame seeds. Bake at 375° until light golden brown, 10-12 minutes. Remove from pans to wire racks.
1 TWIST: 84 cal., 4g fat (2g sat. fat), 17mg chol., 140mg sod., 10g carb. (1g sugars, 1g fiber), 3g pro.

YOGURT CORNBREAD

My husband doesn't like traditional Texas cornbread, so I came up with this recipe using yogurt. Now it's the only kind he'll eat.
—*Amanda Andrews, Mansfield, TX*

TAKES: 30 min. • **MAKES:** 9 servings

- 1 cup yellow cornmeal
- ¼ cup all-purpose flour
- 2 tsp. baking powder
- ½ tsp. salt
- ¼ tsp. baking soda
- 1 large egg, lightly beaten, room temperature
- 1 cup fat-free plain yogurt
- ½ cup fat-free milk
- ¼ cup canola oil
- 1 Tbsp. honey

Preheat oven to 425°. In a medium bowl, combine the first 5 ingredients. In another medium bowl, combine the remaining ingredients. Stir into dry ingredients just until moistened. Pour into an 8-in. square baking dish coated with cooking spray. Bake until a toothpick comes out clean, 16-20 minutes.
1 PIECE: 157 cal., 7g fat (1g sat. fat), 24mg chol., 349mg sod., 20g carb. (0 sugars, 1g fiber), 4g pro. **DIABETIC EXCHANGES:** 1½ starch, 1 fat.

HAM & BROCCOLI CORNBREAD

Leftovers haunt me. Often nobody wants to eat them, and I hate to see them go to waste. A skillet cornbread is an excellent way to leverage many combinations of leftover meat and veggies into an exciting new side dish everyone will love.
—*Fay Moreland, Wichita Falls, TX*

PREP: 15 min. • **BAKE:** 35 min. + standing • **MAKES:** 12 servings

- 5 Tbsp. butter, divided
- 2 large eggs, room temperature
- 1 cup 2% milk
- ½ cup sour cream
  Pinch cayenne pepper
- 2 pkg. (8½ oz. each) cornbread/muffin mix
- 2 cups chopped fresh broccoli
- 1½ cups shredded sharp cheddar cheese
- 1½ cups cubed fully cooked ham
- 3 green onions, thinly sliced

1. Preheat oven to 375°. Place 3 Tbsp. butter in a 12-in. cast-iron skillet; place pan in oven until butter is melted, 3-5 minutes. Carefully tilt pan to coat bottom and sides with butter.
2. Melt remaining 2 Tbsp. butter. In a large bowl, whisk together eggs, milk, sour cream, cayenne pepper and melted butter until blended. Add both packages muffin mix; stir just until moistened. Fold in remaining ingredients. Pour into hot pan.
3. Bake until top is golden brown and a toothpick inserted in center comes out clean, 35-40 minutes. Let stand 15 minutes before serving.
1 PIECE: 338 cal., 18g fat (9g sat. fat), 73mg chol., 700mg sod., 31g carb. (10g sugars, 3g fiber), 12g pro.

⑤î
EASY POPOVERS

Popovers have a brown crisp exterior with an almost hollow interior. As they bake, the heat causes the liquid in the batter to turn to steam, making the batter puff up. After baking, prick the tops to let the steam escape.
—*Lourdes Dewick, Fort Lauderdale, FL*

PREP: 20 min. • **BAKE:** 45 min. • **MAKES:** 6 popovers

- 1 Tbsp. shortening
- 2 large eggs, room temperature
- 1 cup whole milk
- 1 Tbsp. butter, melted
- 1 cup all-purpose flour
- ½ tsp. salt

1. Preheat oven to 450°. Using ½ tsp. shortening for each cup, grease the bottom and sides of six 6-oz. custard cups or the cups of a popover pan. If using custard cups, place on a 15x10x1-in. baking pan.
2. In a small bowl, beat eggs; blend in milk and butter. Beat in flour and salt until smooth (do not overbeat).
3. Fill cups half full. Bake 15 minutes. Reduce heat to 350°; bake until very firm, about 30 minutes longer. Remove from oven and prick each popover to allow steam to escape. Serve immediately.
1 POPOVER: 160 cal., 7g fat (3g sat. fat), 71mg chol., 253mg sod., 18g carb. (2g sugars, 1g fiber), 6g pro.

TIP

WHAT CAN I SERVE WITH POPOVERS?
On their own, popovers are delicious spread with butter and jam or drizzled with honey. They're terrific with afternoon tea. As part of a meal, popovers can be served with pretty much anything, but they are wonderful vehicles for soaking up gravy. Try them with beef stew, pot roast or chicken and dumplings.

QUICK ORANGE ROLLS

This recipe is so dependable—I make it a lot during the holidays because it's quick and delicious. There are never leftovers!
—*Angela Sheridan, Opdyke, IL*

PREP: 15 min. • **BAKE:** 35 min.
MAKES: 1 dozen

- 1 pkg. (8 oz.) cream cheese, softened
- ¼ cup orange marmalade
- 2 Tbsp. orange juice
- ½ cup chopped pecans

DOUGH

- 3½ cups biscuit/baking mix
- 2 Tbsp. sugar
- 1 pkg. (¼ oz.) quick-rise yeast
- 1 cup warm water
- 2 Tbsp. butter, melted

GLAZE

- ½ cup confectioners' sugar
- ¼ cup orange marmalade, warmed

1. In a small bowl, beat cream cheese, orange marmalade and orange juice until blended; stir in pecans.

2. In a large bowl, combine baking mix, sugar and yeast. Stir in the warm water to form a soft dough. Turn dough onto a lightly floured surface; knead until smooth and elastic, about 5 minutes. Cover and let rest 10 minutes. Roll into an 11x8-in. rectangle. Spread cream cheese mixture to within ½ in. of edges. Roll up jelly-roll style, starting with a long side; pinch seam to seal. Cut into 12 slices.

3. Place in a greased 13x9-in. baking dish, cut side down. Cover with a kitchen towel. Let rise in a warm place until doubled, about 1 hour.

4. Preheat oven to 350°. Brush tops with melted butter. Bake until golden brown, 35-40 minutes. Cool slightly in pan on a wire rack. For glaze, stir together confectioners' sugar and marmalade; drizzle over warm rolls.

1 ROLL: 311 cal., 15g fat (6g sat. fat), 24mg chol., 445mg sod., 42g carb. (17g sugars, 2g fiber), 5g pro.

TIP
To ease prep, use a stand mixer to knead the dough. Attach a dough hook to the mixer and knead on medium speed for 4 minutes or until the dough is soft and elastic, and doesn't break when a small amount of dough is gently pulled.

PISTACHIO QUICK BREAD

I love making many of these special loaves to give away for the holidays. They also freeze well, so it is easy to pull one out for unexpected guests.
—*Judy Fischer, Green Bay, WI*

- -

PREP: 20 min. • **BAKE:** 35 min. + cooling
MAKES: 2 loaves (12 pieces each)

  1 **pkg. white cake mix (regular size)**
  1 **pkg. (3.4 oz.) instant pistachio pudding mix**
  4 **large eggs, room temperature**
  1 **cup sour cream**
  ¼ **cup water**
  ¼ **cup canola oil**
  ⅓ **cup sugar**
  ¾ **tsp. ground cinnamon**

1. Preheat oven to 350°. In a large bowl, combine dry cake and pudding mixes. Add the eggs, sour cream, water and oil; beat until blended (batter will be thick).
2. Combine sugar and cinnamon. Spoon half the batter into 2 greased 8x4-in. loaf pans; sprinkle each with 2 Tbsp. cinnamon sugar. Spread remaining batter over top; sprinkle with remaining cinnamon sugar.
3. Bake until a toothpick inserted in the center comes out clean, 35-40 minutes. Cool for 10 minutes before removing from pans to wire racks.
1 PIECE: 169 cal., 7g fat (2g sat. fat), 42mg chol., 218mg sod., 24g carb. (16g sugars, 0 fiber), 2g pro.

QUICK BUTTERMILK CORNBREAD

The tattered recipe card for this cornbread proves it's been a family favorite for years. It's my daughter's top request.
—*Judy Sellgren, Grand Rapids, MI*

- -

TAKES: 30 min. • **MAKES:** 9 servings

  1¼ **cups cornmeal**
  1 **cup all-purpose flour**
  ⅔ **cup packed brown sugar**
  ⅓ **cup sugar**
  1 **tsp. baking soda**
  ½ **tsp. salt**
  1 **large egg, room temperature**
  1 **cup buttermilk**
  ¾ **cup canola oil**

1. In a large bowl, combine the cornmeal, flour, sugars, baking soda and salt. In another bowl, whisk the egg, buttermilk and oil; stir into dry ingredients just until moistened. Pour into a greased 9-in. round or square baking pan (pan will be full).
2. Bake at 425° until a toothpick inserted in the center comes out clean, 20-25 minutes. Cool on a wire rack for 5 minutes. Serve bread warm.
NOTE: To substitute for 1 cup buttermilk, use 1 Tbsp. white vinegar or lemon juice plus enough milk to measure 1 cup. Stir, then let stand 5 min. Or, use 1 cup plain yogurt or 1¾ tsp. cream of tartar plus 1 cup milk.
1 PIECE: 390 cal., 19g fat (3g sat. fat), 25mg chol., 314mg sod., 50g carb. (25g sugars, 2g fiber), 5g pro.

TIP

IS IT OK IF SOME LUMPS REMAIN IN THE BUTTERMILK CORNBREAD BATTER?

It's fine if some lumps remain because you don't want to overmix the batter. Overmixing can lead to a tough texture when baked.

SKILLET HERB BREAD

We had a lot of family get-togethers while I was growing up. My grandmother, aunts and mom were all good cooks, and each had her own specialty when it came to bread. Mom's was my favorite— she created this recipe more than 40 years ago. The flavors call to mind the taste of cornbread stuffing!
—*Shirley Smith, Yorba Linda, CA*

PREP: 10 min. • **BAKE:** 35 min. • **MAKES:** 10 servings

- 1½ cups all-purpose flour
- 2 Tbsp. sugar
- 4 tsp. baking powder
- 1½ tsp. salt
- 1 tsp. rubbed sage
- 1 tsp. dried thyme
- 1½ cups yellow cornmeal
- 1½ cups chopped celery
- 1 cup chopped onion
- 1 jar (2 oz.) chopped pimientos, drained
- 3 large eggs, room temperature, beaten
- 1½ cups fat-free milk
- ⅓ cup vegetable oil

Preheat oven to 400°. In a large bowl, combine the flour, sugar, baking powder, salt, sage and thyme. Combine cornmeal, celery, onion and pimientos; add to dry ingredients and mix well. Add eggs, milk and oil; stir just until moistened. Pour into a greased 10- or 11-in. ovenproof skillet. Bake until the bread tests done, 35-45 minutes. Serve warm.

1 PIECE: 275 cal., 9g fat (2g sat. fat), 57mg chol., 598mg sod., 40g carb. (6g sugars, 2g fiber), 7g pro.

HOMEMADE IRISH SODA BREAD

Some people consider bread to be the most important part of a meal ... and this Irish bread satisfies! This recipe is by far the best soda bread I've ever tried. It has plentiful raisins, making it moist and delicious.
—*Evelyn Kenney, Trenton, NJ*

PREP: 20 min. • **BAKE:** 1 hour • **MAKES:** 1 loaf

- 4 cups all-purpose flour
- ¼ cup sugar
- 1 tsp. salt
- 1 tsp. baking powder
- 1 tsp. baking soda
- ¼ cup cold butter, cubed
- 1⅓ cups buttermilk
- 1 large egg
- 2 cups raisins
- 3 to 4 Tbsp. caraway seeds
- 2 Tbsp. 2% milk

1. Preheat oven to 375°. In a large bowl, combine flour, sugar, salt, baking powder and baking soda. Cut in the butter until mixture resembles coarse crumbs. In a separate bowl, whisk buttermilk and egg; stir into the dry ingredients just until moistened. Stir in the raisins and caraway seeds.

2. Turn out onto a floured surface. Knead gently 8-10 times. Shape into a ball and place on a greased baking pan. Pat into a 7-in. round loaf. Cut a 4-in. cross about ¼ in. deep on top to allow for expansion. Brush top with milk.

3. Bake until golden brown, about 1 hour. Remove from pan to wire rack.

1 PIECE: 223 cal., 4g fat (2g sat. fat), 20mg chol., 326mg sod., 43g carb. (15g sugars, 2g fiber), 5g pro.

GARLIC POTATO BISCUITS

The beauty of biscuits is that you can enjoy the aroma of oven-fresh bread with less work than yeast breads.
—*Diane Hixon, Niceville, FL*

PREP: 25 min. • **BAKE:** 10 min. • **MAKES:** 15 biscuits

- 1 large potato (½ lb.), peeled and diced
- 3 to 4 garlic cloves, peeled
- ⅓ cup butter, softened
- 1 tsp. salt
- ¼ tsp. pepper
- 2 cups all-purpose flour
- 3 tsp. baking powder
- ⅓ cup 2% milk

1. Place potato and garlic in a saucepan; cover with water. Bring to a boil. Reduce heat; cover and simmer until tender. Drain. Add butter, salt and pepper to potato and garlic; mash. In a large bowl, combine flour and baking powder; stir in potato mixture until mixture resembles coarse crumbs. Add milk and stir well.
2. Turn dough onto a lightly floured surface. Roll out to ½-in. thickness. Cut with a floured 2-in. biscuit cutter. Place dough rounds 1 in. apart on an ungreased baking sheet. Bake at 450° until golden brown, 10-12 minutes. Serve warm.
1 BISCUIT: 120 cal., 4g fat (3g sat. fat), 12mg chol., 283mg sod., 18g carb. (1g sugars, 1g fiber), 2g pro.

CINNAMON ROLLS WITH COOKIE BUTTER FILLING

I created this recipe when I had a jar of cookie butter on hand and I was craving cinnamon rolls. Using a frozen bread dough cuts down on time and effort, and the cookie butter makes a nice even filling with a touch of something special.
—*Kallee Krong-Mccreery, Escondido, CA*

PREP: 20 min. + rising • **BAKE:** 15 min. • **MAKES:** 1 dozen

- ½ cup Biscoff creamy cookie spread
- 3 Tbsp. butter, softened
- ½ tsp. vanilla extract
- ⅓ cup sugar
- 1 Tbsp. ground cinnamon
- 1 loaf (1 lb.) frozen bread dough, thawed

ICING
- 1⅓ cups confectioners' sugar
- 1 to 2 Tbsp. 2% milk
- 2 tsp. light corn syrup
- 1 tsp. vanilla extract

1. In a small bowl, mix the first 5 ingredients. On a lightly floured surface, roll dough into a 12x7-in. rectangle. Spread butter mixture over dough to within ½ in. of edges. Roll up jelly-roll style, starting with a long side; pinch seam to seal. Cut into 12 slices. Place in a greased 13x9-in. baking pan, cut side down. Cover dough slices and let rise in a warm place until doubled, about 45 minutes.
2. Preheat oven to 350°. Bake until edges are lightly browned, 15-20 minutes. Place pan on a wire rack. Combine icing ingredients; drizzle over warm rolls. Let stand until set.
1 ROLL: 272 cal., 8g fat (3g sat. fat), 8mg chol., 236mg sod., 44g carb. (25g sugars, 2g fiber), 4g pro.

AIR-FRYER RASPBERRY CRUMBLE COFFEE CAKE

With a ribbon of fresh homemade fruit filling, this homey coffee cake is perfect for breakfast. It is also equally delicious warm out of the air fryer for a weeknight dessert.
—*Shirley Boyken, Mesa, AZ*

PREP: 25 min. • **COOK:** 30 min.
MAKES: 8 servings

FILLING
- ⅓ cup sugar
- 2 Tbsp. cornstarch
- 6 Tbsp. water or cranberry-raspberry juice
- 1 cup fresh or frozen unsweetened raspberries
- 1½ tsp. lemon juice

COFFEE CAKE
- 1½ cups all-purpose flour
- ½ cup sugar
- 1½ tsp. baking powder
- ½ tsp. salt
- ½ tsp. ground cinnamon
- ⅛ tsp. ground mace
- ½ cup cold butter, cubed
- 1 large egg, room temperature, lightly beaten
- ½ cup 2% milk
- ½ tsp. vanilla extract

TOPPING
- 2 Tbsp. cold butter, cubed
- ¼ cup all-purpose flour
- ¼ cup sugar
- 2 Tbsp. sliced almonds

1. For filling, in a saucepan, combine sugar, cornstarch and water until smooth. Bring to a boil over medium heat. Cook and stir until thickened, 1-2 minutes. Add berries and lemon juice. Set aside to cool.
2. In a large bowl, combine flour, sugar, baking powder, salt, cinnamon and mace. Cut in butter to form fine crumbs. Stir in egg, milk and vanilla until blended.
3. Spread half the batter into a greased 8-in. round baking pan that fits into air fryer. Spread filling evenly over top. Drop remaining batter by small spoonfuls and spread evenly over filling.
4. Preheat air fryer to 325°. For topping, cut butter into flour and sugar; stir in almonds. Sprinkle over top. Place pan in air fryer; cook until a toothpick inserted in center comes out with moist crumbs and top is golden brown, 30-35 minutes.

NOTE: In our testing, we find cook times vary dramatically between brands of air fryers. As a result, we give wider than normal ranges on suggested cook times. Begin checking at the first time listed and adjust as needed.
1 PIECE: 376 cal., 17g fat (10g sat. fat), 63mg chol., 368mg sod., 53g carb. (29g sugars, 2g fiber), 5g pro.

BAKING POWDER DROP BISCUITS

One day I had company coming and realized I had run out of biscuit mix. I'd never made biscuits from scratch before, but I decided to give this recipe a try. Now this is the only way I make them!
—*Sharon Evans, Clear Lake, IA*

TAKES: 20 min. • **MAKES:** 1 dozen

- 2 cups all-purpose flour
- 2 Tbsp. sugar
- 4 tsp. baking powder
- ½ tsp. cream of tartar
- ½ tsp. salt
- ½ cup shortening
- ⅔ cup 2% milk
- 1 large egg, room temperature

1. Preheat oven to 450°. In a large bowl, combine the first 5 ingredients. Cut in shortening until the mixture resembles coarse crumbs. In a small bowl, whisk milk and egg. Stir into crumb mixture just until moistened.
2. Drop by ¼ cupfuls 2 in. apart onto an ungreased baking sheet. Bake until golden brown, 10-12 minutes. Serve warm.
1 BISCUIT: 170 cal., 9g fat (2g sat. fat), 17mg chol., 271mg sod., 19g carb. (3g sugars, 1g fiber), 3g pro.

CHEDDAR SKILLET CORNBREAD

Here's a tasty spin on traditional cornbread. It may become your new favorite!
—Terri Adrian, Lake City, FL

TAKES: 30 min. • **MAKES:** 1 loaf (12 wedges)

    2   Tbsp. butter
    2   pkg. (8½ oz. each) cornbread/muffin mix
    2   large eggs, room temperature, lightly beaten
    ½   cup 2% milk
    ½   cup plain yogurt
    1   can (14¾ oz.) cream-style corn
    ½   cup shredded cheddar cheese
HONEY BUTTER
    ½   cup butter, softened
    2   Tbsp. honey

1. Place butter in a 10-in. cast-iron or other ovenproof skillet. Place in a 400° oven until melted, 4-6 minutes.
2. Meanwhile, in a large bowl, combine the cornbread mix, eggs, milk and yogurt until blended. Stir in corn and cheese. Pour into hot skillet.
3. Bake at 400° until a toothpick inserted in the center comes out clean, 20-25 minutes. Cut into wedges.
4. In a small bowl, cream the butter and honey. Serve with warm cornbread.
1 PIECE: 332 cal., 18g fat (9g sat. fat), 64mg chol., 547mg sod., 38g carb. (13g sugars, 3g fiber), 6g pro.

HERBED PARMESAN BREAD

I've been making my Parmesan bread for so many years, I can no longer recall where I got the recipe! Thanks to a convenient baking mix, a freshly made loaf gets in the oven fast.
—Lesley Archer, Chapala, Mexico

PREP: 10 min. • **BAKE:** 35 min. + cooling • **MAKES:** 1 loaf (12 pieces)

    3¾ cups biscuit/baking mix
    1   cup plus 2 Tbsp. grated Parmesan cheese, divided
    1   tsp. Italian seasoning
    ½   tsp. salt
    1   large egg, room temperature
    1   can (5 oz.) evaporated milk
    ¾   cup water

1. Preheat oven to 350°. In a large bowl, combine biscuit mix, 1 cup cheese, Italian seasoning and salt. In a small bowl, whisk egg, milk and water. Stir into dry ingredients just until moistened. Transfer to a greased 8x4-in. loaf pan. Sprinkle with remaining 2 Tbsp. cheese.
2. Bake until a toothpick inserted in center comes out clean, 35-40 minutes. Cool 10 minutes before removing from pan to a wire rack.
1 PIECE: 207 cal., 9g fat (4g sat. fat), 28mg chol., 702mg sod., 25g carb. (2g sugars, 1g fiber), 7g pro.

BREAD MACHINE NAAN

Chewy yeast-raised flatbread is a snap to make in a bread machine. Serve naan with your favorite Indian dishes to soak up all the mouthwatering sauces.
—*Shannon Ventresca, Middleboro, MA*

- -

PREP: 1½ hours • **COOK:** 5 min./batch • **MAKES:** 6 servings

  ¾ **cup warm 2% milk (70° to 80°)**
  ¾ **cup plain yogurt**
  1 **large egg, room temperature, beaten**
  2 **Tbsp. canola oil**
  2 **tsp. sugar**
  1 **tsp. salt**
  1 **tsp. baking powder**
  4 **cups bread flour**
  2 **tsp. active dry yeast**

1. In bread machine pan, place all ingredients in order suggested by the manufacturer. Select the dough setting (check dough after 5 minutes of mixing; add 1-2 Tbsp. of water or flour if needed).
2. When cycle is completed, turn dough onto a lightly floured surface. Divide into 6 portions; shape into balls. Roll each ball into a ¼-in. thick oval. Let rest for 5 minutes.
3. Brush tops with water. In a greased large skillet over medium-high heat, cover and cook dough, wet side down, for 1 minute. Turn dough; cover and cook for 30 seconds longer or until golden brown. Repeat with remaining dough.
1 NAAN: 363 cal., 7g fat (2g sat. fat), 42mg chol., 502mg sod., 64g carb. (4g sugars, 2g fiber), 14g pro.

AIR-FRYER BANANA BREAD

Yes you can make banana bread in the air fryer! This easy recipe is a cinch to put together. Eat the bread while it's still warm or at room temperature with a schmear of butter.
—*Peggy Woodward, Shullsburg, WI*

- -

PREP: 10 min. • **COOK:** 35 min. + cooling • **MAKES:** 8 servings

  ¼ **cup butter, softened**
  ¾ **cup sugar**
  1 **large egg, room temperature**
  1 **cup all-purpose flour**
  ½ **tsp. baking soda**
  ¼ **tsp. salt**
  ⅔ **cup mashed ripe banana (about 1 medium)**
  ½ **cup chopped pecans**

1. Preheat air fryer to 325°. In a large bowl, cream butter and sugar until light and fluffy, 5-7 minutes. Beat in egg. In another bowl, whisk flour, baking soda and salt; add to creamed mixture alternately with banana, beating well after each addition. Fold in the pecans.
2. Transfer to a greased 8-in. round baking pan that will fit in the air fryer. Cover with foil. Cook 25 minutes. Uncover; cook until a toothpick inserted in center comes out clean, 8-10 minutes. Cool in pan on a wire rack for 10 minutes before removing from pan.
NOTE: In our testing, we find cook times vary dramatically between brands of air fryers. As a result, we give wider than normal ranges on suggested cook times. Begin checking at the first time listed and adjust as needed.
1 PIECE: 254 cal., 11g fat (4g sat. fat), 39mg chol., 208mg sod., 36g carb. (22g sugars, 2g fiber), 3g pro.

TIP

WHAT ELSE CAN YOU PUT IN AIR-FRYER BANANA BREAD?
Swap out the pecans for walnuts, or add chocolate chips instead of nuts to go with those ripened bananas. It's always nice to mix in a little cinnamon and vanilla too.

LEMONY ZUCCHINI BREAD

Flecks of zucchini give a third dimension to the popular lemon and poppy seed combination in this moist quick bread. We enjoy this all year long.
—*Carol Funk, Richard, SK*

PREP: 25 min. • **BAKE:** 50 min. + cooling
MAKES: 2 loaves (16 pieces each)

- 4 cups all-purpose flour
- 1½ cups sugar
- 1 pkg. (3.4 oz.) instant lemon pudding mix
- 1½ tsp. baking soda
- 1 tsp. baking powder
- 1 tsp. salt
- 4 large eggs, room temperature
- 1¼ cups 2% milk
- 1 cup canola oil
- 3 Tbsp. lemon juice
- 1 tsp. lemon extract
- 2 cups shredded zucchini
- ¼ cup poppy seeds
- 2 tsp. grated lemon zest

1. In a large bowl, combine the flour, sugar, pudding mix, baking soda, baking powder and salt. In another bowl, whisk the eggs, milk, oil, lemon juice and extract. Stir into the dry ingredients just until moistened. Fold in the zucchini, poppy seeds and lemon zest.

2. Pour into 2 greased 9x5-in. loaf pans. Bake at 350° for 50-55 minutes or until a toothpick inserted in the center comes out clean. Cool loaves for 10 minutes before removing from baking pans to wire racks to cool completely.

1 PIECE: 187 cal., 8g fat (1g sat. fat), 28mg chol., 195mg sod., 25g carb. (12g sugars, 1g fiber), 3g pro.

ROSEMARY-GARLIC FOCACCIA BREAD

This bread smells wonderful when it's baking in the oven. I make it most often during the summer when rosemary is abundant in the garden, but also around the holidays when rosemary plants are available in stores.
—*Tammy Bollman, Minatare, NE*

PREP: 1½ hours + rising • **BAKE:** 15 min.
MAKES: 1 loaf (12 wedges)

- ¾ cup warm 2% milk (70° to 80°)
- ¼ cup water (70° to 80°)
- ¼ cup butter, softened
- 1 egg
- 2¾ cups bread flour
- 2 Tbsp. sugar
- 2 tsp. kosher salt, divided
- 2 tsp. active dry yeast
- 4 tsp. olive oil
- 4 garlic cloves, minced
- 1 Tbsp. minced fresh rosemary

1. In bread machine pan, place the milk, water, butter, egg, flour, sugar, 1 tsp. salt and yeast in the order suggested by the manufacturer. Select dough setting (check dough after 5 minutes of mixing; add 1-2 Tbsp. of water or flour if needed).

2. When cycle is completed, turn dough onto a lightly floured surface. Punch dough down. Cover dough and let rest for 10 minutes. Shape into an 11-in. circle; place on a baking sheet coated with cooking spray. Cover and let rise until doubled, about 30 minutes. Using the end of a wooden spoon handle, make several ¼-in. indentations in dough.

3. Brush with oil. Sprinkle with garlic, rosemary and remaining 1 tsp. salt. Bake at 400° for 15-20 minutes or until golden brown. Cut into wedges.

1 SLICE: 162 cal., 6g fat (3g sat. fat), 28mg chol., 353mg sod., 24g carb. (3g sugars, 1g fiber), 5g pro.

DRIED CRANBERRY SCONES

I go on vacation with my best friend to Michigan every July. Her cousin is allowed to come, too—but only if she brings her special cherry scones! I make them with cranberries for the holidays. Don't double this recipe. If you need more than 12, make two separate batches of dough.
—Sherry Leonard, Whitsett, NC

PREP: 20 min. • **BAKE:** 15 min. • **MAKES:** 1 dozen

- 2 cups all-purpose flour
- ¼ cup sugar
- 2½ tsp. baking powder
- ½ tsp. salt
- 6 Tbsp. cold butter
- ¾ cup buttermilk
- 1 large egg, room temperature
- ¾ cup white baking chips
- ¾ cup dried cranberries
- 1 Tbsp. turbinado (washed raw) sugar

1. Preheat oven to 400°. In a large bowl, whisk flour, sugar, baking powder and salt. Cut in butter until mixture resembles coarse crumbs. In another bowl, whisk buttermilk and egg; stir into crumb mixture just until moistened. Stir in the baking chips and cranberries.
2. Drop dough by ¼ cupfuls 2 in. apart onto parchment-lined baking sheet. Sprinkle with turbinado sugar. Bake until golden brown, 12-15 minutes.
1 SCONE: 247 cal., 10g fat (6g sat. fat), 34mg chol., 290mg sod., 36g carb. (20g sugars, 1g fiber), 4g pro.

BRIE & CARAMELIZED ONION FLATBREAD

Saute the onions and garlic for this flatbread a day ahead so it's easy to put together on the day of the party. Prepared pizza dough makes this recipe a snap.
—Trisha Kruse, Eagle, ID

PREP: 45 min. • **BAKE:** 20 min. + standing
MAKES: 1 flatbread (12 pieces)

- 2 Tbsp. butter
- 3 large sweet onions, halved and thinly sliced (about 6 cups)
- 2 garlic cloves, minced
- 1 Tbsp. brown sugar
- 1 Tbsp. balsamic vinegar
- ½ tsp. salt
- ¼ tsp. pepper
- 1 loaf (1 lb.) frozen pizza dough, thawed
- 8 oz. Brie cheese, cut into ½-in. pieces

1. Grease a 15x10x1-in. baking pan; set aside. In a large skillet, heat butter over medium heat. Add the onions; cook and stir for 4-6 minutes or until softened. Reduce heat to medium-low; cook 25-30 minutes or until deep golden brown, stirring occasionally. Add garlic; cook and stir 1 minute longer.
2. Preheat oven to 425°. Add the brown sugar, vinegar, salt and pepper to onion mixture. Cook and stir 5 minutes longer. Press dough into a 12x10-in. rectangle on prepared pan. Top with onion mixture and cheese. Bake 20-25 minutes or until golden brown. Let stand 10 minutes before cutting.
1 PIECE: 206 cal., 9g fat (5g sat. fat), 24mg chol., 333mg sod., 25g carb. (6g sugars, 1g fiber), 8g pro.

BREAD MACHINE CANDIED SWEET BREAD

The dough for this traditional panettone is conveniently made in a bread machine. Every tender, moist slice is filled with candied fruit and raisins.
—*Josephine Bianchi, Bristol, NH*

PREP: 1½ hours + rising • **BAKE:** 25 min. • **MAKES:** 1 loaf

- ⅔ cup water (70° to 80°)
- 1 large egg, room temperature
- 1 tsp. vanilla extract
- ¼ cup butter, softened
- ¾ tsp. salt
- 2¼ cups bread flour
- 2 Tbsp. sugar
- 1 Tbsp. nonfat dry milk powder
- 1½ tsp. active dry yeast
- ½ cup chopped mixed candied fruit
- ½ cup golden raisins

1. In bread machine pan, place the first 9 ingredients in order suggested by the manufacturer. Select dough setting (check dough after 5 minutes of mixing; add 1-2 Tbsp. of water or flour if needed).

2. Just before the dough cycle is completed, add candied fruit and raisins.

3. When dough cycle is completed, turn dough onto a lightly floured surface. Shape into a 9-in. round loaf; place in a greased 9-in. springform pan. Cover and let rise in a warm place until doubled, about 40 minutes.

4. Preheat oven to 350°; bake until golden brown, 25-30 minutes. Cool on a wire rack. Remove sides of pan; cut loaf into 10 wedges.

1 WEDGE: 231 cal., 6g fat (3g sat. fat), 31mg chol., 237mg sod., 41g carb. (15g sugars, 2g fiber), 5g pro.

🄢 BACON PULL-APART BREAD

I made this tender and tasty bread for my husband, and he loved it! When I'm out of bacon, I use bacon bits.
—*Terri Christensen, Montague, MI*

PREP: 15 min. • **BAKE:** 25 min. • **MAKES:** 12 servings

- 12 bacon strips, diced
- 2 tubes (12 oz. each) refrigerated buttermilk biscuits
- 2 cups shredded part-skim mozzarella cheese
- 1 Tbsp. Italian salad dressing mix
- 2 tsp. olive oil

1. Preheat oven to 375°. In a large skillet, cook bacon over medium heat until cooked but not crisp. Using a slotted spoon, remove to paper towels to drain. Separate biscuits; cut each biscuit into quarters.

2. In a large bowl, combine the cheese, dressing mix, oil and bacon. Place half the biscuit pieces in a greased 10-in. fluted tube pan; sprinkle with half the cheese mixture. Top with remaining biscuit pieces and cheese mixture.

3. Bake until golden brown, 25-30 minutes. Cool 5 minutes before inverting onto a serving plate. Serve immediately.

1 SERVING: 227 cal., 8g fat (3g sat. fat), 18mg chol., 800mg sod., 28g carb. (1g sugars, 0 fiber), 11g pro.

REVIEW

"My mom started making this years ago when I still lived at home, and now this is our family's Christmas breakfast tradition. So yummy!"

—CIVALWAR, TASTEOFHOME.COM

FAVORITE IRISH BREAD

Serve this classic from the Emerald Isle as part of a St. Patrick's Day meal or as a snack with butter, jam and a cup of tea.
—*Sadie Rotondo, Rockland, MA*

PREP: 10 min. • **BAKE:** 40 min. • **MAKES:** 16 servings

- 3 cups all-purpose flour
- 1 cup sugar
- 3 tsp. baking powder
- ¼ tsp. salt
- 1 large egg, room temperature
- 2 cups 2% milk, room temperature
- ½ cup butter, melted
- 1½ cups raisins
- 2 Tbsp. caraway seeds, optional

1. Preheat oven to 350°. In a large bowl, whisk flour, sugar, baking powder and salt. In a small bowl, whisk egg, milk and butter. Stir into dry ingredients just until moistened. Fold in raisins and, if desired, caraway seeds.

2. Transfer to a greased 9-in. square baking pan. Bake until a toothpick inserted in the center comes out clean, 40-45 minutes. Remove from pan onto a wire rack. Serve warm.

1 PIECE: 245 cal., 7g fat (4g sat. fat), 29mg chol., 193mg sod., 43g carb. (22g sugars, 1g fiber), 4g pro.

CARAWAY CHEESE BREAD

We enjoy cheese in a variety of ways. In this savory bread, cheddar blends beautifully with just the right amount of caraway.
—*Homer Wooten, Ridgetown, ON*

PREP: 10 min. • **BAKE:** 30 min. + cooling • **MAKES:** 1 loaf (16 pieces)

- 2½ cups all-purpose flour
- 2 cups shredded cheddar cheese
- 1½ to 2 tsp. caraway seeds
- ¾ tsp. salt
- ½ tsp. baking powder
- ½ tsp. baking soda
- 2 large eggs, room temperature
- 1 cup plain yogurt
- ½ cup butter, melted
- 1 Tbsp. Dijon mustard

1. Preheat the oven to 375°. In a large bowl, combine the first 6 ingredients. In another bowl, combine remaining ingredients. Stir into dry ingredients just until moistened.

2. Pour batter into a greased 9x5-in. loaf pan. Bake until a toothpick comes out clean, 30-35 minutes. Cool 10 minutes before removing from pan to a wire rack. Serve bread warm. Refrigerate leftovers.

1 PIECE: 199 cal., 12g fat (7g sat. fat), 55mg chol., 338mg sod., 16g carb. (1g sugars, 1g fiber), 7g pro.

TIP
You can make this bread with pre-grated bagged cheese if you like. However, since a block of cheese is usually less expensive, you'll get more bang for your buck if you shred it yourself at home. Also, since freshly grated cheese doesn't contain added preservatives and chemicals and since you're shredding it on the spot, it will have a fresher, creamier taste. And fewer additives is always a healthier option.

- GREAT GARLIC BREAD -

Try this classic garlic bread the next time you serve your favorite pasta or pizza dish. Dip in marinara sauce for extra yum!

Preheat oven to 350°. Cut 1 loaf (1 lb.) **French bread** in half lengthwise. In a small bowl, mix ½ cup **butter**, ¼ cup **grated Romano cheese** and 4 minced **garlic cloves**; brush over cut sides of bread. Place bread halves, cut side up, on a baking sheet. Sprinkle with 2 Tbsp. minced **fresh parsley.** Bake 7-9 minutes or until light golden brown. Cut into pieces; serve warm.

6

30-MINUTE DINNERS

Short on time and not sure what to make for dinner tonight?
Serve up homemade flavor in a jiffy with one of these easy family meals.
Recipes like stir-fry, pasta, tacos, pizza, pork chops, fish and other
delicious mainstays satisfy in 30 minutes or less!

QUICK TACOS AL PASTOR

My husband and I tried pork and pineapple tacos at a truck stand in Hawaii. They were so tasty that I decided to make my own version at home.
—*Lori McLain, Denton, TX*

- -

TAKES: 25 min. • **MAKES:** 4 servings

- 1 pkg. (15 oz.) refrigerated cooked pork roast au jus
- 1 cup well-drained unsweetened pineapple chunks, divided
- 1 Tbsp. canola oil
- ½ cup enchilada sauce
- 8 corn tortillas (6 in.), warmed
- ½ cup finely chopped onion
- ¼ cup chopped fresh cilantro
  Optional toppings: Crumbled queso fresco, salsa verde and lime wedges

1. Coarsely shred pork, reserving juices. In a small bowl, crush half the pineapple chunks with a fork.
2. In a large nonstick skillet, heat oil over medium-high heat. Add remaining whole pineapple chunks; cook until lightly browned, 2-3 minutes, turning occasionally. Remove from pan.
3. Add the enchilada sauce and crushed pineapple to same skillet; stir in pork and reserved juices. Cook over medium-high heat until the liquid is evaporated, about 4-6 minutes, stirring occasionally.
4. Serve in tortillas with pineapple chunks, onion and cilantro. If desired, top with queso fresco and salsa, and serve with lime wedges.
2 TACOS: 317 cal., 11g fat (3g sat. fat), 57mg chol., 573mg sod., 36g carb. (12g sugars, 5g fiber), 24g pro. **DIABETIC EXCHANGES:** 3 lean meat, 2 starch, 1 fat.

WEEKNIGHT CHICKEN CHOP SUEY

If you'd like a little extra crunch, serve this chop suey with chow mein noodles.
—*George Utley, South Hill, VA*

- -

TAKES: 30 min. • **MAKES:** 6 servings

- 4 tsp. olive oil
- 1 lb. boneless skinless chicken breasts, cut into 1-in. cubes
- ½ tsp. dried tarragon
- ½ tsp. dried basil
- ½ tsp. dried marjoram
- ½ tsp. grated lemon zest
- 1½ cups chopped carrots
- 1 can (8 oz.) sliced water chestnuts, drained
- 1 medium tart apple, chopped
- ½ cup chopped onion
- 1 cup unsweetened pineapple tidbits plus 3 Tbsp. pineapple juice
- 1 cup cold water, divided
- 3 Tbsp. reduced-sodium teriyaki sauce
- 2 Tbsp. cornstarch
- 3 cups hot cooked brown rice

1. In a large cast-iron or other heavy skillet, heat oil over medium heat. Add chicken, herbs and lemon zest; saute until lightly browned. Add next 4 ingredients. Stir in pineapple tidbits, pineapple juice, ¾ cup water and teriyaki sauce; bring to a boil. Reduce heat; simmer, covered, until chicken is no longer pink and carrots are tender, 10-15 minutes.
2. Combine cornstarch and remaining ¼ cup water; gradually stir into chicken mixture. Bring to a boil; cook and stir until thickened, about 2 minutes. Serve with rice.
1 CUP WITH ½ CUP RICE: 330 cal., 6g fat (1g sat. fat), 42mg chol., 227mg sod., 50g carb. (14g sugars, 5g fiber), 20g pro.

TIP

WHAT OTHER INGREDIENTS CAN YOU ADD TO CHOP SUEY?

This dish is a great way to eat more veggies. Toss in whatever you have on hand, like green pepper, bok choy, broccoli or kale. You could also drizzle on some Sriracha sauce for a spicy kick.

SALMON GRILLED IN FOIL

This tender salmon steams up in foil packets, meaning easy cleanup later.
—*Merideth Berkovich, The Dalles, OR*

- -

TAKES: 20 min. • **MAKES:** 4 servings

4   salmon fillets (4 oz. each)
1   tsp. garlic powder
1   tsp. lemon-pepper seasoning
1   tsp. curry powder
½   tsp. salt
1   small onion, cut into rings
2   medium tomatoes, seeded and chopped

1. Place each salmon fillet, skin side down, on a double thickness of heavy-duty foil (about 18x12 in.). Combine garlic powder, lemon pepper, curry powder and salt; sprinkle over salmon. Top with onion and tomatoes. Fold foil over fish and seal tightly.

2. Grill, covered, over medium heat for 10-15 minutes or until fish flakes easily with a fork. Open foil carefully to allow steam to escape.

1 PACKET: 232 cal., 13g fat (3g sat. fat), 67mg chol., 482mg sod., 5g carb. (3g sugars, 1g fiber), 24g pro. **DIABETIC EXCHANGES:** 3 lean meat.

TIP

HOW CAN YOU TELL WHEN THE GRILLED SALMON IN FOIL IS COOKED?

Checking the internal temperature is the easiest way to tell if your salmon is cooked just right—the salmon needs to reach 140°F.

SAUCY SKILLET FISH

The main industry here on Kodiak Island is fishing, so I'm always on the lookout for new seafood recipes. This is my favorite way to fix halibut since it's quick and tasty. I often get recipe requests when I serve this to guests.
—*Merle Powell, Kodiak, AK*

TAKES: 20 min. • **MAKES:** 8 servings

- ½ cup all-purpose flour
- 1¼ tsp. salt
- 1 tsp. paprika
- ⅛ tsp. pepper
- 2 lbs. halibut, haddock or salmon fillets or steaks
- 1 medium onion, sliced
- ⅓ cup butter, cubed
- 1½ cups sour cream
- 1 tsp. dried basil
- 1 Tbsp. minced fresh parsley

1. In a large bowl, combine the flour, salt, paprika and pepper. Add fish and toss to coat (if using fillets, cut into serving-size pieces first).
2. In a large cast-iron or other heavy skillet, saute onion in butter until tender; remove and set aside. Add fish to the skillet, cook over medium heat until fish just begins to flake easily with a fork, 3-5 minutes on each side. Remove fish to a serving plate and keep warm.
3. Add the sour cream, basil and onion to the skillet; heat through (do not boil). Serve sauce over fish. Garnish with parsley.
1 SERVING: 319 cal., 18g fat (10g sat. fat), 87mg chol., 531mg sod., 9g carb. (3g sugars, 1g fiber), 26g pro.

SKILLET PIZZA

I created this recipe during a hot spell one summer. With the temperature in the 90s every day, I didn't want to turn on the oven. So I decided to make our favorite family pizza in an electric skillet instead! It's great to take along to get-togethers, too—you can prepare it at home, then just plug in the skillet when you arrive.
—*Darlene Brenden, Salem, OR*

TAKES: 30 min. • **MAKES:** 6 servings

- 1 pkg. (6½ oz.) pizza crust mix
- 1 can (8 oz.) tomato sauce
- 1 tsp. Italian seasoning
- ½ cup pepperoni slices
- ¼ cup chopped onion
- ¼ cup chopped green pepper
- ¼ cup sliced ripe olives
- 2 cups shredded mozzarella cheese

1. Grease a 12-in. electric or stovetop skillet. Prepare pizza crust according to package directions.
2. Line bottom and ½ in. up the side of the skillet with dough. Combine tomato sauce and Italian seasoning; spread over dough. Layer pepperoni, onion, green pepper and olives over sauce; sprinkle with cheese.
3. Cover and cook over medium heat (set electric skillet to 375°) until crust is brown on bottom and the cheese is melted, about 15 minutes. Slide pizza onto a cutting board. Serve immediately.
1 PIECE: 298 cal., 16g fat (7g sat. fat), 40mg chol., 847mg sod., 26g carb. (3g sugars, 2g fiber), 15g pro.

SPAGHETTI WITH FOUR CHEESES

Creamy and cheesy, this spaghetti dish is my mainstay whenever company's coming. The recipe, handed down from my aunt, is on the table in 30 minutes, so as cook and hostess, I don't feel hurried.
—*Nella Parker, Hersey, MI*

TAKES: 25 min. • **MAKES:** 6 servings

- 8 oz. uncooked spaghetti
- ¼ cup butter, cubed
- 1 Tbsp. all-purpose flour
- ¼ tsp. salt
- ¼ tsp. pepper
- 1½ cups half-and-half cream
- 1 cup shredded part-skim mozzarella cheese
- 4 oz. fontina cheese, shredded
- ½ cup shredded provolone cheese
- ¼ cup shredded Parmesan cheese
- 2 Tbsp. minced fresh parsley

1. Cook spaghetti according to package directions. Meanwhile, in a large saucepan, melt butter. Stir in the flour, salt and pepper until smooth. Gradually stir in cream. Bring to a boil; cook and stir for 2 minutes or until thickened. Remove from the heat; stir in cheeses until melted.

2. Drain spaghetti; toss with cheese sauce and parsley.

¾ CUP: 470 cal., 28g fat (17g sat. fat), 94mg chol., 622mg sod., 32g carb. (4g sugars, 1g fiber), 20g pro.

QUICK ALMOND CHICKEN STIR-FRY

I make this dish often because it is so quick and easy to prepare. My family likes the flavor that the sugar snap peas and almonds add. Sometimes I top it with chow mein noodles for extra crunch.
—*Darlene Brenden, Salem, OR*

TAKES: 20 min. • **MAKES:** 4 servings

- 1 cup whole unblanched almonds
- ¼ cup canola oil
- 1 lb. boneless skinless chicken breasts, cut into cubes
- 1 Tbsp. cornstarch
- ½ cup chicken broth
- 3 Tbsp. soy sauce
- 2 tsp. honey
- 1 tsp. ground ginger
- 1 pkg. (14 oz.) frozen sugar snap peas
   Hot cooked pasta or rice

1. In a large skillet over medium heat, cook almonds in oil for 3 minutes. Add the chicken; cook until meat is no longer pink, 5-7 minutes.

2. In a small bowl, combine cornstarch, broth, soy sauce, honey and ginger until smooth; add to chicken mixture. Bring to a boil; cook and stir until thickened, about 2 minutes. Reduce heat; add peas. Cook and stir until heated through. Serve with pasta or rice.

1 CUP: 526 cal., 35g fat (4g sat. fat), 63mg chol., 871mg sod., 21g carb. (8g sugars, 8g fiber), 35g pro.

PIZZA POTATO TOPPERS

Not only is this recipe quick and easy to make, but it's an economical dinner as well. I don't know of a more satisfying way to stretch a half pound of meat!
—*Sheila Friedrich, Antelope, MT*

TAKES: 25 min. • **MAKES:** 4 servings

- 4 medium baking potatoes
- ½ lb. ground beef
- ½ cup chopped green pepper
- 1 small onion, chopped
- 1 tomato, chopped
- ½ to ¾ cup pizza sauce
- 1 cup shredded part-skim mozzarella cheese
- Optional: Fresh oregano, basil or parsley

1. Prick potatoes with a fork; cook in a microwave until tender. Meanwhile, in a large skillet, cook and stir beef and green pepper with onion, crumbling beef, until meat is no longer pink; drain. Stir in tomato and pizza sauce; heat through.
2. Split potatoes lengthwise; flake potato centers with a fork. Spoon meat mixture into each; top with mozzarella cheese. Sprinkle with herbs if desired.

1 SERVING: 486 cal., 11g fat (5g sat. fat), 44mg chol., 325mg sod., 74g carb. (10g sugars, 7g fiber), 26g pro.

TIP

Italian sausage also tastes great in this recipe. If you have leftover potatoes from last night's dinner, this is a good way to repurpose them. Baked sweet potatoes will work too!

STEAK FAJITAS

Zesty salsa and tender strips of steak make these traditional fajitas extra special.
—*Rebecca Baird, Salt Lake City, UT*

- -

TAKES: 30 min. • **MAKES:** 6 servings

  2 **large tomatoes, seeded and chopped**
  ½ **cup diced red onion**
  ¼ **cup lime juice**
  1 **jalapeno pepper, seeded and minced**
  3 **Tbsp. minced fresh cilantro**
  2 **tsp. ground cumin, divided**
  ¾ **tsp. salt, divided**
  1 **beef flank steak (about 1½ lbs.)**
  1 **Tbsp. canola oil**
  1 **large onion, halved and sliced**
  6 **whole wheat tortillas (8 in.), warmed**
      Optional: Sliced avocado and lime wedges

1. For salsa, place first 5 ingredients in a small bowl; stir in 1 tsp. cumin and ¼ tsp. salt. Let stand until serving.
2. Sprinkle steak with the remaining 1 tsp. cumin and ½ tsp. salt. Grill, covered, over medium heat or broil 4 in. from heat until meat reaches desired doneness (for medium-rare, a thermometer should read 135°), 6-8 minutes. Let stand 5 minutes.
3. Meanwhile, in a skillet, heat oil over medium-high heat; saute onion until crisp-tender. Slice steak thinly across the grain; serve in tortillas with onion and salsa. If desired, serve with avocado and lime wedges.
NOTE: Wear disposable gloves when cutting hot peppers; the oils can burn skin. Avoid touching your face.
1 FAJITA: 329 cal., 12g fat (4g sat. fat), 54mg chol., 498mg sod., 29g carb. (3g sugars, 5g fiber), 27g pro. **DIABETIC EXCHANGES:** 3 lean meat, 2 starch, ½ fat.

SWEET-AND-SOUR PORK

After my sister moved away to university, I used to visit her on weekends. She often made this wonderful and tangy pork dish. Now, every time I make it for my family, it reminds me of those special visits with her. Everyone who tries this dish loves it.
—*Cherry Williams, St. Albert, AB*

- -

TAKES: 25 min. • **MAKES:** 4 servings

  1 **can (14 oz.) pineapple tidbits**
  2 **Tbsp. cornstarch**
  2 **Tbsp. brown sugar**
  ¾ **tsp. salt**
  ¼ **tsp. ground ginger**
  ¼ **tsp. pepper**
  ⅓ **cup water**
  ⅓ **cup ketchup**
  2 **Tbsp. white vinegar**
  2 **Tbsp. reduced-sodium soy sauce**
  1 **lb. pork tenderloin, cut into 1½x¼-in. strips**
  1 **medium onion, chopped**
  2 **Tbsp. canola oil**
  1 **green pepper, cut into thin strips**
      Hot cooked rice
      Sesame seeds, optional

1. Drain pineapple, reserving juice; set aside. In a small bowl, combine the cornstarch, brown sugar, salt, ginger and pepper. Stir in the water, ketchup, vinegar, soy sauce and reserved juice until smooth.
2. In a large skillet or wok, stir-fry pork and onion in oil for 4-8 minutes or until tender. Stir pineapple juice mixture; add to skillet. Bring to a boil; cook and stir for 1-2 minutes or until thickened.
3. Add green pepper and reserved pineapple. Reduce heat; cover and cook 5 minutes or until pepper is tender. Serve with rice and, if desired, sesame seeds.
1 SERVING: 333 cal., 11g fat (2g sat. fat), 63mg chol., 1190mg sod., 35g carb. (24g sugars, 2g fiber), 25g pro.

SPEEDY CHICKEN MARSALA

Since this is one of our favorite dishes to order in restaurants, I created an at-home version that can be made in a flash.
—*Trisha Kruse, Eagle, ID*

TAKES: 30 min. • **MAKES:** 4 servings

- 8 oz. uncooked whole wheat or multigrain angel hair pasta
- 4 boneless skinless chicken breast halves (5 oz. each)
- ¼ cup all-purpose flour
- 1 tsp. lemon-pepper seasoning
- ½ tsp. salt
- 2 Tbsp. olive oil, divided
- 4 cups sliced fresh mushrooms
- 1 garlic clove, minced
- 1 cup dry Marsala wine

1. Cook pasta according to package directions. Pound chicken with a meat mallet to ¼-in. thickness. In a bowl or shallow dish, mix the flour, lemon pepper and salt. Add the chicken, 1 piece at a time, and turn to coat.
2. In a large skillet, heat 1 Tbsp. oil over medium heat. Add the chicken; cook for 4-5 minutes on each side or until no longer pink. Remove from pan.
3. In the same skillet, heat remaining 1 Tbsp. oil over medium-high heat. Add mushrooms; cook and stir until tender. Add garlic; cook 1 minute longer. Add the wine; bring to a boil. Cook for 5-6 minutes or until liquid is reduced by half, stirring to loosen the browned bits from pan. Return chicken to the pan, turning to coat with sauce; heat through.
4. Drain pasta; serve with chicken and mushroom mixture.

1 SERVING: 493 cal., 11g fat (2g sat. fat), 78mg chol., 279mg sod., 50g carb. (4g sugars, 7g fiber), 40g pro.

> *"Really easy and everyone, including the kids, liked it. I used a cast-iron skillet that was smoking hot to give the chicken some really beautiful brown color. I added a lot of fresh ground pepper too."*
>
> —SHANNONDOBOS, TASTEOFHOME.COM

REVIEW

CHICKEN FLORENTINE PIZZA

On pizza night, we like to switch things up with this version featuring chicken, spinach and ricotta cheese. One taste and you won't miss traditional sauce one bit.
—*Pam Corder, Monroe, LA*

TAKES: 25 min. • **MAKES:** 8 servings

- 1 tsp. Italian seasoning
- ½ tsp. garlic powder
- 3 cups cooked chicken breasts (about 1 lb.), cubed
- 1 cup whole-milk ricotta cheese
- 1 prebaked 12-in. pizza crust
- 1 pkg. (10 oz.) frozen chopped spinach, thawed and squeezed dry
- 2 Tbsp. oil-packed sun-dried tomatoes, drained and chopped
- ½ cup shredded fresh mozzarella cheese
- ¼ cup grated Parmesan cheese

Preheat oven to 425°. Stir together Italian seasoning and garlic powder; toss with chicken. Spread ricotta cheese on pizza crust. Top with chicken, spinach and tomatoes. Sprinkle with mozzarella and Parmesan cheese. Bake 10-15 minutes or until crust is golden and cheese is melted.

1 SLICE: 311 cal., 11g fat (5g sat. fat), 65mg chol., 423mg sod., 26g carb. (3g sugars, 2g fiber), 28g pro.

TIP

> This pizza is wonderful for dinner but can also be cut into bite-sized pieces and served as a fun appetizer at your next party. Feel free to add a few of your favorite toppings, such as mushrooms or chopped fresh tomatoes.

PORK CHOPS WITH RHUBARB

A surprising rhubarb sauce makes these tender chops extra special. I like this fruity sauce on the tangy side, but you can always add more honey to sweeten it up a bit if it's too puckery for your family.
—*Bonnie Bufford, Nicholson, PA*

- -

TAKES: 25 min. • **MAKES:** 2 servings

- 1 Tbsp. all-purpose flour
  Salt and pepper to taste
- 2 bone-in pork loin chops (½ to ¾ in. thick)
- 2 Tbsp. butter
- ½ lb. fresh or frozen rhubarb, chopped
- 1 Tbsp. honey
- ⅛ tsp. ground cinnamon
- 1½ tsp. minced fresh parsley

In a shallow dish, combine the flour, salt and pepper; add pork chops and turn to coat. In a skillet, melt butter over medium heat. Add the pork chops; cook 4-5 minutes on each side or until a thermometer reads 145°. Remove and keep warm. Add rhubarb, honey and cinnamon to the skillet; cook until rhubarb is tender, about 5 minutes. Serve the sauce over the pork chops. Sprinkle with minced parsley.

1 PORK CHOP: 492 cal., 30g fat (14g sat. fat), 142mg chol., 173mg sod., 17g carb. (10g sugars, 2g fiber), 38g pro.

SAUCY MAC & CHEESE

I love the curly noodles in this creamy recipe. Cavatappi, also sold under the name cellentani, is a corkscrew pasta, but any type of spiral pasta will work. This dish is fun to make and looks so pretty topped with extra cheese and crunchy, golden crumbs. I like to add ground pepper to my serving.
—*Sara Martin, Brookfield, WI*

- -

TAKES: 25 min. • **MAKES:** 4 servings

- 2 cups cavatappi or other spiral pasta
- 3 Tbsp. butter, divided
- ⅓ cup panko bread crumbs
- 2 Tbsp. all-purpose flour
- 1½ cups 2% milk
- ¾ lb. Velveeta, cubed
- ¼ cup shredded cheddar cheese

1. Cook pasta according to package directions. Meanwhile, in a large nonstick skillet, melt 1 Tbsp. butter over medium-high heat. Add bread crumbs; cook and stir until golden brown. Remove to a small bowl and set aside.
2. In the same skillet, melt remaining 2 Tbsp. butter. Stir in flour until smooth. Gradually add milk; bring to a boil. Cook and stir until thickened, about 2 minutes. Reduce heat. Stir in Velveeta until melted.
3. Drain pasta; add to cheese mixture. Cook and stir until heated through, 3-4 minutes. Sprinkle with cheddar cheese and toasted bread crumbs.

1¼ CUPS: 661 cal., 36g fat (21g sat. fat), 121mg chol., 1267mg sod., 58g carb. (11g sugars, 2g fiber), 27g pro.

> **TIP**
>
> Turn up the fun on pasta night by serving this family favorite as the main attraction in a mac-and-cheese bar. Make it hearty with meaty toppings like crumbled bacon, shredded rotisserie chicken or taco meat, and pile on the freshness with chopped tomatoes, bell peppers, green onions and more.

DELISH PESTO PASTA WITH CHICKEN MARSALA

This is my easy go-to chicken and pasta recipe. It is ready in less than 30 minutes and fabulous on a weeknight.
—*Lorraine Stevenski, Land O' Lakes, FL*

TAKES: 30 min. • **MAKES:** 6 servings

- 4 cups uncooked penne pasta
- 2 Tbsp. olive oil, divided
- 2 lbs. boneless skinless chicken breasts, cut into thin strips, divided
- 3 garlic cloves, minced
- 2 tsp. grated lemon zest
- 1 cup Marsala wine
- 2 Tbsp. lemon juice
- 1 cup grated Parmesan cheese
- 1 cup 2% milk
- 1 envelope creamy pesto sauce mix
- 1 Tbsp. minced fresh basil
- 1 Tbsp. minced fresh parsley

1. Cook pasta according to package directions. In a Dutch oven, heat 1 Tbsp. oil over medium-high heat. Add half of the chicken; cook and stir until no longer pink. Remove from the pan. Repeat with remaining oil and chicken; remove from the pan.
2. Add garlic and lemon zest to the same pan; cook and stir for 30 seconds. Add wine and lemon juice, stirring to loosen browned bits from the pan. Bring to a boil; cook until liquid is reduced by half. Stir in the cheese, milk and sauce mix. Add chicken; cook until sauce is slightly thickened.
3. Drain pasta; add to chicken mixture and toss to combine.
4. Sprinkle with herbs.
1¼ CUPS: 539 cal., 14g fat (4g sat. fat), 98mg chol., 622mg sod., 49g carb. (8g sugars, 2g fiber), 43g pro.

FRESH CORN & TOMATO FETTUCCINE

This recipe combines delicious whole wheat pasta with the best of fresh garden produce. It's tossed with heart-healthy olive oil, and a little feta cheese adds a nice bite.
—*Angela Spengler, Niceville, FL*

TAKES: 30 min. • **MAKES:** 4 servings

- 8 oz. uncooked whole wheat fettuccine
- 2 medium ears sweet corn, husked
- 2 tsp. plus 2 Tbsp. olive oil, divided
- ½ cup chopped sweet red pepper
- 4 green onions, chopped
- 2 medium tomatoes, chopped
- ½ tsp. salt
- ½ tsp. pepper
- 1 cup crumbled feta cheese
- 2 Tbsp. minced fresh parsley

1. In a Dutch oven, cook fettuccine according to package directions, adding corn during the last 8 minutes of cooking.
2. Meanwhile, in a small skillet, heat 2 tsp. oil over medium-high heat. Add red pepper and green onions; cook and stir until tender.
3. Drain pasta and corn; transfer pasta to a large bowl. Cool corn slightly; cut corn from cobs and add to pasta. Add tomatoes, salt, pepper, remaining 2 Tbsp. oil and the red pepper mixture; toss to combine. Sprinkle with cheese and parsley.
2 CUPS: 527 cal., 17g fat (5g sat. fat), 84mg chol., 1051mg sod., 75g carb. (7g sugars, 9g fiber), 21g pro.

CHICKEN BISCUIT SKILLET

My mother always made this when we were growing up. Now I make it for my own husband and kids. I use the small biscuits because they brown up so nicely on top. I also add mushrooms because my family loves 'em.

—*Keri Boffeli, Monticello, IA*

TAKES: 30 min. • **MAKES:** 6 servings

- 1 Tbsp. butter
- ⅓ cup chopped onion
- ¼ cup all-purpose flour
- 1 can (10½ oz.) condensed chicken broth, undiluted
- ¼ cup fat-free milk
- ⅛ tsp. pepper
- 2 cups shredded cooked chicken breast
- 2 cups frozen peas and carrots (about 10 oz.), thawed
- 1 tube (12 oz.) refrigerated buttermilk biscuits, quartered

1. Preheat oven to 400°. Melt butter in a 10-in. cast-iron or other ovenproof skillet over medium-high heat. Add onion; cook and stir until tender, 2-3 minutes.

2. In a small bowl, mix flour, broth, milk and pepper until smooth; stir into pan. Bring to a boil, stirring constantly; cook and stir until thickened, 1-2 minutes. Add the chicken and vegetables; heat through. Arrange quartered biscuits over stew. Bake until the biscuits are golden brown, 15-20 minutes.

1 SERVING: 320 cal., 11g fat (4g sat. fat), 42mg chol., 861mg sod., 36g carb. (4g sugars, 2g fiber), 22g pro.

> **TIP**
>
> This is a satisfying and delicious way to use leftover chicken (or turkey, during the holiday season). The biscuits are plentiful, making this a hearty dish that's perfect for chilly weather.

CRISPY FISH & CHIPS

A British pub classic turns crown jewel when you add horseradish, panko and Worcestershire. You can also try it with a white fish like cod or haddock.

—*Linda Schend, Kenosha, WI*

TAKES: 30 min. • **MAKES:** 4 servings

- 4 cups frozen steak fries
- 4 salmon fillets (6 oz. each)
- 1 to 2 Tbsp. prepared horseradish
- 1 Tbsp. grated Parmesan cheese
- 1 Tbsp. Worcestershire sauce
- 1 tsp. Dijon mustard
- ¼ tsp. salt
- ½ cup panko bread crumbs
  Cooking spray

1. Preheat oven to 450°. Arrange steak fries in a single layer on a baking sheet. Bake on lowest oven rack 18-20 minutes or until light golden brown.

2. Meanwhile, place salmon on a foil-lined baking sheet coated with cooking spray. In a small bowl, mix horseradish, cheese, Worcestershire sauce, mustard and salt; stir in panko. Press mixture onto fillets. Spritz tops with cooking spray.

3. Bake salmon on middle oven rack 8-10 minutes or until fish just begins to flake easily with a fork. Serve with fries.

1 FILLET WITH ¾ CUP FRIES: 416 cal., 19g fat (4g sat. fat), 86mg chol., 698mg sod., 26g carb. (2g sugars, 2g fiber), 32g pro. **DIABETIC EXCHANGES:** 5 lean meat, 1½ starch.

> **REVIEW**
>
> *"Absolutely delicious! Loved the crunchy coating. I substituted sweet potato fries for the steak fries and sprinkled malt vinegar on both my fish and my chips."*
>
> —IMMANDA, TASTEOFHOME.COM

BAKED LEMON HADDOCK

After testing out a ton of haddock recipes, I've decided that this baked version is the best. The combination of crunchy topping and lemon is just delicious.
—*Jean Ann Perkins, Newburyport, MA*

TAKES: 30 min. • **MAKES:** 6 servings

- 2 **lbs. haddock fillets**
- 1 **cup seasoned dry bread crumbs**
- ¼ **cup butter, melted**
- 2 **Tbsp. dried parsley flakes**
- 2 **tsp. grated lemon zest**
- ½ **tsp. garlic powder**

Preheat oven to 350°. Cut the fish into 6 serving-sized pieces. Place in a greased 11x7-in. baking dish. Combine remaining ingredients; sprinkle over fish. Bake until fish just begins to flake easily with a fork, 20-25 minutes.

4 OZ. COOKED FISH: 269 cal., 9g fat (5g sat. fat), 108mg chol., 446mg sod., 13g carb. (1g sugars, 1g fiber), 32g pro. **DIABETIC EXCHANGES:** 4 lean meat, 2 fat, 1 starch.

IS IT BETTER TO BAKE HADDOCK COVERED OR UNCOVERED?

TIP

This baked haddock recipe does not need to be covered while it's baking. The bread crumb mixture will help lock in some moisture, while at the same time getting a nice and crispy texture from being uncovered in the oven.

BEEFY FRENCH ONION POTPIE

I came up with this dish knowing that my husband loves French onion soup. It makes a perfect base for this hearty, beefy potpie.
—*Sara Hutchens, Du Quoin, IL*

TAKES: 30 min. • **MAKES:** 4 servings

- 1 lb. ground beef
- 1 small onion, chopped
- 1 can (10½ oz.) condensed French onion soup
- 1½ cups shredded part-skim mozzarella cheese
- 1 tube (12 oz.) refrigerated buttermilk biscuits

1. Preheat oven to 350°. In a large skillet, cook beef and onion over medium heat 6-8 minutes or until beef is no longer pink, breaking beef into crumbles; drain. Stir in soup; bring to a boil.
2. Transfer to an ungreased 9-in. deep-dish pie plate; sprinkle with cheese. Bake for 5 minutes or until cheese is melted. Top with biscuits. Bake 15-20 minutes longer or until the biscuits are golden brown.

1 SERVING: 553 cal., 23g fat (10g sat. fat), 98mg chol., 1550mg sod., 47g carb. (4g sugars, 1g fiber), 38g pro.

ASPARAGUS HAM DINNER

I've been making this light meal for my family for years now, and it's always well received. With asparagus, tomato, pasta and chunks of ham, it's a tempting blend of tastes and textures.
—*Rhonda Zavodny, David City, NE*

TAKES: 25 min. • **MAKES:** 6 servings

- 2 cups uncooked corkscrew or spiral pasta
- ¾ lb. fresh asparagus, cut into 1-in. pieces
- 1 medium sweet yellow pepper, julienned
- 1 Tbsp. olive oil
- 6 medium tomatoes, diced
- 6 oz. boneless fully cooked ham, cubed
- ¼ cup minced fresh parsley
- ½ tsp. salt
- ½ tsp. dried oregano
- ½ tsp. dried basil
- ⅛ to ¼ tsp. cayenne pepper
- ¼ cup shredded Parmesan cheese

Cook pasta according to package directions. Meanwhile, in a large cast-iron or other heavy skillet, saute asparagus and yellow pepper in oil until crisp-tender. Add the tomatoes and ham; heat through. Drain pasta; add to mixture. Stir in the parsley and seasonings. Sprinkle with cheese.

1⅓ CUPS: 204 cal., 5g fat (1g sat. fat), 17mg chol., 561mg sod., 29g carb. (5g sugars, 3g fiber), 12g pro. **DIABETIC EXCHANGES:** 1½ starch, 1 vegetable, 1 lean meat, ½ fat.

CHICKEN-FRIED STEAKS

Folks gush over these crispy beef steaks. My husband asks me to prepare them regularly, and they're so easy to make.
—*Denice Louk, Garnett, KS*

TAKES: 25 min. • **MAKES:** 4 servings

- 2 cups all-purpose flour, divided
- 2 tsp. baking powder
- ¾ tsp. each salt, onion powder, garlic powder, chili powder and pepper
- 1 large egg, lightly beaten
- 1¼ cups buttermilk, divided
- 4 beef cubed steaks (4 oz. each)
  Oil for frying
- 1½ cups 2% milk

1. In a shallow bowl, combine 1¾ cups flour, baking powder and seasonings. In another shallow bowl, combine egg and ¾ cup buttermilk. Pat steaks dry with a paper towel. Dip each steak in buttermilk mixture, then roll in flour mixture. Let stand 5 minutes.

2. In a large cast-iron or other heavy skillet, heat ½ in. of oil over medium-high heat. Fry steaks for 5-7 minutes. Turn carefully; cook until coating is crisp and meat is no longer pink, about 5 minutes longer. Remove steaks and keep warm.

3. Drain, reserving ⅓ cup drippings; stir remaining ¼ cup flour into drippings until smooth. Cook and stir over medium heat for 2 minutes. Gradually whisk in the milk and remaining ½ cup buttermilk. Bring to a boil; cook and stir until thickened, 2 minutes. Serve with steaks.

1 STEAK WITH ½ CUP GRAVY: 537 cal., 11g fat (5g sat. fat), 186mg chol., 865mg sod., 64g carb. (11g sugars, 2g fiber), 43g pro.

TIP

HOW DO YOU KEEP THE BREADING ON CHICKEN-FRIED STEAK FROM FALLING OFF?

A key step is starting with meat that has been patted dry. Then, dredge the steak as the recipe directs—first in the milk mixture and then the seasoned flour, shaking off any excess. Letting the meat stand after dredging also helps the coating adhere.

SHRIMP ALFREDO

Instead of buying a jar of Alfredo sauce, make it from scratch with this simple recipe. The enticing garlic aroma will call your family to the table.
—*Taste of Home Test Kitchen*

TAKES: 30 min. • **MAKES:** 4 servings

- 8 oz. uncooked fettuccine
- ¼ cup butter, cubed
- 1½ cups heavy whipping cream
- 1 lb. cooked medium shrimp, peeled and deveined
- ¾ cup grated Parmesan cheese
- 1 garlic clove, minced
- ¼ tsp. pepper
- 1 tsp. minced fresh parsley

1. Cook the fettuccine according to the package directions. Meanwhile, in a large saucepan, melt the butter over medium heat. Stir in the cream. Bring to a gentle boil. Reduce the heat; simmer, uncovered, for 3 minutes, stirring constantly.

2. Add the shrimp, cheese, garlic and pepper; cook and stir until heated through. Drain fettuccine; toss with shrimp mixture. Sprinkle with parsley.

1 CUP: 794 cal., 52g fat (31g sat. fat), 337mg chol., 616mg sod., 44g carb. (5g sugars, 2g fiber), 39g pro.

SAUSAGE POTATO SKILLET

While I was growing up, both my parents worked, so I often went home for lunch with my Italian girlfriend. Lunch was always the same—sausage, fried potatoes, green peppers and onions—but I could never get enough of my favorite meal.
—Amelia Bordas, Springfield, VA

TAKES: 30 min. • **MAKES:** 2 servings

- 2　fresh Italian sausage links
- 1　Tbsp. canola oil
- 1　small onion, sliced
- ¼　cup each sliced green and sweet red pepper
- 2　small potatoes, sliced
　　Salt and pepper to taste

In a large skillet, brown sausage in oil until a thermometer reads 160°. Add onion and peppers; saute until vegetables are tender. Add potatoes and 2 cups water; bring to a boil. Reduce heat; cover and simmer for 15 minutes or until potatoes are tender. Drain; add salt and pepper.

1 SERVING: 416 cal., 22g fat (6g sat. fat), 45mg chol., 544mg sod., 40g carb. (6g sugars, 4g fiber), 15g pro.

WHAT ELSE GOES WELL WITH SAUSAGE?
Sausage pairs well with other veggies, like zucchini, tomatoes and broccoli. Feel free to toss some extra vegetables into your skillet.

PORK VEGGIE STIR-FRY

Even kids find this colorful combo of vegetables, pork strips, seasonings and peanuts very appealing. Serve it over rice for a main dish that needs no sides.
—Laurel Reisinger, Saskatoon, SK

TAKES: 20 min. • **MAKES:** 6 servings

- 3　cups sliced cauliflower
- 3　Tbsp. vegetable oil, divided
- 2　medium carrots, julienned
- 1　can (15 oz.) whole baby corn, rinsed and drained
- ½　cup frozen peas, thawed
- 1　lb. boneless pork, cut into thin strips
- 2　green onions, thinly sliced
- 2　garlic cloves, minced
- 1　Tbsp. minced fresh gingerroot
- ½ to 1 tsp. chili powder
- 1　cup water
- ¼　cup soy sauce
- 4　tsp. honey
- 2　tsp. chicken bouillon granules
- 4　tsp. cornstarch
- 2　Tbsp. cold water
- ¼　cup salted peanuts
　　Hot cooked rice, optional

1. In a skillet or wok, stir-fry cauliflower in 2 Tbsp. oil for 3 minutes. Add carrots; stir-fry for 2 minutes. Add corn and peas; stir-fry until vegetables are crisp-tender. Remove; keep warm.
2. Stir-fry the pork in remaining 1 Tbsp. oil for 2 minutes. Add onions, garlic, ginger and chili powder; stir-fry until pork is no longer pink. Remove; keep warm.
3. Combine 1 cup water, soy sauce, honey and bouillon in same pan. Combine the cornstarch and cold water; gradually add to pan. Bring to a boil; cook and stir for 2 minutes or until thickened.
4. Return vegetables and pork mixture to pan; heat through. Stir in peanuts. If desired, serve with rice.

1 SERVING: 277 cal., 14g fat (3g sat. fat), 45mg chol., 1131mg sod., 16g carb. (8g sugars, 4g fiber), 22g pro.

HEARTY VEGETABLE BEEF RAGU

This recipe is healthy yet satisfying, quick yet delicious. I can have a hearty meal on the table in under 30 minutes, and it's one that my children will gobble up! If you are not fond of kale, stir in baby spinach or chopped broccoli instead.
—Kim Van Dunk, Caldwell, NJ

TAKES: 30 min. • **MAKES:** 8 servings

4	cups uncooked whole wheat spiral pasta
1	lb. lean ground beef (90% lean)
1	large onion, chopped
3	garlic cloves, minced
2	cans (14½ oz. each) Italian diced tomatoes, undrained
1	jar (24 oz.) meatless spaghetti sauce
2	cups finely chopped fresh kale
1	pkg. (9 oz.) frozen peas, thawed
¾	tsp. garlic powder
¼	tsp. pepper
	Grated Parmesan cheese, optional

1. Cook pasta according to package directions; drain. Meanwhile, in a Dutch oven, cook beef, onion and garlic over medium heat, crumbling beef, until meat is no longer pink, 6-8 minutes; drain.
2. Stir in tomatoes, spaghetti sauce, kale, peas, garlic powder and pepper. Bring to a boil. Reduce heat; simmer, uncovered, until kale is tender, 8-10 minutes. Stir pasta into sauce. If desired, serve with cheese.

1½ CUPS: 302 cal., 5g fat (2g sat. fat), 35mg chol., 837mg sod., 43g carb. (15g sugars, 7g fiber), 20g pro. **DIABETIC EXCHANGES:** 2 starch, 2 vegetable, 2 lean meat.

HAMBURGER STROGANOFF

This easy ground beef stroganoff makes a quick weeknight dinner. I serve with a side salad for a complete meal.
—Deb Helmer, Lynden, WA

TAKES: 30 min. • **MAKES:** 6 servings

1½	lbs. ground beef
½	cup chopped onion
	Dash garlic salt
2	Tbsp. all-purpose flour
1	cup water or beef broth
1	can (10¾ oz.) condensed cream of mushroom soup, undiluted
1	can (4½ oz.) mushrooms, drained
1	cup sour cream
	Salt and pepper to taste
	Cooked noodles or rice
	Chopped fresh parsley, optional

1. In a skillet, cook the beef over medium heat, breaking into crumbles, until no longer pink, 5-7 minutes; drain. Add onion and garlic salt to beef; continue to cook until onion is soft. Stir in the flour; cook and stir 2-3 minutes. Add water, condensed soup and mushrooms; bring to a simmer. Reduce heat; cook, stirring occasionally, 8-10 minutes.
2. Gently fold in sour cream; heat only until warm. Add salt and pepper to taste. Serve over noodles or rice. If desired, top with chopped parsley.

1 SERVING: 318 cal., 19g fat (10g sat. fat), 84mg chol., 561mg sod., 10g carb. (3g sugars, 1g fiber), 23g pro.

- ZESTY CHICKEN SOFT TACOS -

You can serve these in corn or flour tortillas instead of naan flatbread if you prefer. Set out toppings to let guests customize their tacos.

In a small bowl, mix 1 cup **reduced-fat sour cream,** 2 Tbsp. **Sriracha chili** sauce, 2 Tbsp. **lime juice,** 1½ tsp. grated **lime zest,** ½ tsp. **salt** and ⅛ tsp. **pepper.** Spread over 6 warm **naan flatbreads.** Top with shredded meat from 1 **rotisserie chicken,** skin removed. If desired, sprinkle each with minced **fresh cilantro.**

- 7 -

COOKING FOR ONE OR TWO

Forget prepackaged meals or endless leftovers. Whether you're a newlywed, an empty nester or simply the main cook for a small household, this mouthwatering collection offers all the classics you love, sized just right for one or two diners.

SHRIMP PASTA PRIMAVERA

They say the way to a man's heart is through his stomach. So when I invite a special guy to dinner, I prepare something I know will impress. This well-seasoned pasta dish has tons of flavor, and it won't hurt your budget!
—*Shari Neff, Takoma Park, MD*

TAKES: 15 min. • **MAKES:** 2 servings

- 4 oz. uncooked angel hair pasta
- 8 jumbo shrimp, peeled and deveined
- 6 fresh asparagus spears, trimmed and cut into 2-in. pieces
- ¼ cup olive oil
- 2 garlic cloves, minced
- ½ cup sliced fresh mushrooms
- ½ cup chicken broth
- 1 small plum tomato, peeled, seeded and diced
- ¼ tsp. salt
- ⅛ tsp. crushed red pepper flakes
- 1 Tbsp. each minced fresh basil, oregano, thyme and parsley
- ¼ cup grated Parmesan cheese

1. Cook pasta according to package directions. Meanwhile, in a large skillet, saute shrimp and asparagus in oil until shrimp turn pink, 3-4 minutes. Add garlic; cook 1 minute longer. Add the mushrooms, broth, tomato, salt and red pepper flakes; simmer, uncovered, for 2 minutes.
2. Drain pasta. Add the pasta and fresh herbs to skillet; toss to coat. Sprinkle with cheese.
1 SERVING: 581 cal., 32g fat (6g sat. fat), 89mg chol., 783mg sod., 49g carb. (4g sugars, 3g fiber), 24g pro.

CREAMY HAM & POTATOES

If you love scalloped potatoes and have a small household, this downsized version with tender chunks of ham is just for you.
—*Wendy Rowley, Green River, WY*

PREP: 20 min. • **COOK:** 5 hours • **MAKES:** 2 servings

- 2 large red potatoes, cubed
- ⅓ cup cubed Velveeta
- ¾ cup cubed fully cooked ham
- 1 Tbsp. dried minced onion
- ⅔ cup condensed cream of celery soup, undiluted
- ⅔ cup 2% milk
- 1 Tbsp. all-purpose flour
- ¼ tsp. pepper

1. In a greased 1½-qt. slow cooker, layer the potatoes, cheese, ham and onion.
2. In a small bowl, combine soup and milk; whisk in flour and pepper. Pour over potatoes. Cover and cook on low until potatoes are tender, 5-6 hours. Stir before serving.
1½ CUPS: 398 cal., 15g fat (6g sat. fat), 52mg chol., 1534mg sod., 45g carb. (8g sugars, 4g fiber), 20g pro.

HONEY-DIJON SALMON & ASPARAGUS

Here's our favorite salmon recipe. It's easy to make, nutritious and delicious. The best part is that cleanup is a snap!
—*Betty Stewart, Leola, PA*

TAKES: 25 min. • **MAKES:** 2 servings

1½ tsp. cornstarch
2¼ tsp. butter, melted
1 tsp. Worcestershire sauce
2 Tbsp. honey
1 Tbsp. Dijon mustard
Dash white pepper
2 salmon fillets (4 oz. each)
¼ cup chopped walnuts
½ lb. fresh asparagus, trimmed

1. In a bowl, combine cornstarch, butter and Worcestershire sauce until smooth. Stir in the honey, mustard and pepper.
2. Place each salmon fillet on a double thickness of heavy-duty foil (about 18x12-in.). Drizzle with honey mixture and sprinkle with walnuts. Place asparagus around salmon. Fold foil around salmon and seal tightly. Grill foil packets, covered, over medium heat for 15-20 minutes or until fish flakes easily with a fork.
1 SERVING: 437 cal., 26g fat (6g sat. fat), 78mg chol., 335mg sod., 25g carb. (17g sugars, 2g fiber), 28g pro.

SIMPLE SALSA CHICKEN

My husband and I prefer our food a little spicier than our children like it, so one evening I baked plain chicken for the kids and created this dish for us. It's now a regular menu item at our house.
—*Jan Cooper, Troy, AL*

PREP: 10 min. • **BAKE:** 25 min. • **MAKES:** 2 servings

2 boneless skinless chicken breast halves (5 oz. each)
⅛ tsp. salt
⅓ cup salsa
2 Tbsp. taco sauce
⅓ cup shredded Mexican cheese blend
Optional: Lime wedges and sliced avocado

1. Place the chicken in a shallow 2-qt. baking dish coated with cooking spray. Sprinkle with salt. Combine salsa and taco sauce; drizzle over chicken. Sprinkle with cheese.
2. Cover and bake chicken at 350° for 25-30 minutes or until a thermometer reads 165°. If desired, serve with lime wedges and sliced avocado.
1 SERVING: 226 cal., 7g fat (3g sat. fat), 92mg chol., 628mg sod., 3g carb. (2g sugars, 0 fiber), 34g pro. **DIABETIC EXCHANGES:** 5 lean meat, 1 fat.

TIP

CAN YOU MAKE THIS SIMPLE SALSA CHICKEN AHEAD OF TIME?

The dish tastes best the day it's made; however, there are no food safety issues with making it 1-2 days in advance (as long as it's stored properly in the fridge). When ready to serve, place the cooked chicken breasts in a 2-qt. baking dish and reheat in a 350° oven for 10-15 minutes. Add additional salsa and cheese to keep the chicken moist, and remove the dish from the oven as soon as the chicken reaches an internal temperature of 165°.

ASPARAGUS-STUFFED CHICKEN ROLLS

With its pretty presentation and succulent flavors, this rich entree makes any meal feel like a special occasion.
—*Louise Ambrose, Kingston, NY*

PREP: 20 min. • **BAKE:** 20 min.
MAKES: 2 servings

- 8 fresh asparagus spears
- 2 boneless skinless chicken breast halves (5 oz. each)
- 1 Tbsp. Dijon mustard
- 4 fresh sage leaves
- 2 slices provolone cheese (1 oz. each)
- 2 slices deli ham (¾ oz. each)
- ¼ cup all-purpose flour
- 1 large egg, lightly beaten
- ½ cup dry bread crumbs
- ¼ cup grated Parmesan cheese
- 1½ tsp. butter
- 1½ tsp. olive oil
- ¼ cup white wine or chicken broth

1. In a large skillet, bring ½ in. of water to a boil. Add asparagus; cover and boil for 3 minutes. Drain and immediately place asparagus in ice water. Drain and pat dry.
2. Flatten the chicken to ¼-in. thickness. Spread Dijon mustard over 1 side of each chicken breast. Down the center of each, place 2 sage leaves, 1 provolone cheese slice, 1 ham slice and 4 asparagus spears. Fold chicken over the asparagus; secure with toothpicks.
3. Place flour and egg in separate shallow bowls. In another shallow bowl, combine bread crumbs and Parmesan cheese. Coat chicken with flour, dip in egg, then coat with bread crumb mixture.
4. In a large skillet, brown chicken on all sides in butter and oil. Transfer to an 8-in. square baking dish coated with cooking spray. Add wine to the skillet, stirring to loosen browned bits from pan. Pour over the chicken.
5. Bake at 350° for 20-25 minutes or until the chicken is no longer pink. Discard the toothpicks before serving.
1 STUFFED CHICKEN BREAST HALF: 459 cal., 21g fat (9g sat. fat), 174mg chol., 873mg sod., 14g carb. (2g sugars, 1g fiber), 46g pro.

STEAK STRIPS WITH DUMPLINGS

You'll love the aroma when you come home to this delicious slow-cooked specialty. Homemade dumplings make it wonderful.
—*John Smalldridge, Princeton, ID*

PREP: 25 min. • **COOK:** 5 hours
MAKES: 2 servings

- ¾ lb. beef top round steak, cut into ½-in. strips
- ¼ tsp. pepper
- 2 tsp. canola oil
- ⅔ cup condensed cream of chicken soup, undiluted
- ½ cup beef broth
- 4 large fresh mushrooms, sliced
- ¼ cup each chopped onion, green pepper and celery

DUMPLINGS
- ½ cup all-purpose flour
- ¾ tsp. baking powder
- ¼ tsp. salt
- 2 Tbsp. beaten egg
- 3 Tbsp. 2% milk
- ½ tsp. dried parsley flakes

1. Sprinkle steak with pepper. In a small skillet, brown steak in oil over medium-high heat. Transfer to a 1½-qt. slow cooker. Combine the soup, broth and vegetables; pour over steak. Cover and cook on low for 4-5 hours.
2. For dumplings, in a small bowl, combine the flour, baking powder and salt. Stir in egg and milk just until blended. Drop by tablespoonfuls onto the meat mixture. Sprinkle with parsley.
3. Cover and cook on high until a toothpick inserted in a dumpling comes out clean, about 1 hour. (Do not lift the slow cooker's cover while cooking.)
¾ CUP BEEF MIXTURE WITH 3 DUMPLINGS: 506 cal., 17g fat (4g sat. fat), 168mg chol., 1372mg sod., 36g carb. (5g sugars, 3g fiber), 49g pro.

AIR-FRYER TILAPIA FILLETS

Get dinner on the table in less than half an hour. The air fryer makes it quick and easy, and it doesn't dry out the delicate fillets.
—*Dana Alexander, Lebanon, MO*

TAKES: 20 min. • **MAKES:** 2 servings

- 2 tilapia fillets (6 oz. each)
- 1 Tbsp. butter, melted
- 1 tsp. Montreal steak seasoning
- ½ tsp. dried parsley flakes
- ¼ tsp. paprika
- ¼ tsp. dried thyme
- ⅛ tsp. onion powder
- ⅛ tsp. salt
- ⅛ tsp. pepper
  Dash garlic powder

1. Preheat air fryer to 400°. Brush fillets with butter. In a small bowl, mix remaining ingredients; sprinkle over fillets.
2. Place fillets in a single layer on greased tray in air-fryer basket. Cook until fish just begins to flake easily with a fork, 6-8 minutes.
NOTE: In our testing, we find cook times vary dramatically between brands of air fryers. As a result, we give wider than normal ranges on suggested cook times. Begin checking at the first time listed and adjust as needed.
1 FILLET: 193 cal., 7g fat (4g sat. fat), 98mg chol., 594mg sod., 0 carb. (0 sugars, 0 fiber), 32g pro. **DIABETIC EXCHANGES:** 5 lean meat, 1½ fat.

GOUDA TURKEY CLUB

Take the humble turkey and cheese sandwich to new heights with this tasty version. All you need to add is the ambiance for a bistro meal at home.
—*Karen Harris, Littleton, CO*

TAKES: 15 min. • **MAKES:** 2 servings

- ½ cup shredded smoked Gouda cheese
- 4 tsp. mayonnaise
- 1 Tbsp. thinly sliced green onion
- ¼ tsp. garlic powder
- ¼ tsp. coarsely ground pepper
- 4 slices whole wheat bread, toasted
- 2 tsp. butter, softened
  Romaine leaves
- 4 slices tomato
- 4 oz. sliced deli smoked turkey
- ½ medium ripe avocado

1. Mix first 5 ingredients. Spread 2 slices of toast with butter, then with cheese mixture. Layer with lettuce, tomato and turkey.
2. Peel and mash avocado; spread over remaining 2 slices toast. Place toast, avocado side down, over turkey.
1 SANDWICH: 464 cal., 27g fat (10g sat. fat), 63mg chol., 995mg sod., 30g carb. (4g sugars, 6g fiber), 27g pro.

JUICY AIR-FRYER CORNISH HENS

This easy air-fryer recipe will help you put a gourmet meal on the table in 30 minutes. Perfect for weeknights!
—Katrina Adams, Mount Olive, AL

- -

PREP: 15 min. • **COOK:** 20 min. + standing • **MAKES:** 2 servings

- 4 tsp. salt-free seasoning blend
- 4 tsp. everything seasoning blend
- 2 tsp. lemon-pepper seasoning
- 2 tsp. paprika
- 1 tsp. salt
- ¼ tsp. pepper
- 2 Cornish game hens (20 to 24 oz. each)
- 2 Tbsp. olive oil

Combine the first 6 ingredients. Tuck wings under hens; tie legs together. Rub oil over hens; sprinkle with seasonings. Place hens, breast side down, on greased tray in air-fryer basket. Cook at 375° until a thermometer inserted in thickest part of thigh reads 170°-175°, 18-20 minutes, turning once. (Cover loosely with foil if hens brown too quickly.) Let stand 10 minutes before carving.
NOTE: In our testing, we find cook times vary dramatically between brands of air fryers. As a result, we give wider than normal ranges on suggested cook times. Begin checking at the first time listed and adjust as needed.
1 HEN: 860 cal., 63g fat (15g sat. fat), 351mg chol., 2313mg sod., 9g carb. (0 sugars, 1g fiber), 60g pro.

BROCCOLI-STUFFED CHICKEN

I was born in 1936 to a family of eight. Much of our food came from our garden and the henhouse at the back of our city lot. Mother served fried chicken every Sunday, but sometimes she surprised us with this creation. This version is sized perfectly for two.
—Donald Laugherty, Connelsville, PA

- -

PREP: 15 min. • **BAKE:** 40 min. • **MAKES:** 2 servings

- 2 boneless skinless chicken breast halves (6 oz. each)
- 1 tsp. poultry seasoning
- ½ tsp. white pepper
- ½ tsp. curry powder
- ½ tsp. garlic powder
- ¼ tsp. salt
- 1 cup finely chopped fresh broccoli
- ½ cup shredded cheddar cheese
- ½ cup chicken broth

1. Preheat oven to 350°. Flatten chicken to ¼-in. thickness. Combine poultry seasoning, pepper, curry powder, garlic powder and salt; sprinkle over chicken. Combine broccoli and cheese; place half the mixture in the center of each chicken breast. Fold long sides over filling; fold ends up and secure with toothpicks.
2. Place, seam side down, in an 8-in. square baking pan; add broth. Cover pan loosely with foil. Bake 30 minutes. Remove foil; baste the chicken with pan juices. Bake, uncovered, until chicken is no longer pink, about 10 minutes longer. Remove toothpicks before serving. If desired, thicken pan juices for gravy.
1 STUFFED CHICKEN BREAST HALF: 324 cal., 14g fat (7g sat. fat), 123mg chol., 822mg sod., 6g carb. (1g sugars, 2g fiber), 43g pro.

> **TIP**
>
> **HOW DO YOU THICKEN THE PAN JUICES TO MAKE GRAVY FOR THIS BROCCOLI-STUFFED CHICKEN?**
> In a small bowl, whisk together equal parts cornstarch or flour and cold water to make a paste (also called a slurry). Whisk this into the warm pan juices, heating until thick. For a slightly richer gravy, mash together equal parts flour and room temperature butter, then stir this mixture into the pan juices until thickened.

CRUMB-COATED CHICKEN & BLACKBERRY SALSA

Maple lends a sweet touch to blackberry salsa. Besides chicken, it's also great with fried fish.
—*Tammy Thomas, Morrisville, VT*

TAKES: 25 min. • **MAKES:** 2 servings

- ½ cup fresh blackberries, halved
- 1 jalapeno pepper, seeded and minced
- 2 Tbsp. minced fresh cilantro
- 2 Tbsp. chopped red onion
- 2 Tbsp. maple syrup
- 2 Tbsp. balsamic vinegar
- 2 boneless skinless chicken breast halves (5 oz. each)
- ⅛ tsp. salt
- ⅛ tsp. pepper
- ¼ cup all-purpose flour
- 1 large egg, beaten
- ½ cup panko bread crumbs
- 1 Tbsp. olive oil

1. In a small bowl, combine the first 6 ingredients. Cover and refrigerate until serving.
2. Flatten chicken to ¼-in. thickness; sprinkle with salt and pepper. Place the flour, egg and bread crumbs in separate shallow bowls. Coat chicken with flour, dip in egg, then coat with crumbs.
3. In a large skillet, heat oil over medium heat; add chicken. Cook chicken until no longer pink, 4-6 minutes on each side. Serve with salsa.
NOTE: Wear disposable gloves when cutting hot peppers; the oils can burn skin. Avoid touching your face.
1 CHICKEN BREAST HALF WITH ¼ CUP SALSA: 411 cal., 13g fat (3g sat. fat), 175mg chol., 150mg sod., 37g carb. (17g sugars, 3g fiber), 35g pro.

AIR-FRYER PECAN STRAWBERRY RHUBARB COBBLER

Chock-full of berries and rhubarb, this pretty cobbler is the perfect finale for a dinner for two. The pecans in the topping and the delicious dessert sauce make it extra special.
—*Lily Julow, Lawrenceville, GA*

PREP: 20 min. + standing • **COOK:** 25 min.
MAKES: 2 servings

- 1 cup sliced fresh or frozen rhubarb
- 1 cup sliced fresh strawberries
- ¼ cup sugar
- 1 Tbsp. quick-cooking tapioca
- 1 tsp. lemon juice
- Dash salt

TOPPING
- ⅓ cup all-purpose flour
- ¼ cup chopped pecans
- 3 Tbsp. sugar
- ⅛ tsp. baking powder
- Dash salt
- 2 Tbsp. cold butter
- 1 large egg, room temperature

SAUCE
- ½ cup vanilla ice cream
- 2¼ tsp. Marsala wine

1. Preheat air fryer to 375°. Combine the first 6 ingredients; divide between 2 greased 8-oz. ramekins or custard cups. Let stand for 15 minutes.
2. In a small bowl, combine the flour, pecans, sugar, baking powder and salt; cut in butter until mixture resembles coarse crumbs. Stir in egg. Drop by spoonfuls over fruit mixture; spread evenly.
3. Place ramekins on tray in air-fryer basket. Cook until filling is bubbly and a toothpick inserted in topping comes out clean, 25-30 minutes.
4. In a microwave-safe bowl, combine ice cream and wine. Cook, uncovered, at 50% power for 1-2 minutes or until heated through; stir until blended. Serve with warm cobbler.
1 COBBLER: 615 cal., 28g fat (11g sat. fat), 138mg chol., 335mg sod., 85g carb. (57g sugars, 5g fiber), 9g pro.

AIR-FRYER SWEET & SOUR PORK

Whether you're serving a party of two or making a bigger batch for company, you'll find this pork tenderloin a succulent choice.
—*Leigh Rys, Herndon, VA*

PREP: 25 min. • **COOK:** 20 min. • **MAKES:** 2 servings

- ½ cup unsweetened crushed pineapple, undrained
- ½ cup cider vinegar
- ¼ cup sugar
- ¼ cup packed dark brown sugar
- ¼ cup ketchup
- 1 Tbsp. reduced-sodium soy sauce
- 1½ tsp. Dijon mustard
- ½ tsp. garlic powder
- 1 pork tenderloin (¾ lb.), halved
- ⅛ tsp. salt
- ⅛ tsp. pepper
  Cooking spray
  Sliced green onions, optional

1. In a small saucepan, combine the first 8 ingredients. Bring to a boil; reduce the heat. Simmer, uncovered, until thickened, 6-8 minutes, stirring occasionally.

2. Preheat air fryer to 350°. Sprinkle pork with salt and pepper. Place pork on greased tray in air-fryer basket; spritz with cooking spray. Cook until the pork begins to brown around the edges, 7-8 minutes. Turn; pour 2 Tbsp. sauce over the pork. Cook until a thermometer inserted into pork reads at least 145°, 10-12 minutes longer. Let pork stand 5 minutes before slicing. Serve with remaining sauce. If desired, top with green onions.

5 OZ. COOKED PORK WITH ½ CUP SAUCE: 502 cal., 7g fat (2g sat. fat), 95mg chol., 985mg sod., 72g carb. (69g sugars, 1g fiber), 35g pro.

BROCCOLI CHEDDAR SOUP

My husband and I love this cheesy recipe. It is proof that soup doesn't need to be made in big batches to be good.
—*Cheryl McRae, West Valley, UT*

TAKES: 20 min. • **MAKES:** 2 servings

- ¼ cup chopped onion
- ¼ cup butter, cubed
- ¼ cup all-purpose flour
- ¼ tsp. salt
- ¼ tsp. pepper
- 1½ cups 2% milk
- ¾ cup chicken broth
- 1 cup cooked chopped fresh or frozen broccoli
- ½ cup shredded cheddar cheese

1. In a small saucepan, saute onion in butter until tender. Stir in the flour, salt and pepper until blended; gradually add milk and broth. Bring to a boil; cook and stir until thickened, about 2 minutes.

2. Add broccoli. Cook and stir until heated through. Remove from the heat; stir in cheese until melted.

1 CUP: 494 cal., 37g fat (24g sat. fat), 116mg chol., 1145mg sod., 26g carb. (11g sugars, 2g fiber), 16g pro.

> ### HOW DO YOU KEEP BROCCOLI CHEDDAR SOUP FROM CURDLING?
> Curdling usually occurs when the milk or cream is added at too high of a heat. As you incorporate the milk and broth into the cooked onion and flour mixture, keep the heat at medium and stir continuously with a whisk. Once all is combined, you can proceed to heat to a boil.

TIP

BAKED HAMBURGERS

Don't fire up the grill tonight. Baking hamburgers in the oven is a fun and easy twist. The burgers are hearty and moist, and the onion gives them a special flavor. The sweet sauce further enhances the taste. I serve these burgers as an entree with accompanying vegetables, or you can serve them on buns.
—Marg Bisgrove, Widewater, AB

PREP: 10 min. • **BAKE:** 35 min. • **MAKES:** 2 servings

- 1   small onion, chopped
- ¼   cup dry bread crumbs
- 2   Tbsp. 2% milk
- ¾   tsp. salt, divided
- ¼   tsp. pepper
- ½   lb. ground beef
- ⅓   cup water
- 2   Tbsp. brown sugar
- 2   Tbsp. ketchup
- ½   tsp. ground mustard
- ½   tsp. white vinegar
- 2   hamburger buns, optional
      Sliced red onion, optional

1. In a small bowl, combine the onion, bread crumbs, milk, ½ tsp. salt and pepper. Crumble beef over mixture and mix lightly but thoroughly. Shape into 2 patties. Place the patties in a greased 11x7-in. baking dish.
2. Combine the water, brown sugar, ketchup, mustard, vinegar and remaining ¼ tsp. salt; pour over patties.
3. Bake, uncovered, at 350° until a thermometer reads 160°, 35-40 minutes. If desired, serve on buns with red onion.
1 BURGER: 363 cal., 15g fat (6g sat. fat), 77mg chol., 1240mg sod., 30g carb. (20g sugars, 1g fiber), 25g pro.

AIR-FRYER EGGS LORRAINE

Whenever I'm looking to impress overnight guests, this is the recipe I serve for breakfast. It's easy to assemble, and it cooks quickly in the air fryer.
—Sandra Woolard, DeLand, FL

TAKES: 25 min. • **MAKES:** 2 servings

- 4   slices Canadian bacon
- 2   slices Swiss cheese
- 4   large eggs
- 2   Tbsp. sour cream
- ⅛   tsp. salt
- ⅛   tsp. pepper
      Minced chives, optional

1. Preheat air fryer to 325°. Coat 2 shallow oval 1½-cup baking dishes that fit in air fryer with cooking spray. Line with Canadian bacon; top with cheese. Carefully break 2 eggs into each dish.
2. In a small bowl, whisk sour cream, salt and pepper until smooth; drop by teaspoonfuls onto eggs. Place dishes in air fryer. Cook until the eggs are set, 10-15 minutes. If desired, sprinkle with chives.
NOTE: In our testing, we find cook times vary dramatically between brands of air fryers. As a result, we give wider than normal ranges on suggested cook times. Begin checking at the first time listed and adjust as needed.
1 SERVING: 258 cal., 18g fat (7g sat. fat), 406mg chol., 687mg sod., 2g carb. (1g sugars, 0 fiber), 22g pro.

CHEESY CHICKEN PARMIGIANA

My husband used to order classic chicken parmigiana at restaurants. Then I found this recipe in our local newspaper, adjusted it for two and began making the beloved dish at home. After more than 50 years of marriage, I still enjoy preparing his favorite recipes from scratch.
—*Iola Butler, Sun City, CA*

- -

PREP: 25 min. • **COOK:** 15 min.
MAKES: 2 servings

1	can (15 oz.) tomato sauce
2	tsp. Italian seasoning
½	tsp. garlic powder
1	large egg
¼	cup seasoned bread crumbs
3	Tbsp. grated Parmesan cheese
2	boneless skinless chicken breast halves (4 oz. each)
2	Tbsp. olive oil
2	slices part-skim mozzarella cheese

Optional: Fresh basil leaves and additional Parmesan cheese

1. In a saucepan, combine the tomato sauce, Italian seasoning and garlic powder. Bring to a boil. Reduce heat; cover and simmer for 20 minutes.
2. Meanwhile, in a shallow bowl, lightly beat the egg. In another shallow bowl, combine bread crumbs and Parmesan cheese. Dip chicken in egg, then coat with crumb mixture.
3. In a large skillet, cook chicken in oil over medium heat until a thermometer reads 165°, about 5 minutes on each side. Top with mozzarella cheese. Cover and cook until cheese is melted, 3-4 minutes longer. Serve with tomato sauce. If desired, sprinkle chicken breasts with basil and additional Parmesan.
1 SERVING: 444 cal., 26g fat (8g sat. fat), 166mg chol., 1496mg sod., 23g carb. (5g sugars, 3g fiber), 29g pro.

PANCAKES FOR TWO

These light and fluffy berry pancakes are perfectly portioned to make a small batch, so there's no need to worry about what to do with leftover batter.
—*Annemarie Pietila, Farmington Hills, MI*

- -

TAKES: 15 min. • **MAKES:** about 8 pancakes

1¼	cups all-purpose flour
1	Tbsp. sugar
1	tsp. baking powder
½	tsp. baking soda
½	tsp. salt
1	large egg, lightly beaten
1¼	cups buttermilk
2	Tbsp. canola oil
1	cup fresh or frozen blueberries, optional

1. In a large bowl, combine flour, sugar, baking powder, baking soda and salt. In another bowl, combine egg, buttermilk and oil; stir into dry ingredients just until blended. If desired, fold in blueberries.
2. Preheat griddle over medium heat. Lightly grease griddle. Pour batter by ¼ cupfuls onto griddle; cook until bubbles on top begin to pop and the bottoms are golden brown. Turn; cook until second side is golden brown.
NOTE: If using frozen blueberries, use without thawing to avoid discoloring the pancake batter.
4 PANCAKES: 527 cal., 18g fat (3g sat. fat), 112mg chol., 1299mg sod., 74g carb. (15g sugars, 2g fiber), 16g pro.

WHAT'S THE BEST WAY TO STORE LEFTOVERS OF THESE PANCAKES?

Store any extra pancakes layered between waxed paper or paper towels in an airtight, lidded container in your refrigerator for 2-3 days. Pancakes also freeze very well, for up to 3 months.

TIP

PRESSURE-COOKER PORK RIBS

When I was growing up, my mom made these delicious ribs for special Saturday dinners. Now I can prepare them any weeknight with the help of an electric pressure cooker.
—*Paula Zsiray, Logan, UT*

PREP: 25 min. • **COOK:** 20 min. + releasing • **MAKES:** 2 servings

- 1 lb. boneless country-style pork ribs, cut into 2-in. chunks
- ½ tsp. onion salt
- ½ tsp. pepper
- ½ tsp. paprika
- 2 tsp. canola oil
- 1 cup water
- 2 Tbsp. ketchup
- 2 tsp. white vinegar
- ½ tsp. Worcestershire sauce
- ½ tsp. prepared mustard
- ⅛ tsp. celery seed

1. Sprinkle pork ribs with onion salt, pepper and paprika. Select saute setting on a 3- or 6-qt. electric pressure cooker. Adjust for medium heat; add oil. When oil is hot, brown meat on all sides; remove from pressure cooker. Add water to pressure cooker. Cook 30 seconds, stirring to loosen browned bits from pan. Press cancel. Whisk in the remaining ingredients. Return ribs to pressure cooker.
2. Lock lid; close pressure-release valve. Adjust to pressure-cook on high for 20 minutes. Let pressure release naturally. If desired, skim fat and thicken cooking juices.

6 OZ. COOKED PORK: 417 cal., 26g fat (8g sat. fat), 131mg chol., 764mg sod., 5g carb. (4g sugars, 0 fiber), 40g pro.

WARM PINEAPPLE SUNDAES WITH RUM SAUCE

Pineapple, rum and sugar are already a flavorful dream together, but adding ginger and butter takes this dessert to another level.
—*Jamie Miller, Maple Grove, MN*

TAKES: 25 min. • **MAKES:** 2 servings

- 4 fresh pineapple spears (about 8 oz.)
- ½ cup packed brown sugar
- 2 Tbsp. dark rum
- ¾ tsp. ground ginger
- 4 tsp. butter, cut into small pieces
- 2 scoops vanilla ice cream or low-fat frozen yogurt
- 4 gingersnap cookies, crushed

1. Preheat oven to 425°. Place pineapple in 1-qt. baking dish. In a small bowl, combine the brown sugar, rum and ginger; spoon over pineapple. Dot with butter.
2. Bake, uncovered, until pineapple is lightly browned and sauce is bubbly, 8-10 minutes. Place the ice cream in 2 dessert dishes; top with pineapple and sauce. Sprinkle with crushed cookies. Serve immediately.

1 SERVING: 536 cal., 16g fat (10g sat. fat), 49mg chol., 221mg sod., 95g carb. (78g sugars, 2g fiber), 4g pro.

REVIEW

"Very yummy! I used rum flavoring instead of rum. This dish makes me think of some amazing desserts we had in the Caribbean. It was a hit with my husband too!"

—BOBANDJESSICA, TASTEOFHOME.COM

BEEF WITH RAMEN NOODLES

I came up this recipe when I was hungry for Chinese food. Everyone who tries it likes it, but each time I make it, I change something slightly. Heat any leftovers in the microwave or in a skillet the next day for lunch.
—*Annette Hemsath, Sutherlin, OR*

TAKES: 25 min. • **MAKES:** 2 servings

- 1 pkg. (3 oz.) beef ramen noodles
- 1 Tbsp. cornstarch
- 1 cup beef broth, divided
- 1 Tbsp. vegetable oil
- ½ lb. beef top sirloin steak, cut into thin strips
- 1 Tbsp. soy sauce
- 1 can (14 oz.) whole baby corn, rinsed and drained
- 1 cup fresh broccoli florets
- ½ cup chopped sweet red pepper
- ½ cup shredded carrot
- 2 green onions, cut into 1-in. pieces
- ¼ cup peanuts

1. Set aside seasoning packet from noodles. Cook noodles according to package directions. Drain and keep warm.
2. In a small bowl, combine cornstarch and ¼ cup broth until smooth; set aside.
3. In a large skillet, heat oil over medium heat; add beef. Cook and stir until beef is no longer pink, 3-5 minutes. Add soy sauce; cook until most liquid has evaporated, about 1 minute. Remove beef and keep warm.
4. In the same skillet over medium heat, add corn, broccoli, red pepper, carrot, onions and remaining ¾ cup broth. Stir in contents of reserved seasoning packets. Cook and stir until vegetables are crisp-tender, 4-6 minutes.
5. Stir reserved cornstarch mixture and add to skillet. Bring to a boil; cook and stir until thickened, 1-2 minutes. Add reserved beef and noodles to skillet; heat through. Top with peanuts.
1½ CUPS: 601 cal., 28g fat (8g sat. fat), 46mg chol., 2086mg sod., 47g carb. (7g sugars, 8g fiber), 40g pro.

SLOW-COOKED PEACH PORK CHOPS

I played around with many variations of this recipe until I came up with one that was just right. The warm peaches make an excellent side dish for the pork.
—*Bonnie Morrow, Spencerport, NY*

PREP: 15 min. • **COOK:** 5 hours • **MAKES:** 2 servings

- 2 bone-in center-cut pork loin chops (7 oz. each)
- 2 tsp. canola oil
- 1 can (8¼ oz.) sliced peaches in extra-light syrup
- 1 can (8 oz.) tomato sauce
- ½ cup water
- 1 tsp. reduced-sodium soy sauce
- ⅛ tsp. dried rosemary, crushed
- ⅛ tsp. dried thyme
- ⅛ tsp. dried basil
  Dash to ⅛ tsp. cayenne pepper

1. In a small skillet, brown pork chops in oil; drain. Transfer to a 1½-qt. slow cooker.
2. Drain peaches, reserving juice. In a bowl, combine the tomato sauce, water, soy sauce, rosemary, thyme, basil, cayenne and reserved peach juice; pour over pork. Top with peaches. Cover and cook on low until pork is tender, about 5 hours.
1 PORK CHOP: 389 cal., 22g fat (6g sat. fat), 97mg chol., 690mg sod., 15g carb. (11g sugars, 3g fiber), 34g pro.

TOAD IN THE HOLE BACON SANDWICH

Switch up the cheese—pepper jack gives a nice kick—or use sliced kielbasa, ham or sausage in place of the bacon in this versatile grilled cheese sandwich.
—*Kallee Krong-Mccreery, Escondido, CA*

TAKES: 15 min. • **MAKES:** 1 serving

- 2 slices sourdough bread
- 1 Tbsp. mayonnaise
- 1 large egg
- 1 slice cheddar cheese
- 2 cooked bacon strips

1. Using a biscuit cutter or round cookie cutter, cut out center from 1 slice of bread (discard center or save for another use). Spread the mayonnaise on 1 side of the bread slices. In a large skillet coated with cooking spray, lightly toast slice with cutout, mayonnaise side down, over medium-low heat. Flip slice; crack egg into center. Add remaining bread slice, mayonnaise side down, to skillet; layer with cheese and bacon.

2. Cook, covered, until egg white is set, yolk is soft-set and cheese begins to melt. If needed, flip bread slice with egg to finish cooking. To assemble sandwich, use solid slice as bottom and cutout slice as top.

1 SANDWICH: 610 cal., 34g fat (11g sat. fat), 240mg chol., 1220mg sod., 46g carb. (4g sugars, 2g fiber), 30g pro.

> **TIP**
> Nothing perks up a grilled cheese sandwich more than a slice of fresh tomato. Go ahead and add it just after the cheese melts but before you assemble the sandwich. Mayo may seem like a strange ingredient to spread on the outside of the bread, but when it's grilled, it melts quickly and creates a beautiful crispy exterior with a golden brown color.

ROSEMARY POT ROAST

Come home to a comforting, ready-to-eat entree with this slow-cooker favorite sized just right for two. It's so easy, and it fills the house with a wonderful aroma.
—*Marcia Schroeder, River Edge, NJ*

PREP: 15 min. • **COOK:** 8 hours
MAKES: 2 servings

- 1 boneless beef chuck steak (¾ in. thick and ¾ lb.)
- 1 to 2 tsp. canola oil
- ¼ cup beef broth
- ¼ cup tomato sauce
- ¼ cup dry red wine or additional beef broth
- 2 Tbsp. chopped onion
- 1 garlic clove, minced
- 1½ tsp. dried parsley flakes
- ¼ tsp. minced fresh rosemary
- ⅛ tsp. salt
- ⅛ tsp. pepper
- 1½ tsp. cornstarch
- 1 Tbsp. water

1. In a large skillet, brown the beef in oil on both sides. Transfer to a 1½-qt. slow cooker. In a small bowl, combine the broth, tomato sauce, wine, onion, garlic, parsley, rosemary, salt and pepper; pour over beef. Cover and cook on low until meat is tender, about 8 hours.

2. Remove beef and keep warm. In a small saucepan, combine cornstarch and water until smooth; stir in cooking juices. Bring to a boil; cook and stir until thickened, about 2 minutes. Serve with beef.

5 OZ. COOKED BEEF: 358 cal., 19g fat (6g sat. fat), 111mg chol., 472mg sod., 6g carb. (1g sugars, 1g fiber), 34g pro.

> **TIP**
> Mashed potatoes and green peas or steamed broccoli with lemon butter make this a hearty meal for two. Leftovers are so tender and tasty, you might want to double this recipe to serve over noodles or in sandwiches the next day.

TOASTED CLUBS WITH DILL MAYO

Simple to prepare, appealing to the eye, and loaded with flavor, this bistro-style sandwich couldn't be better!

—*Jenny Flake, Newport Beach, CA*

TAKES: 20 min. • **MAKES:** 2 servings

- 2 Tbsp. fat-free mayonnaise
- ¼ tsp. dill weed
- ¾ tsp. lemon juice, divided
- ⅛ tsp. pepper
- 4 slices whole wheat bread, toasted
- 4 thin slices deli roast beef
- 4 thin slices deli ham
- 2 slices reduced-fat provolone cheese
- 2 Bibb lettuce leaves
- 2 slices tomato
- 2 center-cut bacon strips, cooked and crumbled
- ¼ cup alfalfa sprouts
- ¼ medium ripe avocado, peeled and sliced

1. In a small bowl, combine mayonnaise, dill, ¼ tsp. lemon juice and pepper; spread over toast. Layer 2 slices with roast beef, ham, cheese, lettuce, tomato, bacon and alfalfa sprouts.

2. Drizzle avocado slices with remaining ½ tsp. lemon juice; place over sprouts. Top with remaining toast.

1 SANDWICH: 328 cal., 13g fat (4g sat. fat), 47mg chol., 1056mg sod., 29g carb. (6g sugars, 6g fiber), 26g pro.

HAWAIIAN BEEF DISH

My dad, who still enjoys experimenting in the kitchen, created this tropical dish when I was a little girl. Sometimes I prepare it the day before and warm it up while I'm cooking the rice.
—*Marilyn Taus, Mississauga, ON*

- -

TAKES: 25 min. • **MAKES:** 2 servings

½	lb. lean ground beef (90% lean)
1	medium onion, halved and sliced
⅓	cup sliced celery
⅓	cup chopped green pepper
1	garlic clove, minced
2	tsp. butter
1	can (8 oz.) unsweetened pineapple chunks
¼	cup packed brown sugar
1	Tbsp. all-purpose flour
1	Tbsp. white wine vinegar
¼	tsp. salt
1	cup hot cooked rice

1. In a small skillet, cook beef over medium heat until no longer pink; crumble beef. Drain beef and set aside; discard dripping. In the same skillet, saute onion, celery, green pepper and garlic in butter until vegetables are crisp-tender, about 5 minutes.

2. Drain pineapple, reserving juice; set pineapple aside. Add enough water to the juice to measure ½ cup. In a bowl, combine the brown sugar, flour, vinegar, salt and pineapple juice mixture until smooth. Add to skillet. Bring to a boil. Cook and stir over medium heat for 2 minutes. Stir in beef and pineapple; heat through. Serve with rice.

1½ CUPS: 515 cal., 12g fat (6g sat. fat), 66mg chol., 440mg sod., 75g carb. (44g sugars, 4g fiber), 26g pro.

BANANA PANCAKE FOR ONE

Get a delicious start to the day with this tender and hearty pancake. Try coconut, strawberry or almond extract in place of the vanilla for a fun change of pace.
—*Carmen Bolar, Bronx, NY*

- -

TAKES: 15 min. • **MAKES:** 1 pancake

¼	cup plus 1 Tbsp. all-purpose flour
½	tsp. baking powder
1	medium ripe banana, mashed
1	large egg, lightly beaten
½	tsp. vanilla extract
	Optional: Maple syrup and additional banana, sliced

1. In a small bowl, combine flour and baking powder. In another bowl, combine mashed banana, egg and vanilla; stir into the dry ingredients just until moistened.

2. Pour batter onto a hot griddle coated with cooking spray; turn when bubbles form on top and pancake is golden brown on 1 side. Cook until the second side is golden brown. If desired, serve with syrup and banana slices.

1 SERVING: 325 cal., 6g fat (2g sat. fat), 186mg chol., 313mg sod., 57g carb. (15g sugars, 4g fiber), 12g pro.

TIP

HOW DO YOU STORE BANANA PANCAKES?
Store pancakes for up to 2-3 days in an airtight container in the refrigerator. You can also freeze any leftover pancakes if you'd like to enjoy them beyond a few days.

MINESTRONE-STYLE SHRIMP SALAD

This shrimp salad is the perfect dish to serve as a small dinner for two. It's light and refreshing.
—*Roxanne Chan, Albany, CA*

PREP: 20 min. • **COOK:** 10 min. • **MAKES:** 2 servings

- 1   cup uncooked tricolor spiral pasta
- 2   Tbsp. lemon juice
- 2   Tbsp. olive oil
- 2   Tbsp. prepared pesto
- 1   garlic clove, minced
- ¼   tsp. salt
- ¼   tsp. pepper

SALAD
- 1   cup canned white kidney or cannellini beans, rinsed and drained
- 1   medium tomato, chopped
- ¼   cup fresh corn
- 2   Tbsp. sliced celery
- 2   Tbsp. diced red onion
- 2   Tbsp. diced carrot
- 2   Tbsp. roasted sweet red peppers, diced
- 2   Tbsp. minced fresh parsley
- 2   cups Italian-blend salad greens
- 8   peeled and deveined cooked large shrimp
     Grated Parmesan cheese, optional

1. Cook pasta according to package directions. Meanwhile, in a small bowl, whisk together the lemon juice, oil, pesto, garlic, salt and pepper; set aside. Rinse pasta with cold water; drain.
2. In a large bowl, combine the pasta, beans, tomato, corn, celery, onion, carrot, red peppers, parsley and dressing. Divide the salad greens between 2 plates; top with pasta mixture and shrimp. If desired, sprinkle with Parmesan cheese.
1 SERVING: 535 cal., 23g fat (4g sat. fat), 48mg chol., 719mg sod., 63g carb. (6g sugars, 10g fiber), 21g pro.

🟢 CATALINA CHICKEN

Using convenient bottled salad dressing and soup mix helps keep the prep time to only 10 minutes. I spoon extra sauce over the baked chicken just before serving.
—*Frances Roberts, Silver Spring, MD*

PREP: 10 min. • **BAKE:** 25 min. • **MAKES:** 2 servings

- 2   boneless skinless chicken breast halves (5 oz. each)
- 2   tsp. canola oil
- ¼   cup Catalina salad dressing
- 4½ tsp. onion soup mix
- 1   Tbsp. grape jelly
     Minced fresh parsley, optional

1. In a large nonstick skillet, brown chicken in oil. Transfer to a shallow baking dish coated with cooking spray. Combine the salad dressing, soup mix and jelly; pour over chicken.
2. Bake chicken, uncovered, at 350° for 25-30 minutes or until a thermometer reads 170°.
1 CHICKEN BREAST HALF: 261 cal., 8g fat (1g sat. fat), 78mg chol., 727mg sod., 17g carb. (8g sugars, 0 fiber), 29g pro.

TIP

WHAT OTHER COOKING METHODS CAN YOU USE TO MAKE CATALINA CHICKEN?

Instead of pan-frying to brown the chicken, try grilling it to allow the sauce to caramelize. Another easy way to prepare this recipe is in a slow cooker, which allows you to set it and forget it!

- STRAWBERRY OVERNIGHT OATS -

These strawberry overnight oats will be ready and waiting for you in the morning. The PB&J-inspired breakfast is free of both gluten and dairy. Use more or less sugar depending on the sweetness of the strawberries.

In a small bowl, combine 1 cup sliced fresh **strawberries** and ½ tsp. **sugar**. Let stand 1 hour; mash if desired. In a pint jar, layer ¼ cup **oats**, 1 Tbsp. **powdered peanut butter**, ½ tsp. **chia seeds** and ⅓ cup strawberry mixture. Repeat layers twice. Pour 1 cup **unsweetened almond milk** over top; seal and refrigerate overnight.

- 8 -

GIVE ME 5 OR FEWER

An effortless weeknight dinner is every cook's dream come true. These five-ingredient recipes really do have five ingredients or fewer (excluding water, salt, pepper and oil). They make cooking (and grocery shopping) easy!

PASTA WITH ROASTED GARLIC & TOMATOES

Here's a simple sauce with just four ingredients, and it's savory enough for a fancy party. I use bow tie pasta, but penne works too.
—*Aysha Schurman, Ammon, ID*

- -

TAKES: 20 min. • **MAKES:** 4 servings

- 1½ lbs. cherry tomatoes
- 12 garlic cloves, peeled
- 3 Tbsp. olive oil
- 3 cups uncooked bow tie pasta
- 4 oz. (½ cup) cream cheese, softened
- ½ tsp. salt

1. Preheat oven to 450°. In a bowl, toss tomatoes and garlic cloves with the oil; transfer to a greased 15x10x1-in. baking pan. Roast 14-16 minutes or until very soft. Meanwhile, cook pasta according to package directions.

2. Cool roasted tomatoes and garlic slightly. Reserve 12 tomatoes for serving with the pasta. Transfer remaining tomato mixture to a food processor. Add cream cheese and salt; process until smooth. Transfer to a large bowl.

3. Drain pasta; add to tomato mixture and toss to coat. Top with reserved tomatoes.

1 CUP: 441 cal., 22g fat (8g sat. fat), 32mg chol., 401mg sod., 52g carb. (7g sugars, 4g fiber), 12g pro.

PRESSURE-COOKER SWISS STEAK

Swiss steak has a been a standby for family cooks for decades, and this no-fuss way to cook it promises to keep the entree popular for years to come. Best of all, it's low in calories and fat.
—*Sarah Burks, Wathena, KS*

- -

PREP: 10 min. • **COOK:** 20 min. + releasing
MAKES: 6 servings

- 1½ lbs. beef round steak, cut into 6 pieces
- ½ tsp. salt
- ¼ tsp. pepper
- 1 medium onion, cut into ¼-in. slices
- 1 celery rib, cut into ½-in. slices
- 2 cans (8 oz. each) tomato sauce

Sprinkle steak with the salt and pepper. Place the onion slices in a 6-qt. electric pressure cooker. Top with celery, tomato sauce and steak. Lock lid; close pressure-release valve. Adjust to pressure-cook on high for 20 minutes. Let pressure release naturally for 5 minutes, then quick-release any remaining pressure. A thermometer inserted in steak should read at least 145°.

1 SERVING: 167 cal., 4g fat (1g sat. fat), 63mg chol., 581mg sod., 6g carb. (2g sugars, 2g fiber), 27g pro. **DIABETIC EXCHANGES:** 3 lean meat, 1 vegetable.

SWEET & SPICY PINEAPPLE CHICKEN SANDWICHES

My kids often ask for chicken sloppy joes, and this version has a bonus of sweet pineapple. It is a perfect recipe to double for a potluck. Try topping the sandwiches with smoked Gouda cheese.
—*Nancy Heishman, Las Vegas, NV*

PREP: 15 min. • **COOK:** 2¾ hours
MAKES: 8 servings

- 2½ lbs. boneless skinless chicken breasts
- 1 bottle (18 oz.) sweet and spicy barbecue sauce, divided
- 2 Tbsp. honey mustard
- 1 can (8 oz.) unsweetened crushed pineapple, undrained
- 8 hamburger buns, split and toasted
  Optional: Bibb lettuce leaves and thinly sliced red onion

1. Place chicken breasts in a 4-qt. slow cooker. Combine ¼ cup barbecue sauce and the mustard; pour over chicken. Cover and cook on low 2½-3 hours or until chicken is tender.
2. Remove chicken; discard liquid. Shred the chicken with 2 forks; return to slow cooker. Add the crushed pineapple and remaining barbecue sauce; cover and cook on high for 15 minutes.
3. Serve on toasted buns. If desired, add lettuce and onion.
FREEZE OPTION: Place shredded chicken in freezer containers. Cool and freeze. To use, partially thaw in the refrigerator overnight. Heat chicken mixture through in a covered saucepan, stirring occasionally; add broth or water if necessary.
1 SANDWICH: 415 cal., 6g fat (1g sat. fat), 78mg chol., 973mg sod., 56g carb. (30g sugars, 2g fiber), 34g pro.

> **TIP**
> The chicken mixture in these sandwiches is more sweet than spicy, making it an ideal meal to serve kids. But if you want more heat, add a jalapeno pepper.

ORANGE-GLAZED HAM

I always thought this delicious ham looked like a sparkling jewel when my mother served it for Easter dinner. The spice rub penetrates every tender slice, and the enticing aroma is only a hint of how good it will taste.
—*Ruth Seitz, Columbus Junction, IA*

PREP: 10 min. • **BAKE:** 2 hours
MAKES: 12 servings

- 1 fully cooked bone-in ham (6 to 8 lbs.)
- 1 Tbsp. ground mustard
- 1 tsp. ground allspice
- ¾ cup orange marmalade

1. Place the ham on a rack in a shallow roasting pan. Score the surface of the ham, making diamond shapes ½ in. deep. Combine the mustard and allspice; rub over ham.
2. Bake, uncovered, at 325° until a thermometer reads 140°, 2-2¼ hours. Spread top of ham with marmalade during the last hour of baking, basting the ham occasionally.
6 OZ. COOKED HAM: 243 cal., 6g fat (2g sat. fat), 100mg chol., 1203mg sod., 14g carb. (13g sugars, 0 fiber), 34g pro.

MARINARA SAUCE

My mother, who was Italian American, called marinara sauce "gravy." She made this sauce in big batches several times a month, so it was a staple on our dinner table. A mouthwatering aroma filled the house each time she cooked it.
—James Grimes, Frenchtown, NJ

PREP: 20 min. • **COOK:** 1 hour
MAKES: 5 cups

- 3   Tbsp. extra virgin olive oil
- 1   large onion, finely chopped
- 4   garlic cloves, minced
- 2   cans (28 oz. each) whole tomatoes
- ¼   cup chopped fresh basil
- 1½ tsp. dried oregano
- ¾   tsp. salt
- ¼   tsp. pepper

In a large saucepan, heat the oil over medium-high heat. Add onions; cook and stir until tender, 3-5 minutes. Add garlic; cook and stir 1 minute longer. Stir in remaining ingredients. Bring to a boil. Reduce heat; cover and simmer until thickened and flavors are blended, 30-45 minutes, stirring occasionally and breaking up tomatoes with wooden spoon.
½ CUP: 44 cal., 4g fat (1g sat. fat), 0 chol., 178mg sod., 2g carb. (1g sugars, 0 fiber), 0 pro.

TIP
For a flavor variation, add roasted garlic, sun-dried tomatoes in oil, roasted red peppers and fresh oregano (instead of dried). You can also add tomato paste to thicken your sauce and add a deeper tomato flavor.

HOMEMADE PASTA DOUGH

Go for it. Once you try your own homemade pasta, you'll be hooked.
—Kathryn Conrad, Milwaukee, WI

PREP: 15 min. + resting
MAKES: 6 servings

- 2   large eggs
- 1   large egg yolk
- ¼   cup water
- 1   Tbsp. olive oil
- ¼   tsp. salt
- ½   tsp. coarsely ground pepper, optional
- 1½ cups all-purpose flour
- ½   cup semolina flour

1. In a bowl, whisk the first 5 ingredients and pepper, if desired. On a clean work surface, mix the all-purpose and semolina flours, forming a mound. Make a large well in the center. Pour egg mixture into the well. Using a fork or your fingers, gradually mix the flour mixture into the egg mixture, forming a soft dough (the dough will be slightly sticky).
2. Lightly dust work surface with flour; knead dough gently 5 times. Divide into 6 portions; cover and let rest 30 minutes.
3. To make fettuccine, roll each ball into a 10x8-in. rectangle, dusting lightly with flour. Roll up jelly-roll style. Cut into ¼-in.-wide strips. Cook in boiling water 1-3 minutes.
1 SERVING: 217 cal., 5g fat (1g sat. fat), 93mg chol., 124mg sod., 34g carb. (0 sugars, 1g fiber), 8g pro.

HOW-TO
HOW DO YOU STORE HOMEMADE PASTA?

Although dried pasta can last indefinitely in your pantry, uncooked fresh pasta will only last for about a day, and it needs to be refrigerated. It's best to make your pasta dough and cook it right away.

If you need to, you can make the pasta dough 1 day ahead of time. If the dough is too sticky when you take it out, dust it with a little more flour.

Once your homemade fresh pasta is cooked, store it in an airtight container in the refrigerator.

CHEESEBURGER POCKETS

Ground beef is my favorite meat to cook with because it's versatile and economical. There's always a fun new recipe to try, like these cheesy burger biscuits.
—*Pat Chambless, Crowder, OK*

PREP: 30 min. • **BAKE:** 10 min.
MAKES: 5 servings

- ½ lb. ground beef
- 1 Tbsp. chopped onion
- ½ tsp. salt
- ⅛ tsp. pepper
- 1 tube (12 oz.) refrigerated buttermilk biscuits
- 5 slices American cheese

1. Preheat oven to 400°. In a large skillet, cook beef, onion, salt and pepper over medium heat, crumbling beef, until meat is no longer pink; drain and cool.
2. Place 2 biscuits overlapping on a floured surface; roll out into a 5-in. oval. Place about ¼ cup of meat mixture on 1 side of oval. Fold a cheese slice to fit over the meat mixture. Fold dough over filling; press edges with a fork to seal. Repeat with the remaining biscuits, meat mixture and cheese.
3. Place on a greased baking sheet. Prick tops with a fork. Bake 10 minutes or until golden brown.
NOTE: Pricking the tops of the pockets helps steam escape during baking. If you don't do this, the pockets will puff up and may break open.
1 POCKET: 299 cal., 10g fat (5g sat. fat), 36mg chol., 1101mg sod., 34g carb. (1g sugars, 0 fiber), 17g pro.

PRESSURE-COOKED MESQUITE RIBS

When we're missing the grill during winter, these tangy ribs give us that same smoky barbecue taste we love. They're so simple, and they're fall-off-the-bone delicious too!
—*Sue Evans, Marquette, MI*

PREP: 15 min. • **COOK:** 40 min. + releasing
MAKES: 8 servings

- 1 cup water
- 2 Tbsp. cider vinegar
- 1 Tbsp. soy sauce
- 4 lbs. pork baby back ribs, cut into serving-sized portions
- 2 Tbsp. mesquite seasoning
- ¾ cup barbecue sauce, divided

1. Combine water, vinegar and soy sauce in a 6-qt. electric pressure cooker. Rub ribs with mesquite seasoning; add to the pressure cooker. Lock lid; close pressure-release valve. Adjust to pressure-cook on high for 35 minutes. Let the pressure naturally release for 10 minutes, then quick-release any remaining pressure.
2. Remove ribs to a foil-lined baking sheet. Preheat broiler. Brush ribs with half the barbecue sauce. Broil 4-6 in. from heat until glazed, 2-4 minutes. Brush with remaining barbecue sauce.
1 SERVING: 329 cal., 21g fat (8g sat. fat), 81mg chol., 678mg sod., 10g carb. (8g sugars, 0 fiber), 23g pro.

PORK TENDERLOIN WITH ZESTY ITALIAN SAUCE

We like to serve this dish with garlic mashed potatoes and fresh green beans or buttery corn on the cob.
—*Joe Vince, Port Huron, MI*

TAKES: 25 min. • **MAKES:** 4 servings

- 1 pork tenderloin (1 lb.), cut into 8 slices
- ½ tsp. salt
- ¼ tsp. pepper
- 1 Tbsp. canola oil
- ½ cup white wine or chicken broth
- ½ cup zesty Italian salad dressing
- 1 Tbsp. butter

1. Sprinkle pork with salt and pepper. In a large skillet, heat oil over medium-high heat. Brown pork, 2 minutes on each side; remove from the pan.

2. Add the wine to pan, stirring to loosen browned bits from the bottom. Bring to a boil; cook until liquid is reduced by about half. Stir in dressing. Reduce the heat; simmer, uncovered, for 1-2 minutes or until slightly thickened.

3. Return pork to pan; simmer, covered, for 3-5 minutes or until a thermometer inserted in pork reads 145°. Stir in butter. Let pork rest for 5 minutes before serving.

2 SLICES PORK WITH 2 TBSP. SAUCE: 273 cal., 15g fat (4g sat. fat), 71mg chol., 664mg sod., 3g carb. (2g sugars, 0 fiber), 23g pro.

15-MINUTE MARINATED CHICKEN

Whenever I serve this grilled chicken to family and friends, I'm bound to be asked for the recipe. It's a fast and tasty meal that I'm happy to share with others.
—*Pam Shinogle, Arlington, TX*

PREP: 15 min. + marinating • **GRILL:** 15 min.
MAKES: 4 servings

- ¼ cup Dijon mustard
- 2 Tbsp. lemon juice
- 1½ tsp. Worcestershire sauce
- ½ tsp. dried tarragon
- ¼ tsp. pepper
- 4 boneless skinless chicken breast halves (4 oz. each)

1. In a shallow dish, combine the first 5 ingredients; add chicken and turn to coat. Marinate at room temperature for 15 minutes or refrigerate up to 4 hours.

2. Drain and discard the marinade. Grill chicken, uncovered, over medium heat, for 8-12 minutes, turning once, or until a thermometer reads 170°.

1 GRILLED CHICKEN BREAST HALF: 141 cal., 3g fat (1g sat. fat), 63mg chol., 436mg sod., 1g carb. (0 sugars, 0 fiber), 23g pro.
DIABETIC EXCHANGES: 3 lean meat.

FRENCH ONION MEAT LOAF

As a teacher and farm wife, I'm always looking for quick and easy menu ideas, especially during planting and harvesting seasons. I keep the ingredients on hand for this simple-to-prepare meat loaf.
—*Jan Peters, Chandler, MN*

PREP: 20 min. • **BAKE:** 1 hour + standing
MAKES: 8 servings

- 3 **eggs**
- 1 **can (10½ oz.) condensed French onion soup, undiluted**
- 1 **pkg. (6 oz.) beef-flavored stuffing mix, crushed**
- 2 **lbs. lean ground beef**
  Beef gravy, optional

In a large bowl, combine the eggs, soup and stuffing crumbs; mix well. Crumble beef over mixture and mix lightly but thoroughly. Shape mixture into a loaf in a greased 13x9-in. baking pan. Bake, uncovered, at 350° for 1 hour or until meat is no longer pink and a thermometer reads 160°. Let stand 10 minutes before slicing. If desired, serve with gravy.

1 SERVING: 304 cal., 12g fat (4g sat. fat), 150mg chol., 749mg sod., 18g carb. (4g sugars, 1g fiber), 27g pro.

TIP

If you're cooking for 1 or 2 people, shape the meat loaf mixture into 2 smaller loaves instead of 1 large one. Bake for about 45 minutes or until a meat thermometer reads 160°. Enjoy 1 loaf and freeze the other to reheat later.

🅕🍎 HAMBURGER CASSEROLE

This recipe is such a hit, it's traveled all over the country! My mother invented the recipe in Pennsylvania, I brought it to Texas when I got married, I'm still making it in California, and my daughter treats her friends to this classic in Colorado.
—*Helen Carmichall, Santee, CA*

PREP: 20 min. • **COOK:** 45 min.
MAKES: 10 servings

- 2 lbs. lean ground beef (90% lean)
- 4 lbs. potatoes, peeled and sliced ¼ in. thick
- 1 large onion, sliced
- 1 tsp. salt
- ½ tsp. pepper
- 1 tsp. beef bouillon granules
- 1 cup boiling water
- 1 can (28 oz.) diced tomatoes, undrained
  Minced fresh parsley, optional

In a Dutch oven, layer half each of the meat, potatoes and onion. Sprinkle with half each of the salt and pepper. Repeat layers. Dissolve bouillon in the boiling water; pour over all. Top with tomatoes. Cover and cook over medium heat until potatoes are tender, 45-50 minutes. If desired, garnish with parsley.
1 CUP: 270 cal., 8g fat (3g sat. fat), 57mg chol., 493mg sod., 30g carb. (5g sugars, 3g fiber), 21g pro. **DIABETIC EXCHANGES:** 3 lean meat, 2 starch.

TIP

To keep parsley fresh for up to a month, trim the stems and place the bunch in a tumbler with an inch of water. Be sure no leaves are in the water. Tie a produce bag around the tumbler to trap humidity; store in the refrigerator. Each time you use the parsley, change the water and turn the produce bag inside out so any moisture that has built up inside the bag can escape.

🅕🍎 BAKED CAESAR CHICKEN

This chicken has a cult following among my friends. One friend ran it in her child's fundraising cookbook as a dish that's so simple, children will enjoy helping to make it. I even prepared it once on a tugboat!
—*Kirsten Norgaard, Astoria, OR*

PREP: 10 min. • **BAKE:** 30 min.
MAKES: 4 servings

- 4 boneless skinless chicken breast halves (6 oz. each)
- ½ cup fat-free creamy Caesar salad dressing
- 1 medium ripe avocado, peeled and cubed
- ¼ cup shredded Parmesan cheese, divided

1. Place chicken in an 11x7-in. baking dish coated with cooking spray.
2. In a small bowl, combine the salad dressing, avocado and 2 Tbsp. cheese; spoon over chicken. Bake, uncovered, at 375° for 30-35 minutes or until a thermometer reads 170°. Sprinkle with remaining 2 Tbsp. cheese.
1 SERVING: 320 cal., 12g fat (3g sat. fat), 98mg chol., 530mg sod., 15g carb. (2g sugars, 4g fiber), 38g pro. **DIABETIC EXCHANGES:** 5 lean meat, 1 starch, 1 fat.

5i 🍲 CHERRY BALSAMIC PORK LOIN

After tasting a wonderful cherry topping for Brie cheese at a local market, I had to create one for pork. If you're really crazy about cherries, add even more to the dish.
—*Susan Stetzel, Gainesville,*

PREP: 20 min. • **COOK:** 3 hours + standing
MAKES: 8 servings (1⅓ cups sauce)

- 1 boneless pork loin roast (3 to 4 lbs.)
- 1 tsp. salt
- ½ tsp. pepper
- 1 Tbsp. canola oil
- ¾ cup cherry preserves
- ½ cup dried cherries
- ⅓ cup balsamic vinegar
- ¼ cup packed brown sugar

1. Sprinkle roast with salt and pepper. In a large skillet, heat oil over medium-high heat. Brown roast on all sides.

2. Transfer to a 6-qt. slow cooker. In a small bowl, mix preserves, cherries, vinegar and brown sugar until blended; pour over roast. Cook, covered, on low until tender (a thermometer inserted in pork should read at least 145°), 3-4 hours.

3. Remove roast from slow cooker; tent with foil. Let stand 15 minutes before slicing. Skim fat from cooking juices. Serve pork with sauce.

5 OZ. COOKED PORK WITH 2 TBSP. SAUCE: 359 cal., 10g fat (3g sat. fat), 85mg chol., 128mg sod., 34g carb. (31g sugars, 0 fiber), 33g pro.

5i DEVILED CHICKEN

My family has always loved this flavorful golden brown chicken. I watch for sales on leg quarters to keep the cost low.
—*Linda Trammell, Kingston, MO*

PREP: 10 min. • **BAKE:** 50 min.
MAKES: 6 servings

- 6 chicken leg quarters
- ¼ cup butter, melted
- 1 Tbsp. lemon juice
- 1 Tbsp. prepared mustard
- 1 tsp. salt
- 1 tsp. paprika
- ¼ tsp. pepper

1. Preheat oven to 375°. Place chicken in a 15x10x1-in. baking pan. In a small bowl, combine remaining ingredients. Pour over the chicken.

2. Bake, uncovered, 50-60 minutes or until a thermometer inserted in thickest part of thigh reads 170°-175°, basting the chicken occasionally with pan juices.

1 LEG QUARTER: 345 cal., 24g fat (9g sat. fat), 125mg chol., 567mg sod., 1g carb. (0 sugars, 0 fiber), 30g pro.

TIP

When it comes to cooking, the term "deviled" has traditionally referred to food that has been prepared with ample spice, zest or savoriness. Ham, sardines, olives and hard-boiled eggs are common deviled foods.

HERBED RIB ROAST

The aromatic mixture of herbs and garlic turns this tender roast into a real treat. Our children and grandchildren look forward to feasting on it at Christmastime and other special occasions.
—*Carol Jackson, South Berwick, ME*

PREP: 10 min. • **BAKE:** 2 hours + standing
MAKES: 10 servings

- 1   beef ribeye roast (4 to 5 lbs.)
- 2   to 3 garlic cloves, thinly sliced
- 1   tsp. salt
- ½   tsp. pepper
- ½   tsp. dried basil
- ½   tsp. dried parsley flakes
- ½   tsp. dried marjoram

Cut 15-20 slits in the roast; insert garlic. Tie the roast at 1½-to-2-in. intervals with kitchen string. Combine salt, pepper, basil, parsley and marjoram; rub over roast. Place fat side up on a rack in a roasting pan. Bake, uncovered, at 325° for 2-2½ hours or until meat reaches the desired doneness (for medium-rare, a thermometer should read 135°; medium, 140°; medium-well, 145°). Let stand for 15 minutes before slicing.

4 OZ. COOKED BEEF: 397 cal., 29g fat (12g sat. fat), 107mg chol., 319mg sod., 0 carb. (0 sugars, 0 fiber), 32g pro.

APRICOT HAM STEAK

Ham is a versatile main menu item—you can enjoy it for breakfast, lunch or dinner. One easy and tasty version is ham steaks topped with a slightly sweet apricot glaze.
—*Scott Woodward, Shullsburg, WI*

TAKES: 10 min. • **MAKES:** 4 servings

- 2 Tbsp. butter, divided
- 4 fully cooked boneless ham steaks (5 oz. each)
- ½ cup apricot preserves
- 1 Tbsp. cider vinegar
- ¼ tsp. ground ginger
  Dash salt

1. In a large skillet, heat 1 Tbsp. butter over medium heat. Cook ham on both sides until lightly browned and heated through. Remove from pan; keep warm.

2. Add remaining 1 Tbsp. butter and remaining ingredients to pan; cook and stir over medium heat until blended and heated through. Serve over ham.

1 SERVING: 299 cal., 11g fat (5g sat. fat), 88mg chol., 1899mg sod., 26g carb. (17g sugars, 0 fiber), 26g pro.

GRILLED APRICOT HAM STEAKS: Melt 1 Tbsp. butter and brush over ham steaks. Grill, covered, over medium heat until lightly browned, 3-5 minutes on each side. Prepare the sauce and serve as directed.

WEEKDAY BEEF STEW

Beef stew capped with flaky puff pastry adds comfort to the weeknight menu—my family is always glad to see this meal. Make a salad and call your crowd to the table.
—*Daniel Anderson, Kenosha, WI*

TAKES: 30 min. • **MAKES:** 4 servings

- 1 sheet frozen puff pastry, thawed
- 1 pkg. (15 oz.) refrigerated beef roast au jus
- 2 cans (14½ oz. each) diced tomatoes, undrained
- 1 pkg. (16 oz.) frozen vegetables for stew
- ¾ tsp. pepper
- 2 Tbsp. cornstarch
- 1¼ cups water

1. Preheat oven to 400°. Unfold puff pastry. Using a 4-in. round cookie cutter, cut out 4 circles. Place 2 in. apart on a greased baking sheet. Bake until golden brown, 14-16 minutes.

2. Meanwhile, shred the beef with 2 forks; transfer to a large saucepan. Add tomatoes, vegetables and pepper; bring to a boil. In a small bowl, mix cornstarch and water until smooth; stir into beef mixture. Return to a boil, stirring constantly. Cook and stir until thickened, 1-2 minutes.

3. Ladle stew into 4 bowls; top each serving with a pastry round.

1½ CUPS WITH 1 PASTRY ROUND: 604 cal., 25g fat (8g sat. fat), 73mg chol., 960mg sod., 65g carb. (10g sugars, 9g fiber), 32g pro.

AIR-FRYER TACO PUFFS

I make these puffs ahead of time and keep the in the refrigerator until I'm ready to pop them in the air fryer. A helpful hint: Plain refrigerated biscuits seal together better than buttermilk types.
—*Jan Schmid, Hibbing, MN*

PREP TIME: 15 min.
COOK TIME: 10 min./batch
MAKES: 8 servings

- 1 lb. ground beef
- ½ cup chopped onion
- 1 envelope taco seasoning
- 2 tubes (16.3 oz. each) large refrigerated flaky biscuits
- 2 cups shredded cheddar cheese

1. In a large skillet, cook beef and onion over medium heat until meat is no longer pink, 5-7 minutes, breaking into crumbles; drain. Add taco seasoning and prepare according to the package directions. Cool meat mixture slightly.
2. Preheat air fryer to 350°. Flatten half the biscuits into 4-in. circles. Spoon ¼ cup meat mixture onto each circle; sprinkle each with ¼ cup cheese. Flatten remaining biscuits; place over filling and pinch edges to seal tightly.
3. In batches, place puffs in a single layer in greased air fryer. Cook until golden brown and puffed, 10-15 minutes.
1 TACO PUFF: 574 cal., 28g fat (13g sat. fat), 63mg chol., 1538mg sod., 55g carb. (9g sugars, 0 fiber), 23g pro.

AIR-FRYER LEMON FETA CHICKEN

This bright, Greek-inspired chicken has only five ingredients—it's a busy-day lifesaver! And popping it into the air fryer makes it even easier.
—*Ann Cain, Morrill, NE*

TAKES: 25 min. • **MAKES:** 2 servings

- 2 boneless skinless chicken breast halves (2 oz. each)
- 1 to 2 Tbsp. lemon juice
- 2 Tbsp. crumbled feta cheese
- ½ tsp. dried oregano
- ¼ tsp. pepper

1. Preheat air fryer to 400°. Place chicken in a lightly greased baking dish that fits into the air fryer. Pour the lemon juice over chicken; sprinkle with feta cheese, oregano and pepper.
2. Cook until a thermometer reads 165°, 20-25 minutes.
1 CHICKEN BREAST HALF : 142 cal., 4g fat (2g sat. fat), 66mg chol., 122mg sod., 1g carb. (0 sugars, 0 fiber), 24g pro.

EASY SLOW-COOKED PORK TENDERLOIN

I've learned that simple dinners make the best comfort foods. Wholesome, everyday ingredients are the key to my success in the kitchen. Three ingredients poured over the pork and—voila, a delicious meal my family of seven devours!
—*Grace Neltner, Lakeside Park, KY*

PREP: 5 min. • **COOK:** 1¾ hours + standing • **MAKES:** 6 servings

- ¼ cup olive oil
- 2 Tbsp. soy sauce
- 1 Tbsp. Montreal steak seasoning
- 2 pork tenderloins (1 lb. each)
  Mashed potatoes or cooked wild rice

In a 5-qt. slow cooker, mix the oil, soy sauce and steak seasoning. Add the pork tenderloins; turn to coat. Cook, covered, on low until a thermometer inserted in pork reads 145°, 1¾-2¼ hours. Let stand 10 minutes before slicing. Serve with mashed potatoes.

5 OZ. COOKED PORK: 259 cal., 14g fat (3g sat. fat), 85mg chol., 707mg sod., 0 carb. (0 sugars, 0 fiber), 31g pro. **DIABETIC EXCHANGES:** 5 lean meat, 2 fat.

GRILLED SHRIMP SCAMPI

When I was in second grade, my class put together a cookbook. I saw this recipe from one of my friends, and I thought my mom would like it. I was right!
—*Peggy Roos, Minneapolis, MN*

PREP: 15 min. + marinating • **GRILL:** 10 min. • **MAKES:** 6 servings

- 2 Tbsp. olive oil
- 2 Tbsp. lemon juice
- 3 garlic cloves, minced
- ¼ tsp. salt
- ¼ tsp. pepper
- 1½ lbs. uncooked jumbo shrimp, peeled and deveined
  Hot cooked jasmine rice
  Minced fresh parsley

1. In a large bowl, whisk the first 5 ingredients. Add shrimp; toss to coat. Refrigerate, covered, 30 minutes.

2. Thread shrimp onto 6 metal or soaked wooden skewers. Grill, covered, over medium heat (or broil 4 in. from heat) 6-8 minutes or until shrimp turn pink, turning once. Serve shrimp with rice; sprinkle with parsley.

1 SKEWER: 118 cal., 4g fat (1g sat. fat), 138mg chol., 184mg sod., 1g carb. (0 sugars, 0 fiber), 18g pro. **DIABETIC EXCHANGES:** 2 meat, ½ fat.

5i 🍎
GRILLED PINEAPPLE CHICKEN

A trip to Hawaii is easy with this juicy grilled pineapple chicken. Simply give it a quick marinade, fire up the grill and let it sizzle. We love this low-carb recipe!
—*Charlotte Rogers, Virginia Beach, VA*

- -

PREP: 10 min. + marinating
GRILL: 10 min.
MAKES: 4 servings

- ¼ **cup unsweetened pineapple juice**
- 2 **Tbsp. sherry**
- 2 **Tbsp. soy sauce**
- ¼ **tsp. ground ginger**
  Dash salt
  Dash pepper
- 4 **boneless skinless chicken breast halves (6 oz. each)**
  Optional: Grilled pineapple and sliced green onions

1. In a large bowl, combine the first 6 ingredients; add chicken and turn to coat. Cover and refrigerate 1-2 hours.
2. Drain and discard marinade. Grill chicken, covered, over medium heat (or broil 4 in. from heat) for 5-7 minutes on each side or until a meat thermometer reads 165°. If desired, serve with grilled pineapple and sliced green onions.
1 SERVING: 187 cal., 4g fat (1g sat. fat), 94mg chol., 209mg sod., 1g carb. (0 sugars, 0 fiber), 35g pro. **DIABETIC EXCHANGES:** 5 lean meat.

DIJON CHICKEN

Here's a fuss-free dish you'll want to add to your weekly dinner rotation. The Dijon mustard adds so much flavor, and the dish comes together very quickly.
—Carol Roberts, Dumas, TX

- -

PREP: 15 min. • **BAKE:** 1 hour
MAKES: 6 servings

- ½ cup Dijon mustard
- ½ cup water
- 1 broiler/fryer chicken (3 to 4 lbs.), cut up
- 4½ cups herb-seasoned stuffing, crushed

1. In a shallow bowl, combine mustard and water; dip the chicken pieces, then roll in stuffing crumbs. Place chicken in a greased 13x9-in. baking pan; sprinkle with the remaining stuffing crumbs.
2. Bake, uncovered, at 350° for 1 hour or until juices run clear.
5 OZ. COOKED CHICKEN: 414 cal., 17g fat (4g sat. fat), 88mg chol., 1122mg sod., 31g carb. (2g sugars, 2g fiber), 33g pro.

> **TIP**
> Dijon mustard, named for its hometown of Dijon in the Burgundy region of France, is a classic French condiment most often made from brown mustard seeds. It's tangy with a slightly spicy or "hot" flavor.

HONEY-FRIED WALLEYE

We enjoy fishing in the summer, so we end up with lots of fresh fillets. Everyone who tries this crisp, golden walleye loves it. It's one of my husband's favorite recipes, and I never have leftovers. Honey gives the coating a deliciously different twist.
—Sharon Collis, Colona, IL

- -

TAKES: 15 min. • **MAKES:** 6 servings

- 1 large egg
- 1 tsp. honey, plus additional for drizzling
- 1 cup coarsely crushed saltines (about 22 crackers)
- ⅓ cup all-purpose flour
- ¼ tsp. salt
- ¼ tsp. pepper
- 6 walleye fillets (about 1½ lbs.)
  Canola oil

1. In a shallow bowl, beat egg and 1 tsp. honey. In another bowl, combine the cracker crumbs, flour, salt and pepper. Dip fillets into the egg mixture, then coat with the crumb mixture.
2. In a large skillet, heat ¼ in. of oil over medium-high heat; fry fish 3-4 minutes on each side or until the fish just begins to flake easily with a fork. Drizzle with additional honey.
1 SERVING: 189 cal., 3g fat (1g sat. fat), 133mg chol., 296mg sod., 14g carb. (1g sugars, 1g fiber), 25g pro.

- GARLIC SHRIMP & RICE -

Here's a quick and simple way to make shrimp. You can use garlic salt instead of the minced garlic cloves and salt.

Cook 1 cup **instant brown rice** according to package directions. Meanwhile, in a large skillet, cook 1 lb. **uncooked medium shrimp**, peeled and deveined, with 2 minced **garlic cloves** and ¾ tsp. **salt** in 3 Tbsp. **reduced-fat butter** and 2 Tbsp. **olive oil** for 1 minute. Add 1 pkg. (6 oz.) **fresh baby spinach**. Cover and cook until shrimp turn pink and spinach is wilted. Stir in rice.

- 9 -

MAKE-AHEAD MARVELS

Conquer weekly recipe prep with these delicious make-ahead meals. From cheesy casseroles that store in the freezer to breakfast bakes that set up the night before, there's a dish for every occasion. You'll even find soups, breads and desserts—all offering make-ahead appeal!

EASY SAUERBRATEN

Here's my simplified take on traditional German fare. The beef roast's definitive pickled flavor is sure to delight fans of Bavarian cuisine.
—*Patricia Rutherford, Winchester, IL*

PREP: 25 min. + marinating
BAKE: 3 hours • **MAKES:** 10 servings

- 4 cups water
- 2 cups red wine vinegar
- 12 whole cloves
- 2 bay leaves
- 3 tsp. salt
- 3 tsp. brown sugar
- 1 boneless beef chuck roast or rump roast (4 lbs.)
- ¼ cup all-purpose flour
- 2 Tbsp. canola oil
- 1 large onion, cut into wedges
- 5 medium carrots, cut into 1½-in. pieces
- 2 celery ribs, cut into 1½-in. pieces

1. In a large bowl, combine the water, vinegar, cloves, bay leaves, salt and brown sugar. Remove 2 cups to a small bowl; cover and refrigerate. Add roast to large bowl with remaining marinade; turn to coat. Cover and refrigerate for 1-2 days, turning twice each day.
2. Discard marinade and spices from large bowl. Pat roast dry; dredge in flour. In a large skillet over medium-high heat, brown roast in oil on all sides. Transfer to a small roasting pan. Add the onion, carrots, celery and reserved marinade.
3. Cover and bake at 325° for 3 to 3½ hours or until meat is tender. With a slotted spoon, remove meat and vegetables to a serving platter. Strain cooking juices; thicken if desired.
1 SERVING: 365 cal., 20g fat (7g sat. fat), 118mg chol., 368mg sod., 9g carb. (3g sugars, 1g fiber), 36g pro.

> **TIP** Sauerbraten is a traditional German beef roast. In English, "sauerbraten" translates to "sour roast" or "pickled roast", referring to the vinegar-based marinade that tenderizes the meat.

SLOW-SIMMERED CHICKEN WITH RAISINS, CAPERS & BASIL

Capers, golden raisins and fresh basil give this dish a sweetly savory flavor. And what is even better than that? The kids love it.
—*Nadine Mesch, Mount Healthy, OH*

PREP: 25 min. • **COOK:** 4 hours
MAKES: 8 servings

- 2 Tbsp. olive oil, divided
- 8 boneless skinless chicken thighs (4 oz. each)
- 1 tsp. salt
- 1 tsp. pepper
- ½ cup Marsala wine
- 8 oz. sliced fresh mushrooms
- 1 medium sweet red pepper, thinly sliced
- 1 medium onion, thinly sliced
- 1 can (14½ oz.) diced tomatoes, undrained
- ½ cup golden raisins
- 2 Tbsp. capers, drained
- ¼ cup chopped fresh basil
  Hot cooked couscous

1. In a large skillet, heat 1 Tbsp. oil over medium-high heat. Sprinkle chicken with salt and pepper; brown chicken on both sides in batches, adding oil as needed. Transfer chicken thighs to a 5- or 6-qt. slow cooker.
2. Add wine to the skillet, stirring to loosen the browned bits; pour into slow cooker. Stir the mushrooms, red pepper, onion, and tomatoes, raisins and capers into slow cooker.
3. Cook, covered, on low until the chicken and vegetables are tender, 4-5 hours. Sprinkle with basil before serving. Serve with couscous.
1 SERVING: 250 cal., 12g fat (3g sat. fat), 76mg chol., 494mg sod., 13g carb. (9g sugars, 2g fiber), 23g pro. **DIABETIC EXCHANGES:** 3 lean meat, 1 vegetable, 1 fat, ½ starch.

> **TIP** Dried apricots work well in place of raisins.

❄ BEEF WELLINGTON FRIED WONTONS

These tasty appetizers scale down classic beef Wellington to an fun party size. They're fancy and delicious!

—*Dianne Phillips, Tallapoosa, GA*

- -

PREP: 35 min. • **COOK:** 25 min.
MAKES: 3½ dozen

- ½ lb. lean ground beef (90% lean)
- 1 Tbsp. butter
- 1 Tbsp. olive oil
- 2 garlic cloves, minced
- 1½ tsp. chopped shallot
- 1 cup each chopped fresh shiitake, baby portobello and white mushrooms
- ¼ cup dry red wine
- 1 Tbsp. minced fresh parsley
- ½ tsp. salt
- ¼ tsp. pepper
- 1 pkg. (12 oz.) wonton wrappers
- 1 large egg
- 1 Tbsp. water
  Oil for deep-fat frying

1. In a small skillet, cook the beef over medium heat until it is no longer pink, breaking into crumbles, 4-5 minutes; transfer to a large bowl. In the same skillet, heat butter and olive oil over medium-high heat. Add garlic and shallot; cook 1 minute longer. Stir in mushrooms and wine. Cook until the mushrooms are tender, 8-10 minutes; add to beef. Stir in parsley, salt and pepper.

2. Place about 2 tsp. filling in the center of each wonton wrapper. Combine egg and water. Moisten wonton edges with egg mixture; fold opposite corners over filling and press to seal.

3. In an electric skillet, heat oil to 375°. Fry wontons, a few at a time, until golden brown, 60-90 seconds on each side. Drain on paper towels. Serve warm.

FREEZE OPTION: Place filled wontons on a baking sheet and place in the freezer until they're firm, then transfer to an airtight container and freeze. Thaw overnight in the fridge and cook as directed.

1 WONTON: 47 cal., 2g fat (1g sat. fat), 9mg chol., 82mg sod., 5g carb. (0 sugars, 0 fiber), 2g pro.

🍎 ❄ 🍲 SLOW-COOKER BEEF BARBACOA

I love this beef barbacoa because the meat is fall-apart tender and the sauce is smoky, slightly spicy and so flavorful. It's a great alternative to ground beef tacos or even pulled pork carnitas. It's also versatile. You can have a soft taco bar and let people make their own—or offer mouthwatering Mexican pizzas or rice bowls.

—*Holly Sander, Lake Mary, FL*

- -

PREP: 20 min. • **COOK:** 6 hours
MAKES: 8 servings

- 1 beef rump or bottom round roast (3 lbs.)
- ½ cup minced fresh cilantro
- ⅓ cup tomato paste
- 8 garlic cloves, minced
- 2 Tbsp. chipotle peppers in adobo sauce plus 1 Tbsp. sauce
- 2 Tbsp. cider vinegar
- 4 tsp. ground cumin
- 1 Tbsp. brown sugar
- 1½ tsp. salt
- 1 tsp. pepper
- 1 cup beef stock
- 1 cup beer or additional stock
- 16 corn tortillas (6 in.)
  Pico de gallo
  Optional toppings: Lime wedges, queso fresco and additional cilantro

1. Cut roast in half. Mix next 9 ingredients; rub over the roast. Place in a 5-qt. slow cooker. Add stock and beer. Cook, covered, until meat is tender, 6-8 hours.

2. Remove roast; shred with 2 forks. Reserve 3 cups cooking juices; discard remaining juices. Skim fat from reserved juices. Return beef and reserved juices to slow cooker; heat through.

3. Serve with tortillas and pico de gallo. If desired, serve with lime wedges, queso fresco and additional cilantro.

FREEZE OPTION: Place shredded beef in freezer containers. Cool and freeze. To use, partially thaw in refrigerator overnight. Heat through in a covered saucepan, stirring gently; add broth if necessary.

2 FILLED TORTILLAS: 361 cal., 10g fat (3g sat. fat), 101mg chol., 652mg sod., 28g carb. (4g sugars, 4g fiber), 38g pro. **DIABETIC EXCHANGES:** 5 lean meat, 2 starch.

5i **PM**
EASY SMOKED SALMON

A magazine featured this recipe years ago, and it's still my favorite salmon. Just add crackers for a super simple yet elegant appetizer.
—*Norma Fell, Boyne City, MI*

PREP: 10 min. + marinating • **BAKE:** 35 min. + chilling
MAKES: 16 servings

- 1 salmon fillet (about 2 lbs.)
- 2 Tbsp. brown sugar
- 2 tsp. salt
- ½ tsp. pepper
- 1 to 2 Tbsp. liquid smoke
  Optional: Capers and lemon slices

1. Place salmon, skin side down, in an 11x7-in. baking pan coated with cooking spray. Sprinkle with brown sugar, salt and pepper. Drizzle with liquid smoke. Cover and refrigerate for 4-8 hours.
2. Drain salmon, discarding liquid. Bake, uncovered, at 350° until the fish flakes easily with a fork, 35-45 minutes. Cool to room temperature. Cover and refrigerate for 8 hours or overnight. If desired, serve with capers and lemon slices.

1½ OZ. COOKED SALMON: 95 cal., 5g fat (1g sat. fat), 28mg chol., 324mg sod., 2g carb. (2g sugars, 0 fiber), 10g pro.

PM
CHEESE & CRAB BRUNCH BAKE

Here's a cheesy seafood casserole that can be pulled together in 30 minutes, refrigerated overnight and baked up the next day.
—*Joyce Conway, Westerville, OH*

PREP: 30 min. + chilling • **BAKE:** 50 min. • **MAKES:** 12 servings

- 2 Tbsp. Dijon mustard
- 6 English muffins, split
- 8 oz. lump crabmeat, drained
- 2 Tbsp. lemon juice
- 2 tsp. grated lemon zest
- 2 cups shredded white cheddar cheese
- 12 large eggs
- 1 cup half-and-half cream
- 1 cup 2% milk
- ½ cup mayonnaise
- 1 tsp. salt
- ½ tsp. cayenne pepper
- ½ tsp. pepper
- 2 cups shredded Swiss cheese
- 1 cup grated Parmesan cheese
- 4 green onions, chopped
- ¼ cup finely chopped sweet red pepper
- ¼ cup finely chopped sweet yellow pepper

1. Spread the mustard over bottom half of muffins. Place in a greased 13x9-in. baking dish. Top with crab, lemon juice and zest. Sprinkle with cheddar cheese. Top with muffin tops.
2. In a large bowl, whisk the eggs, cream, milk, mayonnaise, salt, cayenne and pepper. Pour over muffins; sprinkle with the Swiss cheese, Parmesan cheese, onions and peppers. Cover and refrigerate overnight.
3. Remove from refrigerator 30 minutes before baking. Preheat oven to 375°. Cover and bake 30 minutes. Uncover; bake until set, 20-25 minutes longer. Let stand for 5 minutes before serving. If desired, top with additional chopped green onions.

1 SERVING: 428 cal., 28g fat (13g sat. fat), 286mg chol., 844mg sod., 18g carb. (4g sugars, 1g fiber), 26g pro.

✳ BAKED TWO-CHEESE & BACON GRITS

To a Southerner, grits are a true staple. Combine them with bacon and cheese, and even Northerners will be asking for a second helping.
—*Melissa Rogers, Tuscaloosa, AL*

PREP: 25 min. • **BAKE:** 40 min. + standing
MAKES: 12 servings

- 6 thick-sliced bacon strips, chopped
- 3 cups water
- 3 cups chicken stock
- 1 tsp. garlic powder
- ½ tsp. pepper
- 2 cups quick-cooking grits
- 12 oz. Velveeta, cubed (about 2⅓ cups)
- ½ cup butter, cubed
- ½ cup 2% milk
- 4 large eggs, room temperature, lightly beaten
- 2 cups shredded white cheddar cheese

1. Preheat the oven to 350°. In a large saucepan, cook bacon over medium heat until crisp, stirring occasionally. Remove pan from heat. Remove bacon with a slotted spoon; drain on paper towels.
2. Add water, stock, garlic powder and pepper to bacon drippings; bring to a boil. Slowly stir in grits. Reduce the heat to medium-low; cook, covered, 5-7 minutes or until thickened, stirring occasionally. Remove from heat.
3. Add Velveeta and butter; stir until melted. Stir in milk. Slowly stir in eggs until blended. Transfer to a greased 13x9-in. baking dish. Sprinkle with bacon and shredded cheese. Bake, uncovered, 40-45 minutes or until edges are golden brown and cheese is melted. Let stand 10 minutes before serving.
FREEZE OPTION: Cool unbaked casserole; cover and freeze. To use, partially thaw in refrigerator overnight. Remove casserole from the refrigerator 30 minutes before baking. Bake grits as directed, increasing the time to 50-60 minutes or until heated through and a thermometer inserted in center reads 165°.
¾ CUP: 466 cal., 34g fat (18g sat. fat), 143mg chol., 840mg sod., 23g carb. (3g sugars, 1g fiber), 17g pro.

BAKED NECTARINE CHICKEN SALAD

My nectarine chicken casserole is a fun twist on a classic. Folks love the crunchy chow mein noodles on top. I love that I can make it a day in advance and refrigerate it until it's time to serve. Serve with hot bread or rolls.
—Faye Robinson, Pensacola, FL

PREP: 15 min. • **BAKE:** 20 min. • **MAKES:** 8 servings

- 1⅓ cups mayonnaise
- ½ cup shredded Parmesan cheese
- 2 Tbsp. lemon juice
- 1 tsp. salt
- 1 tsp. onion powder
- 4 cups cubed cooked chicken
- 8 celery ribs, thinly sliced
- 4 medium nectarines, coarsely chopped
- 8 green onions, sliced
- 2 cans (3 oz. each) crispy chow mein noodles

1. Preheat oven to 375°. In a small bowl, mix first 5 ingredients. In a large bowl, combine chicken, celery, nectarines and onions. Add mayonnaise mixture; toss gently to coat.
2. Transfer to a greased 13x9-in. baking dish. Sprinkle with noodles. Bake, uncovered, until heated through, 20-25 minutes. To Make Ahead: This can be made a day in advance. Before adding noodles, cover and refrigerate. Remove from the refrigerator 30 minutes before baking. Sprinkle with noodles. Bake as directed.
1¼ CUPS: 539 cal., 37g fat (7g sat. fat), 69mg chol., 911mg sod., 26g carb. (8g sugars, 3g fiber), 25g pro.

HUNGARIAN GOULASH

Here's a cherished heirloom recipe. My grandmother made this for my mother when she was a child, and then my mom made it for us to enjoy. Paprika and caraway add wonderful flavor, and sour cream gives it a creamy richness. It's simply scrumptious!
—Marcia Doyle, Pompano, FL

PREP: 20 min. • **COOK:** 7 hours • **MAKES:** 12 servings

- 3 medium onions, chopped
- 2 medium carrots, chopped
- 2 medium green peppers, chopped
- 3 lbs. beef stew meat
- ¾ tsp. salt, divided
- ¾ tsp. pepper, divided
- 2 Tbsp. olive oil
- 1½ cups reduced-sodium beef broth
- ¼ cup all-purpose flour
- 3 Tbsp. paprika
- 2 Tbsp. tomato paste
- 1 tsp. caraway seeds
- 1 garlic clove, minced
  Dash sugar
- 12 cups uncooked whole wheat egg noodles
- 1 cup reduced-fat sour cream

1. Place onions, carrots and green peppers in a 5-qt. slow cooker. Sprinkle meat with ½ tsp. salt and ½ tsp. pepper. In a large skillet, brown meat in oil in batches. Transfer to the slow cooker.
2. Add broth to skillet, stirring to loosen browned bits from pan. Combine the flour, paprika, tomato paste, caraway seeds, garlic, sugar and remaining salt and pepper; stir into skillet. Bring to a boil; cook and stir for 2 minutes or until thickened. Pour over meat. Cover and cook on low for 7-9 hours or until meat is tender.
3. Cook noodles according to package directions. Stir sour cream into slow cooker. Drain noodles; serve with goulash.
⅔ CUP GOULASH WITH 1 CUP NOODLES: 388 cal., 13g fat (4g sat. fat), 78mg chol., 285mg sod., 41g carb. (5g sugars, 7g fiber), 31g pro.
DIABETIC EXCHANGES: 3 lean meat, 2 starch, 1 vegetable, 1 fat.

THANKSGIVING'S NOT OVER YET ENCHILADA SOUP

Pumpkin adds a unique richness to this warm soup. You certainly can include Thanksgiving leftovers, but it's a good recipe to turn to anytime you have extra turkey.
—*Denise Pounds, Hutchinson, KS*

PREP: 20 min. • COOK: 20 min. • MAKES: 8 servings (3 qt.)

- 1 large sweet red pepper, finely chopped
- 1 medium onion, chopped
- 1 celery rib, chopped
- 1 Tbsp. olive oil
- 2 cans (14½ oz. each) reduced-sodium chicken broth
- 1 can (28 oz.) green enchilada sauce
- 1 can (15 oz.) pumpkin
- 1½ cups frozen corn
- 2 cans (4 oz. each) chopped green chiles
- 2 Tbsp. ranch salad dressing mix
- 2 cups cubed cooked turkey
  Optional toppings: crumbled queso fresco, shredded cheddar cheese, crushed tortilla chips, cubed avocado and minced fresh cilantro

In a Dutch oven, saute the red pepper, onion and celery in oil until crisp-tender. Add the broth, enchilada sauce, pumpkin, corn, chiles and dressing mix. Bring to a boil. Reduce heat; cover and simmer until vegetables are tender, 10-12 minutes. Stir in turkey and heat through. Garnish servings with toppings of your choice.
1½ CUPS: 209 cal., 6g fat (1g sat. fat), 27mg chol., 1451mg sod., 24g carb. (6g sugars, 4g fiber), 16g pro.

❄ DELUXE HASH BROWN CASSEROLE

My son-in-law gave me the recipe for this hash brown casserole, which my kids say is addictive. Not only is it delicious, it's a great option when you need to prep something in advance.
—*Amy Oswalt, Burr, NE*

PREP: 10 min. • BAKE: 50 min. • MAKES: 12 servings

- 1½ cups sour cream onion dip
- 1 can (10¾ oz.) condensed cream of chicken soup, undiluted
- 1 envelope ranch salad dressing mix
- 1 tsp. onion powder
- 1 tsp. garlic powder
- ½ tsp. pepper
- 1 pkg. (30 oz.) frozen shredded hash brown potatoes, thawed
- 2 cups shredded cheddar cheese
- ½ cup crumbled cooked bacon

Preheat oven to 375°. In a large bowl, mix the first 6 ingredients; stir in potatoes, cheese and bacon. Transfer to a greased 13x9-in. baking dish. Bake until golden brown, 50-60 minutes.
FREEZE OPTION: Cover and freeze unbaked casserole. To use, partially thaw in refrigerator overnight. Remove from refrigerator 30 minutes before baking. Preheat oven to 375°. Bake casserole as directed until top is golden brown and a thermometer inserted in center reads 165°, increasing time to 1¼ to 1½ hours.
⅔ CUP: 273 cal., 17g fat (6g sat. fat), 36mg chol., 838mg sod., 20g carb. (2g sugars, 2g fiber), 10g pro.

PM
TRIPLE BERRY NO-BAKE CHEESECAKE

I love making cheesecakes, but I don't love the time commitment. When I first tried this recipe, my husband told me it was better than the baked ones, and that was a big plus for me!
—Joyce Mummau, Sugarcreek, OH

- -

PREP: 20 min. + chilling
MAKES: 12 servings (3⅓ cups topping)

- 1½ cups graham cracker crumbs
- ⅓ cup packed brown sugar
- ½ tsp. ground cinnamon
- ½ cup butter, melted

FILLING
- 2 pkg. (8 oz. each) cream cheese, softened
- ⅓ cup sugar
- 2 tsp. lemon juice
- 2 cups heavy whipping cream

TOPPING
- 2 cups sliced fresh strawberries
- 1 cup fresh blueberries
- 1 cup fresh raspberries
- 2 Tbsp. sugar

1. In a small bowl, mix cracker crumbs, brown sugar and cinnamon; stir in butter. Press onto the bottom and 1 in. up side of an ungreased 9-in. springform pan. Refrigerate 30 minutes.
2. In a large bowl, beat cream cheese, sugar and lemon juice until smooth. Gradually add cream; beat until stiff peaks form. Transfer to prepared crust. Refrigerate, covered, overnight.
3. In a bowl, gently toss berries with sugar. Let stand until juices are released from berries,15-30 minutes.
4. With a knife, loosen side of cheesecake from pan; remove rim. Serve cheesecake with topping.
1 PIECE WITH ABOUT ¼ CUP TOPPING:
432 cal., 34g fat (21g sat. fat), 109mg chol., 229mg sod., 29g carb. (20g sugars, 2g fiber), 5g pro.

ARTICHOKE CHICKEN

Rosemary, mushrooms and artichokes combine to give chicken a wonderful savory flavor. I've served this dish for a large group by doubling the recipe. It's always a big hit with everyone—especially my family!
—Ruth Stenson, Santa Ana, CA

- -

PREP: 15 min. • **BAKE:** 40 min.
MAKES: 8 servings

- 8 boneless skinless chicken breast halves (4 oz. each)
- 2 Tbsp. butter
- 2 jars (6 oz. each) marinated quartered artichoke hearts, drained
- 1 jar (4½ oz.) whole mushrooms, drained
- ½ cup chopped onion
- ⅓ cup all-purpose flour
- 1½ tsp. dried rosemary, crushed
- ¾ tsp. salt
- ¼ tsp. pepper
- 2 cups chicken broth or 1 cup broth and 1 cup dry white wine
  Hot cooked pasta, optional
  Minced fresh parsley

1. In a large skillet, brown chicken in butter. Remove chicken to an ungreased 13x9-in. baking dish. Arrange artichokes and mushrooms on top of chicken.
2. Saute onion in pan juices until crisp-tender. Combine the flour, rosemary, salt and pepper. Stir into pan until blended. Add chicken broth. Bring to a boil; cook and stir until thickened and bubbly, about 2 minutes. Spoon over chicken.
3. Bake, uncovered, at 350° until a thermometer inserted in the chicken reads 165°, about 40 minutes. If desired, serve with pasta. Sprinkle with parsley.
FREEZE OPTION: Cool unbaked casserole; cover and freeze. To use, partially thaw in refrigerator overnight. Remove from refrigerator 30 minutes before baking. Preheat oven to 350°. Bake casserole as directed, increasing time as necessary to heat through and for a thermometer inserted in the chicken to read 165°.
1 SERVING: 232 cal., 9g fat (3g sat. fat), 81mg chol., 752mg sod., 7g carb. (1g sugars, 1g fiber), 28g pro. **DIABETIC EXCHANGES:** 4 lean meat, 1½ fat, ½ starch.

MALTED CHOCOLATE CHEESECAKE

With an impressive presentation and a scrumptious, classic malt flavor, this cheesecake will make anyone feel special.
—Anna Ginsberg, Chicago, IL

PREP: 30 min. • **BAKE:** 40 min. + cooling
MAKES: 2 servings

- 4 portions refrigerated ready-to-bake sugar cookie dough
- 4 oz. cream cheese, softened
- ½ cup dark chocolate chips, melted
- 2 Tbsp. sugar
- 1 large egg white, room temperature
- ½ tsp. vanilla extract

TOPPING

- 4½ tsp. cream cheese, softened
- 2 tsp. sugar
- 1 tsp. malted milk powder
- 1 tsp. baking cocoa
- ⅔ cup whipped topping
- 1 Tbsp. chocolate syrup

1. Line a 5¾x3x2-in. loaf pan with foil. Press cookie dough onto bottom of pan. Bake at 325° for 15-20 minutes or until golden brown. Cool on a wire rack.

2. In a small bowl, beat the cream cheese, melted chocolate and sugar until smooth. Add egg white; beat on low speed just until combined. Stir in vanilla. Pour over crust.

3. Place loaf pan in a baking pan; add 1 in. of hot water to larger pan. Bake at 325° until center is just set and top appears dull, 40-45 minutes.

4. Remove loaf pan from water bath. Cool on a wire rack for 10 minutes. Carefully run a knife around edge of pan to loosen; cool 1 hour longer.

5. Refrigerate overnight. For topping, in a small bowl, beat the cream cheese, sugar, milk powder and baking cocoa until smooth. Fold in whipped topping. Spread over cheesecake. Cover and refrigerate for 1 hour.

6. Using foil, lift cheesecake out of pan. Cut in half. Drizzle chocolate syrup over each piece. Refrigerate leftovers.

1 PIECE: 934 cal., 58g fat (34g sat. fat), 74mg chol., 350mg sod., 92g carb. (68g sugars, 0 fiber), 14g pro.

FIVE-CHEESE ZITI AL FORNO

SEE PHOTO ON PAGE 199

After tasting the five-cheese ziti at Olive Garden, I made my own version. I always double this and freeze the second casserole.
—*Keri Whitney, Castro Valley, CA*

- -

PREP: 20 min. • **BAKE:** 30 min. + standing • **MAKES:** 12 servings

- 1½ lbs. (about 7½ cups) uncooked ziti or small tube pasta
- 2 jars (24 oz. each) marinara sauce
- 1 jar (15 oz.) Alfredo sauce
- 2 cups shredded part-skim mozzarella cheese, divided
- ½ cup reduced-fat ricotta cheese
- ½ cup shredded provolone cheese
- ½ cup grated Romano cheese

TOPPING
- ½ cup grated Parmesan cheese
- ½ cup panko bread crumbs
- 3 garlic cloves, minced
- 2 Tbsp. olive oil
- Optional: Minced fresh parsley or basil, optional

1. Preheat oven to 350°. Cook the pasta according to package directions for al dente; drain.
2. Meanwhile, in a large Dutch oven, combine the marinara sauce, Alfredo sauce, 1 cup mozzarella and the ricotta, provolone and Romano. Cook over medium heat until sauce begins to simmer and cheeses are melted. Stir in cooked pasta; pour the mixture into a greased 13x9-in. baking dish. Top with remaining 1 cup mozzarella cheese.
3. In a small bowl, stir together Parmesan, bread crumbs, garlic and olive oil; sprinkle over pasta.
4. Bake, uncovered, until mixture is bubbly and topping is golden brown, 30-40 minutes. Let stand 10 minutes before serving. Garnish with fresh parsley or basil if desired.
FREEZE OPTION: Cool the unbaked casserole; cover and freeze. To use, partially thaw in the refrigerator overnight. Remove from the refrigerator 30 minutes before baking. Preheat oven to 350°. Cover casserole with foil; bake 50 minutes. Uncover; bake until heated through and a thermometer inserted in the center reads 165°, 15-20 minutes longer.
1 CUP: 449 cal., 15g fat (8g sat. fat), 32mg chol., 960mg sod., 59g carb. (11g sugars, 4g fiber), 21g pro.

> **TIP**
> Crunchy toppings add a lot of texture to a casserole but will get soggy in the freezer. That doesn't mean you need to skip them, though—just add them on the day you're eating the casserole, or freeze them separately in a zip-top bag and sprinkle them on after thawing your main dish.

OVERNIGHT ASPARAGUS STRATA

I've made this tasty egg dish for breakfast, brunch, even dinner as a side dish. This is not your run-of-the-mill strata.
—*Lynn Licata, Sylvania, OH*

- -

PREP: 15 min. + chilling • **BAKE:** 40 min. • **MAKES:** 8 servings

- 1 lb. fresh asparagus, trimmed and cut into 1-in. pieces
- 4 English muffins, split and toasted
- 2 cups shredded Colby-Monterey Jack cheese, divided
- 1 cup cubed fully cooked ham
- ½ cup chopped sweet red pepper
- 8 large eggs
- 2 cups 2% milk
- 1 tsp. salt
- 1 tsp. ground mustard
- ¼ tsp. pepper

1. In a large saucepan, bring 8 cups water to a boil. Add the asparagus; cook, uncovered, for 2-3 minutes or just until crisp-tender. Drain and immediately drop into ice water. Drain and pat dry.
2. Arrange 6 English muffin halves in a greased 13x9-in. baking dish, cut side up. Trim remaining muffin halves to fill spaces. Layer with 1 cup cheese, asparagus, ham and red pepper.
3. In a large bowl, whisk eggs, milk, salt, mustard and pepper. Pour over top. Refrigerate, covered, overnight.
4. Preheat oven to 375°. Remove strata from refrigerator while oven heats. Sprinkle with remaining 1 cup cheese. Bake, uncovered, 40-45 minutes or until a knife inserted in the center comes out clean. Let stand 5 minutes before cutting.
1 PIECE: 318 cal., 17g fat (9g sat. fat), 255mg chol., 916mg sod., 20g carb. (5g sugars, 1g fiber), 21g pro.

MAKE-AHEAD BUTTERHORNS

Mom loved to make these lightly sweet, golden rolls. They're beautiful and impressive to serve, and they have a wonderful taste that carries with it the best memories of home.
—*Bernice Morris, Marshfield, MO*

PREP: 30 min. + freezing
BAKE: 15 min. • **MAKES:** 32 rolls

- 2 pkg. (¼ oz. each) active dry yeast
- ⅓ cup warm water (110° to 115°)
- 2 cups warm 2% milk (110° to 115°)
- 1 cup shortening
- 1 cup sugar
- 6 large eggs, room temperature
- 2 tsp. salt
- 9 cups all-purpose flour, divided
- 3 to 4 Tbsp. butter, melted

1. In a large bowl, dissolve yeast in water. Add milk, shortening, sugar, eggs, salt and 4 cups flour; beat 3 minutes or until smooth. Add enough remaining flour to form a soft dough.
2. Turn onto a floured surface; knead lightly. Place in a greased bowl, turning once to grease top. Cover and let rise in a warm place until doubled, about 2 hours.
3. Punch dough down; divide into 4 equal parts. Roll each into a 9-in. circle; brush with butter. Cut each dough circle into 8 pie-shaped wedges; roll up each wedge from wide edge to tip of dough and pinch to seal.
4. Place rolls with tip down on baking sheets; freeze. Transfer to airtight freezer containers; freeze up to 4 weeks.
5. To use frozen rolls: Arrange frozen rolls 2 in. apart on greased baking sheets. Cover with lightly greased plastic wrap; thaw in the refrigerator overnight. To bake, preheat oven to 375°. Let rolls rise in a warm place until doubled, about 1 hour. Bake until golden brown, 12-15 minutes. Serve warm.
1 ROLL: 239 cal., 9g fat (3g sat. fat), 39mg chol., 178mg sod., 34g carb. (7g sugars, 1g fiber), 6g pro.
TO BAKE ROLLS WITHOUT FREEZING: Prepare and shape rolls as directed; arrange 2 in. apart on greased baking sheets. Cover with lightly greased plastic wrap; let rise in a warm place until doubled, about 45 minutes. Preheat oven to 350°. Bake until golden brown, 12-15 minutes.

GRANDMA'S OXTAIL STEW

Oxtail stew is a favorite family heirloom recipe. This wonderfully rich soup will warm your soul and tantalize your taste buds. Don't let the name of this dish turn you off. Oxtail describes the meaty part of the tail of an ox (now commonly cow). The portion is delicious but requires long and slow cooking.
—*Bobbie Keefer, Byers, CO*

PREP: 20 min. • **COOK:** 10 hours
MAKES: 8 servings (3 qt.)

- 2 lbs. oxtails, trimmed
- 2 Tbsp. olive oil
- 4 medium carrots, sliced (about 2 cups)
- 1 medium onion, chopped
- 2 garlic cloves, minced
- 2 cans (14½ oz. each) diced tomatoes, undrained
- 1 can (15 oz.) beef broth
- 3 bay leaves
- 1 tsp. salt
- 1 tsp. dried oregano
- ½ tsp. dried thyme
- ½ tsp. pepper
- 6 cups chopped cabbage

1. In a large skillet, brown oxtails in oil over medium heat. Remove from pan; place in a 5-qt. slow cooker.

2. Add carrots and onion to drippings; cook and stir until just softened, about 3-5 minutes. Add garlic; cook 1 minute longer. Transfer the vegetable mixture to slow cooker. Add tomatoes, broth, bay leaves, salt, oregano, thyme and pepper; stir to combine.
3. Cook, covered, on low 8 hours. Add the cabbage; cook until cabbage is tender and meat pulls away easily from bones, about 2 hours longer. Remove oxtails; set aside until cool enough to handle. Remove meat from bones; discard the bones and shred the meat. Return meat to soup. Discard the bay leaves.
FREEZE OPTION: Freeze cooled stew in freezer containers. To use, partially thaw in refrigerator overnight. Heat through in a saucepan, stirring occasionally; add broth if necessary.
1½ CUPS: 204 cal., 10g fat (3g sat. fat), 34mg chol., 705mg sod., 14g carb. (8g sugars, 5g fiber), 16g pro.

TIP

HOW DO YOU TRIM OXTAILS?

Oxtails can be tough to cut, so it's best to ask the butcher to slice them into pieces, if they aren't already. Trimming the thick pieces of excess fat off the oxtails before cooking will ensure a stew that's flavorful with a velvety mouthfeel.

FRENCH MARKET SOUP

An old friend gave me this recipe. I think it tastes best the next day, so I suggest preparing it the day before you plan to serve it. Leftovers also freeze well.
—*Terri Lowe, Lumberton, TX*

PREP: 20 min. + soaking • **COOK:** 4½ hours
MAKES: 12 servings (4½ qt.)

- 3 cups assorted dried beans for soup
- 2 smoked ham hocks
- 12 cups water
- 1½ tsp. salt
- ½ tsp. pepper
- 1 can (28 oz.) crushed tomatoes, undrained
- 2 medium onions, chopped
- ¼ to ⅓ cup lemon juice
- 2 garlic cloves, minced
- ½ tsp. chili powder
- 1 lb. smoked kielbasa, chopped
- 1½ cups cubed cooked chicken
- ½ cup dry red wine or chicken broth
- ½ cup minced fresh parsley

1. Sort beans and rinse in cold water. Place beans in a Dutch oven; add water to cover by 2 in. Bring to a boil; boil for 2 minutes. Remove from the heat; cover and let stand for 1-4 hours or until beans are softened.
2. Drain and rinse beans, discarding liquid; return beans to the pan. Add the ham hocks, water, salt and pepper; bring to a boil. Reduce heat; cover and simmer for 3 hours or until beans are tender.
3. Remove ham hocks; set aside until cool enough to handle. Add tomatoes, onions, lemon juice, garlic and chili powder to the beans. Simmer 1 hour longer.
4. Remove ham from bones and cut into cubes; discard bones. Return ham to soup. Stir in the kielbasa, chicken, wine and parsley. Simmer for 30-40 minutes or until soup is heated through and as thick as desired.
NOTE: This recipe was tested with Bob's Red Mill 13-Bean Soup Mix.
1½ CUPS: 291 cal., 14g fat (5g sat. fat), 52mg chol., 840mg sod., 32g carb. (3g sugars, 18g fiber), 23g pro.

PM
MAKE-AHEAD CORNBREAD DRESSING

My family has always been big vegetable eaters. I wanted to share a little taste of my childhood with my in-laws, so I created this dish. It's a nice make-ahead option and the flavors blend nicely overnight.
—*Patricia Broussard, Lafayette, LA*

PREP: 1½ hours + chilling • **BAKE:** 55 min.
MAKES: 14 servings (¾ cup each)

- 1 medium spaghetti squash (about 4 lbs.)
- 1 pkg. (8½ oz.) cornbread/muffin mix
- 1 medium onion, finely chopped
- 2 celery ribs, thinly sliced
- ½ cup butter, cubed
- 2 garlic cloves, minced
- ½ lb. bulk pork sausage, cooked and drained
- 1 cup frozen corn
- 2 Tbsp. poultry seasoning
- ¾ tsp. salt
- ¼ tsp. pepper
- 1 cup chopped walnuts, toasted
- 1 cup chicken broth
- ¼ cup grated Parmesan cheese

1. Cut squash lengthwise in half; remove and discard the seeds. Place squash in a roasting pan, cut side down; add ½ in. of hot water. Bake, uncovered, at 375° for 45 minutes. Drain water from pan; turn squash cut side up. Bake 5 minutes longer or until squash is tender.
2. Prepare and bake the cornbread mix according to package directions, using an 8-in. square baking dish. Cool to room temperature; crumble bread. Place in an ungreased 13x9-in. baking pan. Bake at 350° for 8-13 minutes or until lightly browned, stirring twice.
3. In a large skillet, cook onion and celery in butter over medium heat for 4 minutes. Add garlic; cook 2 minutes longer. Stir in the sausage, corn, poultry seasoning, salt and pepper; heat through.
4. When squash is cool enough to handle, use a fork to separate the strands. In a large bowl, combine the sausage mixture, cornbread, squash and walnuts. Stir in the chicken broth.
5. Transfer to a greased 13x9-in. baking dish. Cover and refrigerate for 8 hours or overnight. Remove from the refrigerator 30 minutes before baking. Cover and bake at 350° for 45 minutes. Uncover; sprinkle with cheese; bake 10-15 minutes longer or until heated through.
¾ CUP: 269 cal., 19g fat (7g sat. fat), 42mg chol., 528mg sod., 21g carb. (6g sugars, 3g fiber), 6g pro.

FROZEN WALDORF SALAD

While I was growing up on a farm in western Kansas, we always had lots of hungry farm hands around during harvesttime. This salad is one we served often because it was easy to make and we could prepare it ahead of time.
—*Mildred Hall, Topeka, KS*

PREP: 25 min. + freezing • **MAKES:** 12 servings

- 1   can (20 oz.) crushed pineapple
- 1   cup sugar
- 2   large eggs, beaten
-     Dash salt
- 1   cup chopped celery
- 2   medium red apples, chopped
- 1   cup chopped pecans
- 1   cup heavy whipping cream, whipped
-     Lettuce leaves, optional

1. Drain pineapple, reserving the juice. Set pineapple aside. In a saucepan, combine the juice with sugar, eggs and salt. Cook, stirring constantly, over medium-low heat until slightly thickened. Remove from the heat; cool. Stir in pineapple, celery, apples and pecans. Fold in whipped cream.
2. Pour into a 9-in. square pan. Cover and freeze until firm. Let stand at room temperature for about 15 minutes before cutting. Serve on lettuce-lined plates if desired.
1 PIECE: 257 cal., 15g fat (5g sat. fat), 63mg chol., 40mg sod., 30g carb. (26g sugars, 2g fiber), 3g pro.

Ⓟ CHOCOLATE CRUNCH ICE CREAM

Making ice cream goes smoothly when you do the prep work in advance. I prepare the custard ahead and refrigerate it overnight. Plus, I toast the almonds beforehand and separate my add-ins into labeled containers.
—*Rosalie Peters, Caldwell, TX*

PREP: 30 min. + chilling • **PROCESS:** 20 min./batch + freezing
MAKES: 1½ qt.

- 1½ cups milk
- ¾   cup sugar, divided
- 4   egg yolks
- 2½ tsp. instant coffee granules
- 2   cups 60% cacao bittersweet chocolate baking chips, melted and cooled
- 1½ cups heavy whipping cream
- 1   tsp. vanilla extract
- ¾   cup semisweet chocolate chips, melted
- ¾   cup slivered almonds, toasted
- ⅓   cup milk chocolate toffee bits

1. In a large saucepan, heat milk to 175°; stir in ½ cup sugar until dissolved. In a small bowl, whisk egg yolks and remaining sugar. Stir in coffee granules and bittersweet chocolate.
2. In small bowl, whisk a small amount of hot mixture into egg yolks; return all to pan, whisking constantly. Cook over low heat until mixture is just thick enough to coat a metal spoon and a thermometer reads at least 160°, stirring constantly. Do not allow to boil. Remove from heat immediately.
3. Quickly transfer to a large bowl; place bowl in a pan of ice water. Stir gently and occasionally for 2 minutes. Stir in cream and vanilla. Press plastic wrap onto surface of custard. Refrigerate several hours or overnight.
4. Line a baking sheet with waxed paper; spread melted semisweet chocolate to ⅛-in. thickness. Refrigerate for 20 minutes; chop coarsely.
5. Fill cylinder of ice cream freezer two-thirds full with custard; freeze according to manufacturer's directions. (Refrigerate any remaining mixture until ready to freeze.)
6. Transfer ice cream to freezer containers, allowing headspace for expansion. For each batch, stir in some of the chopped chocolate, almonds and toffee bits. Freeze 2-4 hours or until firm.
¾ CUP: 675 cal., 46g fat (25g sat. fat), 182mg chol., 95mg sod., 67g carb. (61g sugars, 5g fiber), 9g pro.

MAKE-AHEAD EGGS BENEDICT TOAST CUPS

When I was growing up, we had eggs Benedict with champagne and orange juice on Christmas morning. I wanted to come up with an easy dish that would mimic the flavors of traditional eggs Benedict and would also freeze well. Friends, all I can say is, this one checks all the boxes!
—*Lyndsay Wells, Ladysmith, BC*

PREP: 30 min. • **BAKE:** 10 min.
MAKES: 1 dozen

- 6   **English muffins, split**
- 1   **envelope hollandaise sauce mix**
- 12 **slices Canadian bacon, quartered**
- 1   **tsp. pepper**
- 1   **Tbsp. olive oil**
- 6   **large eggs**
- 1   **Tbsp. butter**

1. Preheat oven to 375°. Flatten muffin halves with a rolling pin; press into greased muffin cups. Bake until lightly browned, about 10 minutes.

2. Meanwhile, prepare hollandaise sauce according to package directions; cool slightly. Sprinkle bacon with pepper. In a large skillet, cook the bacon in oil over medium heat until partially cooked but not crisp. Remove to paper towels to drain. Divide bacon among muffin cups. Wipe skillet clean.

3. Whisk the eggs and ½ cup cooled hollandaise sauce until blended. In the same skillet, heat butter over medium heat. Pour in egg mixture; cook and stir until eggs are thickened and no liquid egg remains. Divide the egg mixture among muffin cups; top cups with the remaining hollandaise sauce.

4. Bake cups until heated through, about 8-10 minutes. Serve warm. If making cups the night before, refrigerate unbaked cups, covered, overnight. Bake at 375° until golden brown, 10-12 minutes.

FREEZE OPTION: Cover and freeze unbaked cups in muffin cups until firm. Transfer to an airtight container; return to freezer. To use, bake cups in muffin tin as directed, increasing time to 25-30 minutes. Cover muffin cups loosely with foil if needed to prevent overbrowning.

1 TOAST CUP: 199 cal., 11g fat (5g sat. fat), 114mg chol., 495mg sod., 15g carb. (2g sugars, 1g fiber), 9g pro.

PUMPKIN CHEESECAKE EMPANADAS

These cute pumpkin empanadas make the perfect treat—and we love that they are baked and not fried!
—Taste of Home *Test Kitchen*

PREP: 25 min. • **BAKE:** 15 min.
MAKES: 3 dozen

- 1 large egg white
- ½ tsp. vanilla extract
- 1½ tsp. packed brown sugar
- 1½ tsp. aniseed
- ¾ tsp. ground cinnamon
- ¼ tsp. ground nutmeg

EMPANADAS

- 3 oz. cream cheese, softened
- ¼ cup canned pumpkin pie mix
- 1 large egg yolk, room temperature, lightly beaten
- 1 Tbsp. finely chopped pecans, toasted
- 2 sheets refrigerated pie crust

1. Preheat oven to 400°. In a small bowl, whisk egg white and vanilla. In another small bowl, combine brown sugar, aniseed, cinnamon and nutmeg.

2. In a bowl, beat cream cheese and pie mix until smooth. Add the egg yolk; beat on low speed just until blended. Stir in the pecans.

3. On a lightly floured surface, roll each crust to ¼-in. thickness. Cut with a floured 3-in. round biscuit cutter. Place circles 2 in. apart on parchment-lined baking sheets. Place 1 tsp. filling on 1 side of each circle. Brush edges of crust with egg white mixture; fold circles in half. With a fork, press edges to seal. Brush with egg white mixture and sprinkle with spice mixture. Bake until golden brown, 15-20 minutes.

FREEZE OPTION: Cover and freeze unbaked empanadas on parchment-lined baking sheets until firm. Transfer to a freezer container; return to freezer. To use, bake empanadas as directed.

NOTE: To toast nuts, bake in a shallow pan in a 350° oven for 5-10 minutes or cook in a skillet over low heat until lightly browned, stirring occasionally.

1 EMPANADA: 69 cal., 4g fat (2g sat. fat), 10mg chol., 56mg sod., 7g carb. (1g sugars, 0 fiber), 1g pro.

ZUCCHINI PIZZA CASSEROLE

My husband has a hearty appetite, our two kids never tire of pizza, and I grow lots of zucchini. So this tasty, tomatoey casserole is absolute tops with all of us throughout the year. Once you've tried the recipe, you may even decide to grow more zucchini in your own garden next summer!
—*Lynn Bernstetter, White Bear Lake, MN*

PREP: 20 min. • **BAKE:** 40 min. • **MAKES:** 8 servings

- 4 cups shredded unpeeled zucchini
- ½ tsp. salt
- 2 large eggs
- ½ cup grated Parmesan cheese
- 2 cups shredded part-skim mozzarella cheese, divided
- 1 cup shredded cheddar cheese, divided
- 1 lb. ground beef
- ½ cup chopped onion
- 1 can (15 oz.) Italian tomato sauce
- 1 medium green or sweet red pepper, chopped

1. Preheat oven to 400°. Place zucchini in colander; sprinkle with salt. Let stand 10 minutes, then squeeze out moisture.
2. Combine the zucchini with the eggs, Parmesan and half the mozzarella and cheddar cheeses. Press into a greased 13x9-in. or 3-qt. baking dish. Bake 20 minutes.
3. Meanwhile, in a large saucepan, cook beef and onion over medium heat until meat is no longer pink, breaking meat into crumbles; drain. Add tomato sauce; spoon over zucchini mixture. Sprinkle with remaining cheeses; add green pepper. Bake until heated through, about 20 minutes longer.
FREEZE OPTION: Cool baked casserole; cover and freeze. To use, partially thaw in refrigerator overnight. Remove from refrigerator 30 minutes before baking. Preheat the oven to 350°. Unwrap casserole; reheat on a lower oven rack until heated through and a thermometer inserted in center reads 165°.
1 CUP: 315 cal., 20g fat (10g sat. fat), 119mg chol., 855mg sod., 10g carb. (4g sugars, 2g fiber), 25g pro.

SHEET-PAN TILAPIA & VEGETABLE MEDLEY

Unlike some one-pan dinners that require precooking in a skillet or pot, this one uses just the sheet pan, period.
—*Judy Batson, Tampa, FL*

PREP: 20 min. • **BAKE:** 20 min. • **MAKES:** 2 servings

- 2 medium Yukon Gold potatoes, cut into wedges
- 3 large fresh Brussels sprouts, thinly sliced
- 3 large radishes, thinly sliced
- 1 cup fresh sugar snap peas, cut into ½-in. pieces
- 1 small carrot, thinly sliced
- 2 Tbsp. butter, melted
- ½ tsp. garlic salt
- ½ tsp. pepper
- 2 tilapia fillets (6 oz. each)
- 2 tsp. minced fresh tarragon or ½ tsp. dried tarragon
- ⅛ tsp. salt
- 1 Tbsp. butter, softened
  Optional: Lemon wedges and tartar sauce

1. Preheat oven to 450°. Line a 15x10x1-in. baking pan with foil; grease foil.
2. In a large bowl, combine the first 5 ingredients. Add melted butter, garlic salt and pepper; toss to coat. Place vegetables in a single layer in prepared pan; bake until potatoes are tender, about 20 minutes.
3. Remove from oven; preheat broiler. Arrange vegetables on 1 side of sheet pan. Add fish to other side. Sprinkle fillets with tarragon and salt; dot with softened butter. Broil 4-5 in. from heat until fish flakes easily with a fork, about 5 minutes. If desired, serve with lemon wedges and tartar sauce.
1 SERVING: 555 cal., 20g fat (12g sat. fat), 129mg chol., 892mg sod., 56g carb. (8g sugars, 8g fiber), 41g pro.

3. Spread one-fourth of the cheese sauce into a greased 8-in. square baking dish. Layer with each of the following: 2 noodles, one-third of the meat mixture and one-fourth of the cheese sauce. Repeat the layers twice. Sprinkle with the remaining ¼ cup cheese.

4. Bake, covered, 45 minutes. Bake, uncovered, 8-10 minutes longer or until cheese is melted. Let lasagna stand 10 minutes before serving.

FREEZE OPTION: Allow unbaked lasagna to cool; cover and freeze. To use, partially thaw in the refrigerator overnight. Remove from the refrigerator 30 minutes before baking. Preheat oven to 350°. Cover lasagna with foil; bake as directed, increasing the baking time to 55-60 minutes or until heated through and a thermometer inserted in the center reads 165°. Uncover and bake 10-12 minutes longer or until bubbly.

1 PIECE: 470 cal., 31g fat (14g sat. fat), 87mg chol., 896mg sod., 26g carb. (7g sugars, 1g fiber), 22g pro.

5i VODKA-INFUSED CHERRY TOMATOES

These vodka-infused tomatoes need two days to marinate in the refrigerator. They make planning easy because they require little last-minute fuss. They're the perfect way to start a party!
—*Patricia Nieh, Portola Valley, CA*

PREP: 10 min. + chilling • **MAKES:** 5 dozen

- 2 **pints cherry tomatoes**
- 2 **cups vodka**
- ½ **cup coarse sea salt, optional**
- ¼ **cup coarsely ground pepper, optional**

1. Using a skewer, poke a few holes in each tomato. In a container, combine tomatoes and vodka. Cover and refrigerate for 2 days.

2. Pour tomatoes and vodka into a shallow serving dish. Serve tomatoes with toothpicks; if desired, combine sea salt and pepper in a small bowl for dipping.

1 TOMATO: 4 cal., 0 fat (0 sat. fat), 0 chol., 1mg sod., 0 carb. (0 sugars, 0 fiber), 0 pro.

❄ SAUSAGE & SWISS CHARD LASAGNA

This rich and cheesy lasagna is a great way to get kids to eat greens—it's so tasty they'll never know the Swiss chard is there!
—*Candace Morehouse, Show Low, AZ*

PREP: 45 min. • **BAKE:** 55 min. + standing • **MAKES:** 6 servings

- 1 **lb. bulk Italian sausage**
- 1¾ **cups sliced fresh mushrooms**
- 2 **garlic cloves, minced**
- 1 **bunch Swiss chard (about 10 oz.)**
- 3 **Tbsp. butter**
- ¼ **cup all-purpose flour**
- 3 **cups 2% milk**
- 1 **cup shredded Gruyere or Swiss cheese, divided**
- 1 **Tbsp. minced fresh parsley or 1 tsp. dried parsley flakes**
- 1 **Tbsp. minced fresh oregano or 1 tsp. dried oregano**
- 1 **tsp. grated lemon zest**
- ½ **tsp. salt**
- ⅛ **tsp. pepper**
- 6 **no-cook lasagna noodles**

1. Preheat oven to 350°. In a large skillet, cook the sausage, mushrooms and garlic over medium heat 8-10 minutes or until sausage is no longer pink and mushrooms are tender, breaking up sausage into crumbles. Remove from the pan with a slotted spoon. Remove drippings.

2. Remove stems from Swiss chard; coarsely chop leaves. In same skillet, heat butter over medium heat. Stir in flour until smooth; gradually whisk in the milk. Bring to a boil, stirring constantly; cook and stir 1-2 minutes or until thickened. Add ¾ cup cheese, parsley, oregano, lemon zest, salt and pepper; stir until cheese is melted. Stir in Swiss chard leaves.

- PECAN FRENCH TOAST -

Make-ahead convenience is a bonus with this yummy brunch dish.
It tastes like it took all morning but it couldn't be easier to make!

Preheat oven to 350°. In a bowl, whisk 2 large **eggs**, ⅔ cup **2% milk**, ½ tsp. **vanilla extract** and ⅛ tsp. **salt**; pour over 4 slices of 1-in. thick **French bread**. Let stand for 10 minutes, turning once. Meanwhile, in a small saucepan, combine ¼ cup packed **brown sugar**, 2 Tbsp. cubed **butter** and 1 Tbsp. **corn syrup**; cook over medium heat until thickened, 1-2 minutes. Pour into a greased 8-in. square baking dish; sprinkle with ¼ cup chopped **pecans**. Top with bread. Bake, uncovered, until a thermometer reads 160°, 30-35 minutes. Invert onto a serving platter. Serve immediately.

- 10 -

QUICK & EASY COMFORT FOODS

Craving comfort food but need to get dinner on the fast track and with little fuss? Dig into these tried-and-true dishes that prove hearty, homey fare doesn't have to be time-consuming or complicated.

PRESSURE-COOKER TUSCAN CHICKEN PASTA

After the chicken and pasta cook and the milk and cream cheese are added, the mixture will look liquidy. Continue to cook and stir and the dish will come together like magic.
—Amber Gaines, Colorado Springs, CO

- -

PREP/• COOK: 25 minutes • **MAKES:** 4 servings

- 1 lb. boneless skinless chicken breasts, cut into 1-in. pieces
- 8 oz. cellentani or uncooked spiral pasta
- 2 cups chicken broth
- 2 Tbsp. butter
- ¾ cup 2% milk
- 4 oz. cream cheese, cubed
- ½ tsp. garlic powder
- 3 cups fresh baby spinach
- 1 cup grated Parmesan cheese
- 1 pkg. (3 oz.) julienned soft sun-dried tomatoes (not packed in oil)
- 2 Tbsp. chopped fresh basil
- ⅛ tsp. salt
- ⅛ tsp. pepper

In a 6-qt. electric pressure cooker, combine first 4 ingredients. Lock lid; close pressure-release valve. Adjust to pressure-cook on high for 3 minutes. Let the pressure release naturally for 5 minutes; quick-release any remaining pressure. Select saute setting; adjust for medium heat. Add the milk, cream cheese and garlic powder. Cook and stir until cream cheese is melted, 3-5 minutes. Stir in the spinach, Parmesan cheese, sun-dried tomatoes, basil, salt and pepper. Cook and stir until spinach is wilted. Press cancel. Serve immediately. Garnish with additional basil if desired.

1½ CUPS: 660 cal., 26g fat (14g sat. fat), 130mg chol., 1199mg sod., 62g carb. (14g sugars, 7g fiber), 41g pro.

PRESSURE-COOKER STUFFED PEPPERS

Here's a good-for-you dinner that's also a meal-in-one classic. Add a salad and, in just moments, call everyone to the table.
—Michelle Gurnsey, Lincoln, NE

- -

PREP: 15 min. • **COOK:** 5 min. + releasing • **MAKES:** 4 servings

- 4 medium sweet red peppers
- 1 can (15 oz.) black beans, rinsed and drained
- 1 cup shredded pepper jack cheese
- ¾ cup salsa
- 1 small onion, chopped
- ½ cup frozen corn
- ⅓ cup uncooked converted long grain rice
- 1¼ tsp. chili powder
- ½ tsp. ground cumin
   Reduced-fat sour cream, optional

1. Place the trivet insert and 1 cup water in a 6-qt. electric pressure cooker.
2. Cut and discard tops from peppers; remove seeds. In a large bowl, mix beans, cheese, salsa, onion, corn, rice, chili powder and cumin; spoon into peppers. Set peppers on trivet.
3. Lock lid; close pressure-release valve. Adjust to pressure-cook on high for 5 minutes. Let pressure release naturally. If desired, serve with sour cream.

1 STUFFED PEPPER: 333 cal., 10g fat (5g sat. fat), 30mg chol., 582mg sod., 45g carb. (8g sugars, 8g fiber), 15g pro. **DIABETIC EXCHANGES:** 2 starch, 2 lean meat, 2 vegetable, 1 fat.

 PM

SHEET-PAN CAESAR CHICKEN & POTATOES

In our area, we have an abundance of fresh lemons year-round. I used some to make a tasty marinade that gives this meal a burst of flavor. You can also grill the chicken if you prefer.
—*Kallee Krong-Mccreery, Escondido, CA*

PREP: 15 min. + marinating • **BAKE:** 30 min. • **MAKES:** 4 servings

- ¼ cup lemon juice
- ¼ cup Caesar vinaigrette
- 4 bone-in chicken thighs (about 1½ lbs.)
- 3 medium red potatoes (about 1¼ lbs.), each cut into 8 wedges
- ½ lb. medium carrots, cut into 1½-in. pieces
- 1 tsp. garlic salt
- ½ tsp. dill weed
- ¼ tsp. pepper

1. For marinade, in a large bowl, mix lemon juice and dressing; remove 2 Tbsp. mixture for potatoes. Add chicken to remaining marinade; turn to coat. Cover and refrigerate chicken and reserved marinade 4 hours or overnight.

2. Preheat oven to 400°. Place chicken on center of a foil-lined 15x10x1-in. baking pan; discard chicken marinade. Toss potatoes and carrots with reserved marinade and the seasonings; arrange around chicken.

3. Roast until a thermometer inserted in chicken reads 170°-175° and potatoes are tender, 30-40 minutes.

1 CHICKEN THIGH WITH 1 CUP VEGETABLES: 348 cal., 18g fat (5g sat. fat), 80mg chol., 698mg sod., 20g carb. (4g sugars, 3g fiber), 25g pro.

AIR-FRYER ROTISSERIE CHICKEN

This air-fryer chicken is crispy yet succulent. I enjoy it as a main entree cut straight from bone, but you can also shred it and add it to tacos, soups, pasta salads and so much more.
—*Dawn Parker, Surrey, BC*

PREP: 5 min. • **COOK:** 65 min. + standing • **MAKES:** 6 servings

- 1 broiler/fryer chicken (3 to 4 lbs.)
- 1 Tbsp. olive oil
- 2 tsp. seasoned salt

Preheat air fryer to 350°. Brush outside of the chicken with olive oil and sprinkle with seasoned salt. Place chicken, breast side down, on tray in air-fryer basket; cook 30 minutes. Flip chicken and cook until a thermometer inserted in thickest part of thigh reads 170°-175°, 35-40 minutes longer. Remove chicken; let stand for 15 minutes before carving.

NOTE: In our testing, we find cook times vary dramatically between brands of air fryers. As a result, we give wider than normal ranges on suggested cook times. Begin checking at the first time listed and adjust as needed.

5 OZ. COOKED CHICKEN: 313 cal., 19g fat (5g sat. fat), 104mg chol., 596mg sod., 0 carb. (0 sugars, 0 fiber), 33g pro.

WHAT SIZE AIR FRYER SHOULD YOU USE TO COOK A WHOLE CHICKEN?

We recommend using an air fryer with a 5-qt. capacity or larger. This recipe calls for a 3- or 4-pound broiler/fryer chicken, which should fit nicely. If your chicken is too big, cut the chicken into pieces and adjust the cooking time accordingly.

TIP

AIR-FRYER QUICK TATER TOTS BAKE

I prepare this dish when I'm short on time. You can also make the bake a little fancier by assembling it in individual ramekins instead of one large baking dish.
—Jean Ferguson, Elverta, CA

PREP: 15 min. • **COOK:** 30 min. • **MAKES:** 4 servings

- ¾ to 1 lb. ground beef or turkey
- 1 small onion, chopped
  Salt and pepper to taste
- 1 pkg. (16 oz.) frozen Tater Tots
- 1 can (10¾ oz.) condensed cream of mushroom soup, undiluted
- ⅔ cup 2% milk or water
- 1 cup shredded cheddar cheese

1. Preheat air fryer to 350°. In a large skillet, cook beef and onion over medium heat until meat is no longer pink; crumble beef; drain. Season with salt and pepper.
2. Transfer to a greased 2-qt. baking dish that will fit in the air-fryer basket. Top with Tater Tots. Combine soup and milk; pour over potatoes. Sprinkle with cheese. Place baking dish on tray in air-fryer basket. Cook, uncovered, until heated through, 30-40 minutes.

1½ CUPS: 570 cal., 35g fat (12g sat. fat), 87mg chol., 1357mg sod., 37g carb. (5g sugars, 4g fiber), 26g pro.

AUTHENTIC PASTA CARBONARA

I learned on my culinary internship in Tuscany that real Italian cuisine is not as fussy or elaborate as one might expect. This dish is quick, simple and delicious, just the way they like it in Italy.
—Lauren Brien-Wooster, South Lake Tahoe, CA

PREP: 20 min. • **COOK:** 15 min. • **MAKES:** 8 servings

- 1 pkg. (1 lb.) spaghetti or linguine
- 6 bacon strips, chopped
- 1 cup fresh or frozen peas
- 2 Tbsp. lemon juice
- 1½ tsp. grated lemon zest
- 2 large eggs, lightly beaten
- 2 Tbsp. minced fresh parsley
- ½ cup grated Parmigiano-Reggiano cheese
- ¼ tsp. salt
- ¼ tsp. pepper
  Additional grated Parmigiano-Reggiano cheese, optional

1. In a large saucepan, cook the pasta according to the package directions for al dente. Drain pasta, reserving pasta water; keep pasta warm. In the same pot, cook the bacon over medium heat until crisp, stirring occasionally. Add the peas; cook until just heated through.
2. Add pasta to pot; toss to combine. Stir in remaining ingredients, adding enough reserved pasta water for sauce to reach desired consistency. If desired, serve with additional cheese.

1 CUP: 353 cal., 12g fat (4g sat. fat), 65mg chol., 326mg sod., 46g carb. (3g sugars, 3g fiber), 14g pro.

TIP
The heat of the pasta cooks the eggs, but they may not reach 160°, the temperature at which they're considered safe to eat. To prevent any food-borne illness, we recommend using pasteurized eggs in this dish.

AIR-FRYER SAUSAGE PIZZA

I've always loved personal-size pizzas, and when I figured out how to make them in my air fryer, I was in pizza heaven! It's so easy, and now that my boys can customize their own, everyone is happy.
—Margo Zoerner, Pleasant Prairie, WI

PREP: 30 min. • **BAKE:** 10 min./batch • **MAKES:** 4 pizzas

- 1 loaf (1 lb.) frozen bread dough, thawed
- 1 cup pizza sauce
- ½ lb. bulk Italian sausage, cooked and drained
- 1⅓ cups shredded part-skim mozzarella cheese
- 1 small green pepper, sliced into rings
- 1 tsp. dried oregano
  Crushed red pepper flakes, optional

1. On a lightly floured surface, roll and stretch dough into four 4-in. circles. Cover; let rest for 10 minutes.

2. Preheat air fryer to 400°. Roll and stretch each dough into a 6-in. circle. Place 1 crust on greased tray in air-fryer basket. Carefully spread crust with ¼ cup pizza sauce, ⅓ cup sausage, ⅓ cup cheese, a fourth of the green pepper rings and a pinch of oregano. Cook until crust is golden brown, 6-8 minutes. If desired, sprinkle with red pepper flakes. Repeat with the remaining ingredients.

NOTE: In our testing, we find cook times vary dramatically between brands of air fryers. As a result, we give wider than normal ranges on suggested cook times. Begin checking at the first time listed and adjust as needed.

1 PIZZA: 615 cal., 26g fat (9g sat. fat), 58mg chol., 1513mg sod., 64g carb. (9g sugars, 6g fiber), 29g pro.

PRESSURE-COOKER PORK TACOS WITH MANGO SALSA

I've made quite a few tacos in my day, but you can't beat the tender pork filling made in a pressure cooker. Make the mango salsa from scratch if you have time!
—Amber Massey, Argyle, TX

PREP: 25 min. • **COOK:** 5 min. • **MAKES:** 12 servings

- 2 Tbsp. white vinegar
- 2 Tbsp. lime juice
- 3 cups cubed fresh pineapple
- 1 small red onion, coarsely chopped
- 3 Tbsp. chili powder
- 2 chipotle peppers in adobo sauce
- 2 tsp. ground cumin
- 1½ tsp. salt
- ½ tsp. pepper
- 1 bottle (12 oz.) dark Mexican beer
- 3 lbs. pork tenderloin, cut into 1-in. cubes
- ¼ cup chopped fresh cilantro
- 1 jar (16 oz.) mango salsa
- 24 corn tortillas (6 in.), warmed
  Optional toppings: Cubed fresh pineapple, cubed avocado and queso fresco

1. Puree the first 9 ingredients in a blender; stir in beer. In a 6-qt. electric pressure cooker, combine pork and pineapple mixture. Lock lid; close pressure-release valve. Adjust to pressure-cook on high for 3 minutes. Quick-release pressure. A thermometer inserted into pork should read at least 145°. Stir to break up pork.

2. Stir cilantro into salsa. Using a slotted spoon, serve pork mixture in tortillas; add salsa and toppings as desired.

FREEZE OPTION: Freeze cooled meat mixture and cooking juices in freezer containers. To use, partially thaw in refrigerator overnight. Heat through in a saucepan, stirring occasionally.

2 TACOS: 284 cal., 6g fat (2g sat. fat), 64mg chol., 678mg sod., 30g carb. (5g sugars, 5g fiber), 26g pro. **DIABETIC EXCHANGES:** 3 lean meat, 2 starch.

GRAMPA'S GERMAN-STYLE POT ROAST

Grampa was of German heritage and loved the old-world recipes his mother gave him. I made a few changes so I could prepare this dish in the slow cooker and give it a slightly updated flavor.
—*Nancy Heishman, Las Vegas, NV*

PREP: 20 min. • **COOK:** 6 hours + standing
MAKES: 8 servings

- 4 thick-sliced bacon strips
- 1 lb. baby Yukon Gold potatoes
- 4 medium carrots, sliced
- 1 can (14 oz.) sauerkraut, rinsed and well drained
- ¾ cup chopped dill pickles
- 1 tsp. smoked paprika
- 1 tsp. ground allspice
- ½ tsp. kosher salt
- ½ tsp. pepper
- 1 boneless beef chuck roast (3 lbs.)
- 2 pkg. (14.4 oz. each) frozen pearl onions, thawed
- 4 garlic cloves, minced
- ½ cup stout beer or beef broth
- ⅓ cup Dusseldorf mustard
- ½ cup sour cream
- ½ cup minced fresh parsley

1. In a large skillet, cook the bacon over medium heat until crisp. Remove to paper towels to drain.
2. Meanwhile, place potatoes, carrots, sauerkraut and pickles in a 7-qt. slow cooker. Mix paprika, allspice, salt and pepper; rub over roast. Brown roast in bacon drippings over medium heat. Transfer to slow cooker. Add onions and garlic to drippings; cook and stir 1 minute. Stir in beer and mustard; pour over meat. Crumble bacon; add to slow cooker.
3. Cook, covered, on low 6-8 hours, until meat and vegetables are tender. Remove roast; let stand 10 minutes before slicing. Strain cooking juices. Reserve vegetables and juices; skim off fat. Return reserved vegetables and cooking juices to slow cooker. Stir in sour cream; heat through. Serve with roast; sprinkle with parsley.

1 SERVING: 552 cal., 31g fat (12g sat. fat), 127mg chol., 926mg sod., 28g carb. (9g sugars, 6g fiber), 39g pro.

AIR-FRYER CHICKEN PICCATA POCKETS

My husband loves chicken piccata. I made it in a puff pastry pocket with a bit of cream cheese, and it tasted sensational. When he took leftovers to work, everyone asked him what smelled so amazing.
—*Arlene Erlbach, Morton Grove, IL*

PREP: 15 min. • **COOK:** 20 min.
MAKES: 4 servings

- 1 pkg. (8 oz.) cream cheese, softened
- 2 Tbsp. lemon juice
- ¼ tsp. salt
- ¼ tsp. pepper
- 2 Tbsp. capers, drained
- 1 large shallot, finely chopped
- 1 sheet frozen puff pastry, thawed
- 4 chicken tenderloins, cubed
- 1 large egg, well beaten
- 1 Tbsp. water
- 4 thin lemon slices
- 2 Tbsp. chopped fresh parsley

1. Preheat air fryer to 400°. In a bowl, beat cream cheese, lemon juice, salt and pepper on medium speed until well combined. Fold in capers and shallot.
2. Unfold the puff pastry; roll into a 12-in. square. Cut into 4 smaller squares. Spread cream cheese mixture over squares to within ¼ in. of edges; top with chicken.
3. Fold a corner of each pastry square over chicken, forming a triangle. Pinch triangle edges to seal and flatten with a fork for tighter seal. Whisk the egg and water; brush over the pastry pockets, including edges. Discard leftover egg mixture. Pierce each pocket twice with a fork to vent.
4. Place in a single layer on greased tray in air-fryer basket. Cook until golden brown, 18-25 minutes. Remove from the air fryer; cool 5 minutes. Serve pockets with lemon slices and parsley.

FREEZE OPTION: Cover and freeze unbaked pockets on a waxed paper-lined baking sheet until firm. Transfer to an airtight container; return to freezer. To use, air fry as directed, increasing cook time by about 5 minutes.

NOTE: Cook times vary dramatically between brands of air fryers. As a result, we give wider than normal ranges on suggested cook times. Begin checking at the first time listed and adjust as needed.

1 CHICKEN POCKET: 564 cal., 38g fat (16g sat. fat), 120mg chol., 669mg sod., 41g carb. (3g sugars, 5g fiber), 18g pro.

SLOW-COOKER BEEF STEW

When there's a chill in the air, I love to make my slow-cooked stew. It's loaded with tender chunks of beef, potatoes and carrots.
—*Earnestine Wilson, Waco, TX*

PREP: 25 min. • **COOK:** 7 hours • **MAKES:** 8 servings (2 qt.)

- 1½ lbs. potatoes, peeled and cubed
- 6 medium carrots, cut into 1-in. lengths
- 1 medium onion, coarsely chopped
- 3 celery ribs, coarsely chopped
- 3 Tbsp. all-purpose flour
- 1½ lbs. beef stew meat, cut into 1-in. cubes
- 3 Tbsp. canola oil
- 1 can (14½ oz.) diced tomatoes, undrained
- 1 can (14½ oz.) beef broth
- 1 tsp. ground mustard
- ½ tsp. salt
- ½ tsp. pepper
- ½ tsp. dried thyme
- ½ tsp. browning sauce, optional
  Minced fresh thyme

1. Layer the potatoes, carrots, onion and celery in a 5-qt. slow cooker. Place flour in a large shallow dish. Add stew meat; turn to coat evenly. In a large skillet, brown meat in oil in batches. Place over vegetables.
2. In a large bowl, combine the tomatoes, broth, mustard, salt, pepper, thyme and, if desired, browning sauce. Pour over beef. Cover and cook on low for 7-8 hours, or until the meat and vegetables are tender. If desired, sprinkle with fresh thyme before serving.

1 CUP: 272 cal., 12g fat (3g sat. fat), 53mg chol., 541mg sod., 23g carb. (6g sugars, 4g fiber), 19g pro. **DIABETIC EXCHANGES:** 2 lean meat, 1½ starch, 1 fat.

AIR-FRYER BREADED SHRIMP

These quick air-fryer shrimp are so good you won't even miss the fat. Eat them alone with cocktail sauce or put them on a fresh salad or sandwich.
—*Rashanda Cobbins, Milwaukee, WI*

PREP: 25 min. • **COOK:** 10 min./batch • **MAKES:** 4 servings

- ½ cup all-purpose flour
- ½ tsp. seafood seasoning
- ½ tsp. dill weed
- ½ tsp. pepper
- 1 large egg
- ½ cup 2% milk
- 1 tsp. hot pepper sauce
- 1 cup panko bread crumbs
- 1 lb. uncooked shrimp (26-30 per lb.), peeled and deveined
  Cooking spray
  Optional: seafood cocktail sauce and lemon wedges

1. Preheat air fryer to 375°. In a shallow bowl, mix flour, seasoned salt, dill weed and pepper. In a separate shallow bowl, whisk egg, milk and hot pepper sauce. Place bread crumbs in a third shallow bowl. Dip shrimp in flour to coat both sides; shake off excess. Dip in egg mixture, then in bread crumbs, patting to help adhere.
2. In batches, arrange shrimp in a single layer in greased air fryer; spritz with cooking spray. Cook until lightly browned and shrimp turn pink, 3-4 minutes on each side. If desired, serve with cocktail sauce and lemon wedges.

6 SHRIMP: 198 cal., 4g fat (1g sat. fat), 171mg chol., 287mg sod., 15g carb. (2g sugars, 1g fiber), 23g pro. **DIABETIC EXCHANGES:** 3 lean meat, 1 starch.

TEXAS-STYLE LASAGNA

With its spicy flavor, this dish is a real crowd-pleaser. It goes wonderfully with side servings of picante sauce, guacamole and tortilla chips.
—*Effie Gish, Fort Worth, TX*

PREP: 40 min. • **BAKE:** 30 min. + standing • **MAKES:** 12 servings

- 1½ lbs. ground beef
- 1 tsp. seasoned salt
- 1 pkg. (1¼ oz.) taco seasoning
- 1 can (14½ oz.) diced tomatoes, undrained
- 1 can (15 oz.) tomato sauce
- 1 can (4 oz.) chopped green chiles
- 2 cups 4% cottage cheese
- 2 large eggs, lightly beaten
- 12 corn tortillas (6 in.), torn
- 3½ to 4 cups shredded Monterey Jack cheese
  Optional toppings: Crushed tortilla chips, salsa and cubed avocado

1. In a large skillet, cook beef over medium heat until no longer pink; drain. Add the seasoned salt, taco seasoning, tomatoes, tomato sauce and chiles. Reduce heat; simmer, uncovered, for 15-20 minutes. In a small bowl, combine the cottage cheese and eggs.

2. In a greased 13x9-in. baking dish, layer half of each of the following: meat sauce, tortillas, cottage cheese mixture and Monterey Jack cheese. Repeat layers.

3. Bake, uncovered, at 350° for 30 minutes or until bubbly. Let stand 10 minutes before serving. Garnish individual servings with toppings if desired.

FREEZE OPTION: Before baking, cover and freeze lasagna up to 3 months. Thaw in the refrigerator overnight. Remove from refrigerator 30 minutes before baking. Bake as directed, increasing time as necessary for a thermometer to read 160°.

1 PIECE: 349 cal., 18g fat (10g sat. fat), 101mg chol., 1041mg sod., 20g carb. (3g sugars, 2g fiber), 26g pro.

BEEF & SPINACH SKILLET

Over the years, I've tried to instill a love of cooking in our children. We've enjoyed a variety of delicious recipes, including this savory stovetop entree.
—*Nancy Robaidek, Krakow, WI*

PREP: 20 min. • **COOK:** 15 min. • **MAKES:** 6 servings

- 1 lb. ground beef
- 1 medium onion, chopped
- 1 pkg. (10 oz.) frozen chopped spinach, thawed and squeezed dry
- 1 can (4 oz.) mushroom stems and pieces, drained
- 1 tsp. garlic salt
- 1 tsp. dried basil
- ¼ cup butter
- ¼ cup all-purpose flour
- ½ tsp. salt
- 2 cups whole milk
- 1 cup shredded Monterey Jack cheese or part-skim mozzarella cheese
  Biscuits, optional

1. In a 10-in. cast-iron or other ovenproof skillet, cook beef and onion over medium heat until meat is no longer pink; drain. Add the spinach, mushrooms, garlic salt and basil. Cover and cook for 5 minutes.

2. In a saucepan, melt butter over medium heat. Stir in the flour and salt until smooth. Gradually add milk. Bring to a boil; cook and stir until thickened, about 2 minutes. Stir in cheese. Pour over meat mixture; mix well. Reduce heat; cook, covered, until heated through. If desired, serve with biscuits.

1 SERVING: 351 cal., 23g fat (13g sat. fat), 85mg chol., 872mg sod., 13g carb. (6g sugars, 2g fiber), 23g pro.

PUFF PASTRY CHICKEN BUNDLES

Tenderized chicken breasts rolled with spinach, herbed cream cheese and walnuts create a savory surprise inside each of these golden puff pastry bundles. I serve this elegant entree when we have guests or are celebrating a holiday or special occasion.
—*Brad Moritz, Limerick, PA*

PREP: 30 min. • **BAKE:** 20 min.
MAKES: 8 servings

- 8 boneless skinless chicken breast halves (about 6 oz. each)
- 1 tsp. salt
- ½ tsp. pepper
- 40 large spinach leaves
- 1 carton (8 oz.) spreadable chive and onion cream cheese
- ½ cup chopped walnuts, toasted
- 2 sheets frozen puff pastry, thawed
- 1 large egg
- ½ tsp. cold water

1. Preheat oven to 400°. Cut a lengthwise slit in each chicken breast half to within ½ in. of the other side; open meat so it lies flat. Pound with a meat mallet to ⅛-in. thickness. Sprinkle with salt and pepper.
2. Place 5 spinach leaves on each chicken breast half. Spoon a scant 2 Tbsp. of cream cheese down the center of each chicken breast half; sprinkle with 1 Tbsp. walnuts. Roll up chicken; tuck in ends.
3. Unfold puff pastry; cut into 8 portions. Roll each into a 7-in. square. Place chicken on 1 half of each square; fold other half of pastry over chicken. Crimp edges with fork. Combine egg and cold water; brush over edges of pastry.
4. Bake on a greased 15x10x1-in. baking sheet until a thermometer reads 165°, 20-25 minutes.

1 SERVING: 624 cal., 32g fat (10g sat. fat), 136mg chol., 742mg sod., 39g carb. (1g sugars, 6g fiber), 44g pro.

PRESSURE-COOKER TUNA NOODLE CASSEROLE

We tweaked this family-friendly classic to work for the pressure cooker. It's easy, wholesome and totally homemade!
—Taste of Home *Test Kitchen*

PREP: 25 min. • **COOK:** 15 min.
MAKES: 10 servings

- ¼ cup butter, cubed
- ½ lb. sliced fresh mushrooms
- 1 medium onion, chopped
- 1 medium sweet pepper, chopped
- 1 tsp. salt, divided
- 1 tsp. pepper, divided
- 2 garlic cloves, minced
- ¼ cup all-purpose flour
- 2 cups reduced-sodium chicken broth
- 2 cups half-and-half cream
- 4 cups (8 oz.) uncooked egg noodles
- 3 cans (5 oz. each) light tuna in water
- 2 Tbsp. lemon juice
- 2 cups shredded Monterey Jack cheese
- 2 cups frozen peas, thawed
- 2 cups crushed potato chips

1. Select saute setting on a 6-qt. electric pressure cooker and adjust for medium heat. Add butter. When melted, add the mushrooms, onion, sweet pepper, ½ tsp. salt and ½ tsp. pepper; cook and stir until tender, 6-8 minutes. Add garlic; cook for 1 minute longer. Stir in flour until blended. Gradually whisk in broth. Bring to a boil, stirring constantly; cook and stir until thickened, 1-2 minutes.
2. Stir in cream and noodles. Lock lid; close pressure-release valve. Adjust to pressure-cook on high for 3 minutes. Allow the pressure to naturally release for 3 minutes, then quick-release any remaining pressure.
3. Meanwhile, in a small bowl, combine tuna, lemon juice and remaining salt and pepper. Select saute setting and adjust for low heat. Stir cheese, tuna mixture and peas into noodle mixture. Cook until heated through. Just before serving, sprinkle with potato chips.

1 SERVING: 393 cal., 21g fat (12g sat. fat), 84mg chol., 752mg sod., 28g carb. (5g sugars, 3g fiber), 22g pro.

SO-EASY COQ AU VIN

Here's my adaptation of the beloved French dish. I substituted boneless skinless chicken breasts for a lighter version that still showcases the traditional and memorable taste.
—Sonya Labbe, West Hollywood, CA

PREP: 20 min. • COOK: 5 hours • MAKES: 4 servings

- 3   bacon strips, chopped
- 4   boneless skinless chicken breast halves (4 oz. each)
- ½   lb. sliced fresh mushrooms
- 1   medium onion, chopped
- 4   garlic cloves, minced
- 1   bay leaf
- ⅓   cup all-purpose flour
- ½   cup red wine
- ½   cup chicken broth
- ½   tsp. dried thyme
- ¼   tsp. pepper
     Hot cooked noodles, optional

1. In large skillet, cook bacon over medium heat until crisp, stirring occasionally. Remove with a slotted spoon; drain on paper towels. Brown chicken on both sides in drippings over medium heat. Transfer chicken to a 3-qt. slow cooker.
2. Add the mushrooms, onion and garlic to skillet; cook and stir just until tender, 1-2 minutes. Spoon over chicken; add bay leaf.
3. In a small bowl, whisk the flour, wine, broth, thyme and pepper until smooth; pour over chicken.
4. Cover; cook on low until chicken is tender, 5-6 hours. Discard bay leaf. If desired, serve with noodles. Top with bacon.

1 CHICKEN BREAST HALF WITH ½ CUP MUSHROOM SAUCE: 299 cal., 11g fat (3g sat. fat), 75mg chol., 324mg sod., 16g carb. (4g sugars, 2g fiber), 28g pro. **DIABETIC EXCHANGES:** 3 lean meat, 1½ fat, 1 vegetable, ½ starch.

CHICKEN & HASH BROWN BAKE

The first time I served this dish was to a family with five children. The kids and the adults loved it! This is one recipe I often make for potlucks as it goes a long way, and all ages enjoy it.
—Ruth Andrewson, Leavenworth, WA

PREP: 10 min. • BAKE: 50 min. • MAKES: 8 servings

- 1   pkg. (32 oz.) frozen cubed hash brown potatoes, thawed
- 1   tsp. salt
- ¼   tsp. pepper
- 4   cups diced cooked chicken
- 1   can (4 oz.) mushroom stems and pieces, drained
- 1   cup sour cream
- 2   cups chicken broth or stock
- 1   can (10¾ oz.) condensed cream of chicken soup, undiluted
- 2   tsp. chicken bouillon granules
- 2   Tbsp. finely chopped onion
- 2   Tbsp. finely chopped sweet red pepper
- 1   garlic clove, minced
     Paprika
- ¼   cup sliced almonds

1. Preheat oven to 350°. Spread potatoes in an ungreased 13x9-in. baking dish. Sprinkle with salt and pepper. Sprinkle chicken and mushrooms over the top. Combine the sour cream, broth, soup, bouillon granules, onion, red pepper and garlic; pour over mushrooms.
2. Sprinkle with paprika and almonds. Bake, uncovered, until heated through, 50-60 minutes.

1¼ CUPS: 346 cal., 15g fat (6g sat. fat), 73mg chol., 1164mg sod., 27g carb. (3g sugars, 3g fiber), 26g pro.

PRESSURE-COOKER ANDOUILLE RED BEANS & RICE

After my husband's favorite New Orleans takeout restaurant closed, I challenged myself to develop a tasty red beans and rice recipe that I could make at home. This pressure-cooker version is hearty and satisfies his Cajun cravings.
—*Jennifer Schwarzkopf, Oregon, WI*

PREP: 20 min. • **COOK:** 40 min. + releasing • **MAKES:** 8 servings

- 6 cups water
- 1 lb. dried kidney beans
- 1 large onion, chopped
- 1 celery rib, sliced
- ½ medium sweet red pepper, chopped
- ½ medium green pepper, chopped
- 4 garlic cloves, minced
- 1 bay leaf
- 1 tsp. kosher salt
- 1 tsp. dried thyme
- 1 to 2 tsp. Louisiana-style hot sauce
- ½ tsp. pepper
- 1 lb. fully cooked andouille sausage links, sliced
  Hot cooked rice
  Thinly sliced green onions, optional

1. Place the first 12 ingredients in a 6-qt. electric pressure cooker. Lock lid; close the pressure-release valve. Adjust to pressure-cook on high for 20 minutes. Quick-release pressure.
2. Stir in sausage. Lock lid; close pressure-release valve. Adjust to pressure-cook on high for 17 minutes. Let pressure release naturally. Remove bay leaf. Serve with rice and, if desired, sprinkle with green onions.

FREEZE OPTION: Freeze cooled bean mixture in freezer containers. To use, partially thaw in refrigerator overnight. Heat mixture through in a saucepan, stirring occasionally; add water if necessary.

1¼ CUPS: 349 cal., 12g fat (4g sat. fat), 74mg chol., 774mg sod., 40g carb. (3g sugars, 9g fiber), 25g pro.

CHUNKY CHICKEN SALAD WITH GRAPES & PECANS

This chicken salad with grapes is ready in a snap when using rotisserie chicken and a few quick chops of pecans, sweet onion and celery.
—*Julie Sterchi, Campbellsville, KY*

TAKES: 25 min. • **MAKES:** 8 servings

- ½ cup mayonnaise
- 2 Tbsp. sour cream
- 1 Tbsp. lemon juice
- ⅛ tsp. salt
- ⅛ tsp. pepper
- 4 cups shredded rotisserie chicken
- 1¼ cups seedless red grapes, halved
- ½ cup chopped pecans
- ½ cup chopped celery
- ¼ cup chopped sweet onion, optional
  Lettuce leaves or whole wheat bread slices, optional

In a large bowl, combine the first 5 ingredients. Add the chicken, grapes, pecans, celery and, if desired, onion; mix lightly to coat. If desired, serve with lettuce leaves or whole wheat bread.

¾ CUP CHICKEN SALAD: 311 cal., 22g fat (4g sat. fat), 70mg chol., 180mg sod., 6g carb. (5g sugars, 1g fiber), 21g pro.

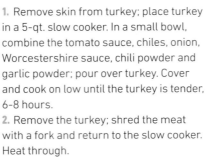

SIMMERED TURKEY ENCHILADAS

I found a new way to serve economical turkey thighs. I simmer them in tomato sauce, green chiles and seasonings until they're tender and flavorful, then tuck the meat in warm tortillas with our favorite fresh toppings.
—Stella Schams, Tempe, AZ

PREP: 10 min. • **COOK:** 6 hours
MAKES: 4 servings

- 2 lbs. turkey thighs or drumsticks
- 1 can (8 oz.) tomato sauce
- 1 can (4 oz.) chopped green chiles
- ⅓ cup chopped onion
- 2 Tbsp. Worcestershire sauce
- 1 to 2 Tbsp. chili powder
- ¼ tsp. garlic powder
- 8 flour tortillas (6 in.), warmed
  Optional toppings: Chopped green onions, sliced ripe olives, chopped tomatoes, shredded cheddar cheese, sour cream and shredded lettuce

1. Remove skin from turkey; place turkey in a 5-qt. slow cooker. In a small bowl, combine the tomato sauce, chiles, onion, Worcestershire sauce, chili powder and garlic powder; pour over turkey. Cover and cook on low until the turkey is tender, 6-8 hours.
2. Remove the turkey; shred the meat with a fork and return to the slow cooker. Heat through.
3. Spoon about ½ cup turkey mixture down the center of each tortilla. Fold bottom of tortilla over filling and roll up. Add toppings of your choice.
FREEZE OPTION: Individually wrap cooled burritos in paper towels and foil; freeze in a freezer container. To use, remove foil; place paper towel-wrapped burrito on a microwave-safe plate. Microwave on high until heated through, 3-4 minutes, turning once. Let stand 20 seconds.
2 ENCHILADAS: 497 cal., 20g fat (4g sat. fat), 114mg chol., 1028mg sod., 34g carb. (3g sugars, 2g fiber), 45g pro.

SHEET-PAN CHICKEN PARMESAN

Saucy chicken, melty mozzarella and crisp-tender broccoli—all in one pan. What could be better?
—Becky Hardin, St. Peters, MO

PREP: 20 min. • **BAKE:** 20 min.
MAKES: 4 servings

- 1 large egg
- ½ cup panko bread crumbs
- ½ cup grated Parmesan cheese
- ½ tsp. salt
- 1 tsp. pepper
- 1 tsp. garlic powder
- 4 boneless skinless chicken breast halves (6 oz. each)
  Olive oil-flavored cooking spray
- 4 cups fresh or frozen broccoli florets (about 10 oz.)
- 1 cup marinara sauce
- 1 cup shredded mozzarella cheese
- ¼ cup minced fresh basil, optional

1. Preheat oven to 400°. Lightly coat a 15x10x1-in. baking pan with cooking spray.
2. In a shallow bowl, whisk egg. In a separate shallow bowl, stir together the next 5 ingredients. Dip chicken breast in egg; allow excess to drip off. Dip in crumb mixture, patting to help coating adhere. Repeat with remaining chicken. Place chicken breasts in center third of baking pan. Spritz with cooking spray.
3. Bake 10 minutes. Remove from oven. Spread broccoli in a single layer along both sides of sheet pan (if broccoli is frozen, break pieces apart). Return to oven; bake 10 minutes longer. Remove from oven.
4. Preheat broiler. Spread marinara sauce over chicken; top with shredded cheese. Broil chicken and broccoli 3-4 in. from heat until the cheese is golden brown and vegetables are tender, 3-5 minutes. If desired, sprinkle with basil.
1 SERVING: 504 cal., 17g fat (7g sat. fat), 147mg chol., 1151mg sod., 27g carb. (10g sugars, 8g fiber), 52g pro.

> **TIP**
> This chicken is delicious with noodles and marinara sauce but you could also serve each breast atop a bed of riced cauliflower. A number of brands are available in the frozen vegetable case.

PIZZA TATER TOT CASSEROLE

For a new spin on the classic Tater Tot casserole, try my tasty pizza-inspired version. It's a cinch to customize by adding your family's favorite toppings!
—*Sharon Skildum, Maple Grove, MN*

- -

PREP: 10 min. • **BAKE:** 35 min. • **MAKES:** 8 servings

  1½ lbs. ground beef
  1   medium green pepper, chopped, optional
  1   medium onion, chopped
  ½   lb. sliced fresh mushrooms
  1   can (15 oz.) pizza sauce
  1   tsp. dried basil
  3   cups shredded part-skim mozzarella cheese
  1   pkg. (32 oz.) frozen Tater Tots
  1   cup shredded cheddar cheese

1. In a large skillet, cook the beef, green pepper if desired, onion and mushrooms over medium heat until meat is no longer pink, breaking meat into crumbles; drain. Add pizza sauce and basil.

2. Transfer to a greased 3-qt. or 13x9-in. baking dish. Top with mozzarella cheese and potatoes. Bake, uncovered, at 400° until potatoes are lightly browned, 30-35 minutes.

3. Sprinkle with cheddar cheese; bake until cheese is melted, about 5 minutes.

1 SERVING: 572 cal., 32g fat (13g sat. fat), 96mg chol., 1081mg sod., 41g carb. (7g sugars, 5g fiber), 36g pro.

SKILLET LASAGNA

My husband loves my simple stovetop lasagna. Loaded with beef and two types of cheese, this easy version makes a super supper.
—*Lucinda Walker, Somerset, PA*

- -

PREP: 25 min. • **COOK:** 40 min. + standing • **MAKES:** 8 servings

  1½ lbs. lean ground beef (90% lean)
  1   small onion, chopped
  1   medium green pepper, chopped
  1   jar (24 oz.) spaghetti sauce with mushrooms
  1   tsp. dried oregano
  1   tsp. dried basil
  6   lasagna noodles, cooked and rinsed
  3   cups shredded mozzarella cheese
  ½   cup grated Parmesan cheese
      Torn fresh basil leaves, optional

1. In a Dutch oven, brown the beef, onion and pepper; drain if necessary. Stir in spaghetti sauce, oregano and basil. Simmer, uncovered, for 10-15 minutes.

2. In a 10-in. cast-iron or other heavy skillet, spread ¼ cup of the meat sauce. Top with 3 noodles, cutting to fit as needed. Layer with half of the remaining sauce and half of the mozzarella and Parmesan cheeses. Top with the remaining noodles, meat sauce and Parmesan.

3. Cover and heat on medium for 3 minutes. Reduce heat to low; cook for 35 minutes. Sprinkle with remaining mozzarella and let stand for 10 minutes with cover ajar. If desired, sprinkle with torn fresh basil leaves.

1 PIECE: 395 cal., 18g fat (9g sat. fat), 78mg chol., 842mg sod., 29g carb. (10g sugars, 3g fiber), 31g pro.

COCONUT CURRY CHICKEN

My husband and I love this yummy dish. It's a breeze to prepare in the slow cooker, and it tastes just like a meal you'd have at your favorite Indian or Thai restaurant.
—*Andi Kauffman, Beavercreek, OR*

PREP: 20 min. • COOK: 5 hours • MAKES: 4 servings

- 2 medium potatoes, peeled and cubed
- 1 small onion, chopped
- 2 tsp. canola oil
- 1 lb. boneless skinless chicken breast halves
- 1 cup light coconut milk
- 4 tsp. curry powder
- 1 garlic clove, minced
- 1 tsp. reduced-sodium chicken bouillon granules
- ¼ tsp. salt
- ¼ tsp. pepper
- 2 cups hot cooked rice
  Optional: Cilantro, shredded coconut, chopped peanuts and thinly sliced red chiles

1. Place potatoes and onion in a 3- or 4-qt. slow cooker. In a large nonstick skillet, heat oil over medium heat; add chicken. Cook until lightly browned, turning once, 3-5 minutes. Transfer to the slow cooker.
2. In a small bowl, combine coconut milk, curry, garlic, bouillon, salt and pepper; pour over chicken. Cover and cook on low until meat is tender, 5-6 hours. Remove chicken to cutting board. Cut into slices.
3. Serve chicken and sauce with rice; if desired top with cilantro, coconut, peanuts and chiles.
1 SERVING: 371 cal., 10g fat (4g sat. fat), 63mg chol., 265mg sod., 42g carb. (3g sugars, 3g fiber), 27g pro. **DIABETIC EXCHANGES:** 3 starch, 3 lean meat, 1½ fat.

SHEET-PAN CHIPOTLE-LIME SHRIMP BAKE

I make this seafood dinner for company because it tastes amazing but takes little effort to throw together. Use asparagus, Broccolini or a mix of the two. For me, it's all about what's available for a decent price.
—*Colleen Delawder, Herndon, VA*

PREP: 10 min. • BAKE: 40 min. • MAKES: 4 servings

- 1½ lbs. baby red potatoes, cut into ¾-in. cubes
- 1 Tbsp. extra virgin olive oil
- ¾ tsp. sea salt, divided
- 3 medium limes
- ¼ cup unsalted butter, melted
- 1 tsp. ground chipotle pepper
- ½ lb. fresh asparagus, trimmed
- ½ lb. Broccolini or broccoli, cut into small florets
- 1 lb. uncooked shrimp (16-20 per lb.), peeled and deveined
- 2 Tbsp. minced fresh cilantro

1. Preheat oven to 400°. Place potatoes in a greased 15x10x1-in. baking pan; drizzle with olive oil. Sprinkle with ¼ tsp. sea salt; stir to combine. Bake for 30 minutes. Meanwhile, squeeze ⅓ cup juice from limes, reserving fruit. Combine the lime juice, melted butter, chipotle and remaining ½ tsp. sea salt.
2. Remove pan from the oven; stir potatoes. Arrange asparagus, Broccolini, shrimp and reserved limes on top of potatoes. Pour lime juice mixture over vegetables and shrimp.
3. Bake until shrimp turn pink and vegetables are tender, about 10 minutes longer. Sprinkle with minced fresh cilantro.
1 SERVING: 394 cal., 17g fat (8g sat. fat), 168mg chol., 535mg sod., 41g carb. (4g sugars, 6g fiber), 25g pro.

SHEET-PAN PORK SUPPER

Here's a delicious meal-in-one, and it's so quick and easy to clean up since you use one pan for everything. Use any variety of small potatoes that suits your tastes—fingerlings or other colored potatoes are a fun and delicious option.
—Debbie Johnson, Centertown, MO

- -

PREP: 10 min. • **BAKE:** 35 min.
MAKES: 8 servings

- ¼ cup butter, softened
- 2 tsp. minced fresh chives or 1 tsp. dried minced chives
- 1 garlic clove, minced
- 1½ lbs. fresh green beans, trimmed
- 2 Tbsp. olive oil
- ¾ tsp. salt
- ½ tsp. pepper
- 1½ lbs. baby red potatoes, halved
- 2 pork tenderloins (about 1 lb. each)
- ½ cup teriyaki glaze or hoisin sauce
  Optional: Toasted sesame seeds and additional fresh minced chives

1. Preheat oven to 450°. In a small bowl, combine butter, chives and garlic. In a second bowl, combine green beans with 1 Tbsp. olive oil, ¼ tsp. salt and ¼ tsp. pepper. Arrange green beans down 1 side of a 15x10x1-in. baking pan. In the same bowl, combine potatoes with remaining 1 Tbsp. olive oil, ½ tsp. salt and ¼ tsp. pepper. Arrange potatoes on other side of pan.
2. Pat pork dry with paper towels; brush with the teriyaki glaze. Place on top of the green beans.
3. Bake until a thermometer inserted in pork reads 145°, 25-30 minutes. Remove tenderloins to a cutting board and top with 2 Tbsp. seasoned butter. Tent pork with aluminum foil; let stand.
4. Stir green beans and potatoes; return to the oven and cook until the vegetables are tender and lightly browned, about 10 minutes longer. Stir remaining seasoned butter into vegetables.
5. Slice the pork; serve with roasted vegetables and pan drippings. If desired, top with sesame seeds and additional minced chives.
3 OZ. COOKED PORK WITH 1¼ CUPS VEGETABLES: 354 cal., 14g fat (6g sat. fat), 79mg chol., 1186mg sod., 30g carb. (9g sugars, 5g fiber), 28g pro.

EASY ARROZ CON POLLO

My children look forward to dinner when they know I'm serving this. I look forward to a meal that easy to make.
—*Debbie Harris, Tucson, AZ*

- -

PREP: 10 min. • **BAKE:** 55 min. • **MAKES:** 6 servings

1¾	cups uncooked instant rice
6	boneless skinless chicken breast halves (4 oz. each)
½	tsp. garlic salt
¼	tsp. pepper
1	can (14½ oz.) chicken broth
1	cup picante sauce
1	can (8 oz.) tomato sauce
½	cup chopped onion
½	cup chopped green pepper
½	cup shredded Monterey Jack cheese
½	cup shredded cheddar cheese

1. Preheat oven to 350°. Spread the rice in a greased 13x9-in. baking dish. Sprinkle both sides of the chicken with garlic salt and pepper; place over rice. In a large bowl, combine the broth, picante sauce, tomato sauce, onion and green pepper; pour over the chicken.

2. Cover and bake for 50-55 minutes or until a thermometer reads 165°. Sprinkle with cheeses. Bake, uncovered, until the cheese is melted, about 5 minutes more.

1 SERVING: 334 cal., 9g fat (4g sat. fat), 80mg chol., 1055mg sod., 30g carb. (3g sugars, 2g fiber), 31g pro.

> **TIP**
>
> **CAN YOU USE OTHER CUTS OF CHICKEN FOR THIS EASY ARROZ CON POLLO RECIPE?**
> Absolutely! Boneless skinless chicken thighs would work well in this recipe. Whatever cut you use, just be sure your chicken is cooked through to a food-safe internal temperature of 165°.

SICILIAN PIZZA (SFINCIONE)

I've loved this pizza since childhood. The crunchy bread-crumb topping sets it apart from its American counterpart.
—*Susan Falk, Sterling Heights, MI*

- -

PREP: 20 min. • **BAKE:** 20 min. • **MAKES:** 12 servings

2	loaves (1 lb. each) fresh or frozen pizza dough, thawed
3	Tbsp. olive oil, divided
1	can (28 oz.) whole tomatoes, drained and crushed
1	medium onion, finely chopped
1	can (2 oz.) anchovy fillets, drained and broken into ¼-in. pieces
1	cup shredded mozzarella cheese
½	cup soft bread crumbs
	Fresh torn basil leaves

1. Preheat oven to 425°. Grease a 15x10x1-in. baking pan. Press dough to fit bottom and ½ in. up sides of pan. Brush with 2 Tbsp. oil; top with tomatoes, onion and anchovies. Sprinkle with mozzarella. Combine bread crumbs and remaining 1 Tbsp. oil; sprinkle over pizza.

2. Bake on a lower oven rack until edges are golden brown and cheese is melted, 20-25 minutes. Sprinkle pizza with fresh basil before serving.

1 PIECE: 277 cal., 9g fat (2g sat. fat), 11mg chol., 527mg sod., 38g carb. (4g sugars, 3g fiber), 11g pro.

EASY JAMBALAYA

I brought this easy jambalaya to a Sunday potluck and it was quickly gobbled up. When friends asked me for the recipe, they couldn't believe how easy it was!
—*Tami Kuehl, Loup City, NE*

- -

PREP: 15 min. • **COOK:** 25 min. • **MAKES:** 4 servings

1   pkg. (8 oz.) jambalaya mix
1   pkg. (14 oz.) hot smoked sausage, cut into ½-in. slices
1   cup uncooked shrimp (16-20 per lb.), peeled and deveined, cut into ¾-in. pieces
3   green onions, thinly sliced
½   cup shredded cheddar cheese
½   cup pico de gallo

Prepare jambalaya mix according to the package directions, adding sausage and shrimp during the last 5 minutes of cooking. Remove from heat. Stir in cheese, pico de gallo and green onions; heat through.

1½ CUPS: 601 cal., 32g fat (14g sat. fat), 127mg chol., 2159mg sod., 48g carb. (3g sugars, 1g fiber), 28g pro.

REVIEW

"Great weeknight meal. Quick and easy to prepare and full of flavor. Nothing to it. Ready in no time. Tastes great."

—RENEEMURBY, TASTEOFHOME.COM

PRESSURE-COOKER WINE-BRAISED BEEF SHANKS

I adapted this from a slow-cooker recipe to one that cooks much faster in a pressure cooker. The aroma reminds me of my Grandma's house. Serve over egg noodles, rice or dumplings.
—*Helen Nelander, Boulder Creek, CA*

- -

PREP: 20 min. • **COOK:** 40 min. + releasing • **MAKES:** 6 servings

3   beef shanks (14 oz. each)
1   tsp. salt
1   tsp. canola oil
1   small onion, chopped
1   medium carrot, chopped
1   medium green pepper, chopped
1   cup dry red wine or beef broth
1   cup beef broth
1   lemon slice
1   Tbsp. cornstarch
1   Tbsp. water

1. Sprinkle beef with salt. Select saute or browning setting on a 6-qt. electric pressure cooker. Adjust for medium heat; add oil. When oil is hot, brown beef in batches. Press cancel. Return all to pressure cooker. Add the onion, carrot, green pepper, wine, broth and lemon.

2. Lock lid; close pressure-release valve. Adjust to pressure-cook on high for 40 minutes. Allow pressure to naturally release for 10 minutes, then quick-release any remaining pressure. Remove meat and vegetables from pressure cooker; keep warm. Discard the lemon.

3. Skim fat from cooking juices. Select saute setting and adjust for low heat. In a small bowl, mix cornstarch and water until smooth; stir into cooking juices. Simmer, stirring constantly, until thickened, 1-2 minutes. Serve with beef and vegetables.

3 OZ. COOKED BEEF WITH ½ CUP SAUCE: 172 cal., 5g fat (2g sat. fat), 51mg chol., 592mg sod., 5g carb. (2g sugars, 1g fiber), 23g pro.
DIABETIC EXCHANGES: 3 lean meat.

CAST-IRON SAUSAGE PIZZA

This shortcut pizza starts with frozen dough in a cast-iron pan. Add your family's favorite toppings for variety.
—Taste of Home *Test Kitchen*

PREP: 30 min. • **BAKE:** 20 min. • **MAKES:** 6 slices

- 1 loaf (1 lb.) frozen bread dough, thawed
- 2 tsp. cornmeal
- 1½ cups pizza sauce
- ½ lb. bulk Italian sausage, cooked and drained
- 1½ cups shredded part-skim mozzarella cheese, divided
- 1 tsp. dried oregano
- 1 small green pepper, sliced into rings
  Crushed red pepper flakes, optional

1. Preheat oven to 425°. On a lightly floured surface, roll and stretch dough into a 10-in. circle. Cover; let rest for 10 minutes. Roll and stretch the dough into a 12-in. circle. Grease a 10-in. cast-iron or other ovenproof skillet; sprinkle with cornmeal. Press dough onto bottom and 1 in. up side of prepared skillet.
2. Spread with pizza sauce; top with sausage, 1 cup cheese, oregano and green pepper. Sprinkle with remaining ½ cup cheese. Bake until crust is golden brown, 20-25 minutes. If desired, sprinkle with red pepper flakes.

1 SLICE: 424 cal., 18g fat (6g sat. fat), 39mg chol., 1092mg sod., 45g carb. (7g sugars, 4g fiber), 20g pro.

EASY SLOW-COOKER CHICKEN ROPA VIEJA

When discussing various methods of cooking ropas, a friend of mine told me her sister adds apple juice. I thought a Granny Smith apple might give the dish an extra kick—and it does. The ropas may also be served with hominy or tortillas, but I think the plantains add a special touch.
—Arlene Erlbach, Morton Grove, IL

PREP: 20 min. • **COOK:** 5 hours • **MAKES:** 6 Servings

- 2 medium sweet red peppers, sliced
- 1 medium Granny Smith apple, peeled and chopped
- 1 cup fresh cilantro leaves
- 1 cup chunky salsa
- 2 Tbsp. tomato paste
- 1 garlic clove, minced
- 1 tsp. ground cumin
- 5 tsp. adobo seasoning, divided
- 1½ lbs. boneless skinless chicken thighs
- 3 to 6 tsp. lime juice
- ¼ cup butter
- 3 ripe plantains, peeled and sliced into thin rounds
  Optional: Hot cooked rice, lime wedges and additional fresh cilantro leaves

1. Place the first 7 ingredients and 1 tsp. adobo in a 5- or 6-qt. slow cooker. Rub the remaining 4 tsp. adobo seasoning over chicken; add to slow cooker. Cook, covered, on low until chicken is tender, 5-6 hours. Using 2 forks, shred chicken. Stir in lime juice to taste; heat through.
2. Meanwhile, heat butter in a large skillet over medium heat. Cook plantains in batches until tender and golden brown, about 3 minutes per side. Drain on paper towels.
3. Serve chicken with plantains using a slotted spoon. If desired, serve with rice, lime wedges and cilantro.

1 SERVING: 387 cal., 16g fat (7g sat. fat), 96mg chol., 1428mg sod., 39g carb. (20g sugars, 4g fiber), 23g pro.

GREEK SPAGHETTI WITH CHICKEN

When this flavorful spaghetti emerges from the oven, it's time for true comfort food. It's so easy to serve a dinner rich with chicken, spinach and two types of cheese.
—*Melanie Dalbec, Inver Grove, MN*

PREP: 25 min. • **BAKE:** 25 min. • **MAKES:** 10 servings

- 1 pkg. (16 oz.) spaghetti, broken into 2-in. pieces
- 4 cups cubed cooked chicken breast
- 2 pkg. (10 oz. each) frozen chopped spinach, thawed and squeezed dry
- 2 cans (10¾ oz. each) condensed cream of chicken soup, undiluted
- 1 cup mayonnaise
- 1 cup sour cream
- 3 celery ribs, chopped
- 1 small onion, chopped
- ½ cup chopped green pepper
- 1 jar (2 oz.) diced pimientos, drained
- ½ tsp. lemon-pepper seasoning
- 1 cup shredded Monterey Jack cheese
- ½ cup soft bread crumbs
- ½ cup shredded Parmesan cheese

1. Cook spaghetti according to package directions; drain. Return the spaghetti to saucepan. Stir in the chicken, spinach, soup, mayonnaise, sour cream, celery, onion, green pepper, pimientos and lemon pepper.
2. Transfer to a greased 13x9-in. baking dish (dish will be full). Top with Monterey Jack cheese, bread crumbs and Parmesan cheese. Bake, uncovered, at 350° for 25-30 minutes or until heated through.
NOTE: To make soft bread crumbs, tear the bread into pieces and place in a food processor or blender. Cover and pulse until crumbs form. One slice of bread yields ½ to ¾ cup crumbs.
1⅓ CUPS: 594 cal., 32g fat (10g sat. fat), 68mg chol., 815mg sod., 45g carb. (4g sugars, 5g fiber), 31g pro.

PRESSURE-COOKER SPANISH CHILI

I prepare this Spanish chili on the weekend so I have an instant weeknight dinner on hand. I love my pressure cooker because it makes mealtime a breeze!
—*Lynn Faria, Southington, CT*

PREP: 10 min. • **COOK:** 15 min. + releasing • **MAKES:** 8 servings

- 1 lb. ground beef
- 1 medium onion, chopped
- 1 medium sweet red pepper, chopped
- 1 medium green pepper, chopped
- 1 can (15 oz.) tomato sauce
- 1 can (14½ oz.) diced tomatoes, undrained
- 1 tsp. packed brown sugar
- 2 tsp. chili powder
- 1 envelope Goya Sazon with coriander and annatto (1 tsp.)
- 1 tsp. baking cocoa
- ½ tsp. pepper
- ¼ tsp. salt
- ¼ tsp. cayenne pepper
- 1 can (16 oz.) chili beans, undrained
- 2 tsp. red wine vinegar
  Optional toppings: Sour cream and green onions

1. Select saute or browning setting on a 6-qt. electric pressure cooker; adjust for medium heat. Cook the beef until no longer pink, 5-7 minutes, breaking it into crumbles; drain. Press cancel. Stir in the onion, sweet red pepper, green pepper, tomato sauce, diced tomatoes, brown sugar, chili powder, Sazon, cocoa, pepper, salt and cayenne. Lock the lid; close pressure-release valve. Adjust to pressure-cook on high for 8 minutes. Let the pressure release naturally.
2. Select saute setting and adjust for low heat. Stir in beans and vinegar. Simmer, stirring occasionally, until heated through and chili reaches desired consistency. If desired, serve chili with optional toppings.
1 CUP: 194 cal., 8g fat (3g sat. fat), 35mg chol., 699mg sod., 20g carb. (6g sugars, 6g fiber), 15g pro. **DIABETIC EXCHANGES:** 2 medium-fat meat, 1 starch.

- EASY SLOW-COOKER TAMALE DINNER -

Here's a quick and easy slow-cooker dinner inspired by Mexican tamales. No need to mess with corn husks here!

In a small skillet, cook 1 lb. **ground turkey** over medium heat until no longer pink, 6-8 minutes, breaking into crumbles; drain. Lightly beat 1 **large egg**. In a large bowl, combine **egg**, 1½ cups **2% milk** and ¾ cup **yellow cornmeal** until smooth. Add 1 can (14½ oz.) undrained **diced tomatoes**, 1 cup thawed **frozen corn**, 4 tsp. **chili powder**, 2 tsp. **ground cumin**, 1 tsp. **salt**, 1 tsp. **garlic powder**, 1 tsp. **onion powder** and **turkey**. Transfer to a greased 3-qt. slow cooker. Cook, covered, on low until edges are brown, 4-5 hours. Serve with shredded **cheddar cheese**, **sour cream** and **salsa**. If desired, sprinkle with chopped **green onions**.

- 11 -

DELECTABLE DESSERTS

Looking for something to satisfy your sweet tooth? For a dessert that goes together in jiffy and will disappear just as fast, try these easy recipes for cookies, pies, brownies, cakes, creamy confections, frosty treats and more.

COOL STRAWBERRY CREAM

This fruity luscious dessert makes a wonderful ending to a special dinner. When fresh strawberries are not available, I substitute two packages of the frozen unsweetened kind, thawed and drained.
—Joyce Cooper, Mount Forest, ON

PREP: 30 min. + freezing • **MAKES:** 12 servings

    2   pkg. (8 oz. each) cream cheese, softened
    ¾   cup sugar
    ½   cup sour cream
    3   cups fresh strawberries, mashed
    1   cup whipped topping
BLUEBERRY SAUCE
    1   pkg. (12 oz.) frozen unsweetened blueberries
    ⅓   cup sugar
    ¼   cup water

1. Line a 9x5-in. loaf pan with a double thickness of foil. In a large bowl, beat the cream cheese, sugar and sour cream until smooth. Fold in strawberries and whipped topping. Pour into prepared pan. Cover and freeze for several hours or overnight.
2. In a small saucepan, bring the blueberries, sugar and water to a boil; cook and stir for 3 minutes. Cool slightly. Transfer to a blender; cover and process until pureed. Refrigerate until chilled.
3. Remove dessert from the freezer 15-20 minutes before serving. Use foil to lift out of pan; remove foil. Cut dessert into slices with a serrated knife. Serve with blueberry sauce.
1 PIECE WITH ABOUT 2 TBSP. SAUCE: 198 cal., 10g fat (6g sat. fat), 27mg chol., 62mg sod., 26g carb. (23g sugars, 2g fiber), 2g pro.

AIR-FRYER APPLE PIE EGG ROLLS

These easy apple pie egg rolls can be prepared as needed, using egg roll wrappers as vessels for the fruit rather than traditional pie crust. The air-fryer method of cooking results in a crispy, crunchy crust with a tender, juicy filling. Flavored cream cheese spread may be used instead of plain, depending on availability.
—Sheila Joan Suhan, Scottdale, PA

PREP: 25 min. • **COOK:** 10 min./batch • **MAKES:** 8 servings

    3   cups chopped peeled tart apples
    ½   cup packed light brown sugar
    2½ tsp. ground cinnamon, divided
    1   tsp. cornstarch
    8   egg roll wrappers
    ½   cup spreadable cream cheese
        Butter-flavored cooking spray
    1   Tbsp. sugar
    ⅔   cup hot caramel ice cream topping

1. Preheat air fryer to 400°. In a small bowl, combine apples, brown sugar, 2 tsp. cinnamon and cornstarch. With a corner of an egg roll wrapper facing you, spread 1 scant Tbsp. cream cheese to within 1 in. of edges. Place ⅓ cup apple mixture just below the center of wrapper. (Cover remaining wrappers with a damp paper towel until ready to use.)
2. Fold bottom corner over filling; moisten remaining wrapper edges with water. Fold side corners toward center over filling. Roll egg roll up tightly, pressing at tip to seal. Repeat.
3. In batches, arrange egg rolls in a single layer on greased tray in air-fryer basket; spritz with cooking spray. Cook until golden brown, 5-6 minutes. Turn; spritz with cooking spray. Cook until golden brown and crisp, 5-6 minutes longer. Combine sugar and remaining ½ tsp. cinnamon; roll hot egg rolls in mixture. Serve with caramel sauce.
1 ROLL: 273 cal., 4g fat (2g sat. fat), 13mg chol., 343mg sod., 56g carb. (35g sugars, 2g fiber), 5g pro.

MOIST CREAM CHEESE POUND CAKE

Warm a slice of this cream cheese pound cake in the microwave for about 25 seconds. Then serve it with a scoop of butter pecan ice cream, fresh fruit or alone.
—*Betty Smith, Evans, GA*

- -

PREP: 15 min. • **BAKE:** 1½ hours + cooling • **MAKES:** 16 servings

- 1½ cups butter, softened
- 3 cups sugar
- 1 pkg. (8 oz.) cream cheese, softened
- 6 large eggs, room temperature
- 3 cups all-purpose flour
- ½ tsp. baking powder
  - Optional: whipped cream, confectioners' sugar and assorted fresh fruit

Preheat oven to 325°. Grease and flour a 10-in. tube pan. In a large bowl, cream butter, sugar and cream cheese until light and fluffy, 5-7 minutes. Add the eggs, 1 at a time, beating well after each addition. In a small bowl, whisk flour and baking powder. Gradually beat into creamed mixture. Transfer to prepare pan. Bake until a toothpick inserted in the center comes out clean, 80-90 minutes. Cool in the pan 10 minutes before removing to a wire rack to cool completely. Serve cake with desired toppings.
1 PIECE: 461 cal., 24g fat (14g sat. fat), 130mg chol., 224mg sod., 57g carb. (38g sugars, 1g fiber), 6g pro.

EASY PIE CRUST

Even novice bakers who shy away from homemade pastry can't go wrong with this easy pie crust recipe. It is simple to roll out and produces a tender, flaky crust every time.
—*Ruth Gritter, Grand Rapids, MI*

- -

PREP: 10 min. + chilling
MAKES: pastry for a single- or double-crust pie (9 or 10 in.)

INGREDIENTS FOR SINGLE-CRUST PIE
- 1 cup all-purpose flour
- ¼ tsp. salt
- ⅓ cup shortening
- 1½ tsp. white vinegar
- 2 to 3 Tbsp. 2% milk

INGREDIENTS FOR DOUBLE-CRUST PIE
- 2 cups all-purpose flour
- ½ tsp. salt
- ⅔ cup shortening
- 1 Tbsp. white vinegar
- 5 to 6 Tbsp. 2% milk

1. In a small bowl, combine the flour and salt; cut in shortening until the mixture is crumbly. Sprinkle with vinegar. Gradually add the milk, tossing with a fork until a ball is formed. Cover and refrigerate for 30 minutes or until easy to handle.
2. For a single crust, roll out pastry on a lightly floured surface to fit a 9-in. or 10-in. pie plate. Transfer pastry to pie plate. Trim pastry ½ in. beyond edge of plate; flute edges. Fill or bake shell according to recipe directions.
3. For a double crust, divide pastry in 2 portions so that 1 ball is slightly larger than the other. Roll out larger ball on a lightly floured surface to fit a 9-in. or 10-in. pie plate. Transfer pastry to pie plate. Trim pastry even with edge of plate. Add filling. Roll out remaining pastry to fit top of pie; place over filling. Trim, seal and flute edges. Cut slits in top. Bake according to recipe directions.
1 PIECE: 132 cal., 8g fat (2g sat. fat), 0 chol., 76mg sod., 12g carb. (0 sugars, 0 fiber), 2g pro.

CRANBERRY-APPLE NUT CRUNCH

My mother gave me the recipe for this dessert, which I think is especially pretty and appropriate for fall. I updated it to use instant oatmeal to make it even easier.
—*Joyce Sheets, Lafayette, IN*

- -

PREP: 15 min. • **BAKE:** 50 min.
MAKES: 8 servings

- 3 cups chopped peeled apples
- 2 cups fresh or frozen cranberries
- 3 Tbsp. all-purpose flour
- 1 cup sugar

TOPPING

- 3 packets (1.51 oz. each) instant oatmeal with cinnamon and spice
- ¾ cup chopped pecans
- ½ cup all-purpose flour
- ½ cup packed brown sugar
- ½ cup butter, melted
    Whole cranberries for garnish
    Vanilla ice cream, optional

In a large bowl, combine first 4 ingredients and mix well. Place in a 2-qt. baking dish. For the topping, combine the oatmeal, nuts, flour, sugar and butter in another bowl. Mix well; spoon evenly over the fruit mixture. Bake, uncovered, at 350° until the fruit is bubbly and tender, 50-60 minutes. Garnish with cranberries. Serve warm with ice cream if desired.

1 CUP: 422 cal., 20g fat (8g sat. fat), 31mg chol., 152mg sod., 62g carb. (47g sugars, 3g fiber), 3g pro.

SIMPLE LEMON MOUSSE

This classic mousse is a refreshing treat after a heavy meal. Garnish with lemon slices and a dollop of whipped cream. This recipe would also work with other citrus fruits such as a blood orange or grapefruit.
—*Taste of Home Test Kitchen*

- -

PREP: 20 min. • **COOK:** 10 min. + chilling
MAKES: 6 servings

- ⅔ cup sugar
- 2 Tbsp. cornstarch
    Dash salt
- 3 large egg yolks
- ⅔ cup whole milk
- ½ cup lemon juice
- 2 tsp. grated lemon zest
- 1 cup heavy whipping cream
    Lemon slices, optional

1. In a small saucepan, mix the sugar, cornstarch and salt; whisk in egg yolks and milk until smooth. Whisk in lemon juice until blended; bring to a boil over medium heat, stirring constantly. Cook and stir until thickened slightly, about 2 minutes longer. Stir in lemon zest.
2. Transfer mixture to a bowl. Cover and refrigerate until cold.
3. To serve, in a small bowl, beat cream on high speed until soft peaks form. Fold into lemon mixture. Spoon into serving dishes. If desired, top with additional whipped cream and lemon slices.

½ CUP: 282 cal., 18g fat (11g sat. fat), 140mg chol., 52mg sod., 29g carb. (25g sugars, 0 fiber), 3g pro.

TIP

CAN YOU MAKE LEMON MOUSSE WITHOUT EGGS?

Traditional lemon mousse needs eggs to achieve the light, creamy texture. Although they aren't mousse, lemon marmalade or lemon jam can be whisked until thinned out, then folded into whipped cream for a tasty lemon dessert if eggs aren't available.

CREAMY PINA COLADA PIES

This is a family favorite and super easy to make. Some like the consistency of this pie right out of the refrigerator and others prefer a softer pie—either way it's delicious!
—*Jenny Hales, Arcadia, OK*

PREP/COOK TIME: 15 min. + chilling
MAKES: 2 pies (8 servings each)

- 1 carton (8 oz.) frozen whipped topping, thawed
- 1 can (10 oz.) frozen nonalcoholic pina colada mix, thawed
- ¾ cup sweetened condensed milk
- ½ cup sweetened shredded coconut
- ½ cup macadamia nuts, chopped
- 1 can (8 oz.) crushed pineapple, well drained
- 2 graham cracker crusts (9 in.)
  Maraschino cherries, optional

In a large bowl, combine first 3 ingredients until smooth. Fold in coconut, nuts and pineapple. Divide and pour the mixture into prepared crusts. Refrigerate, covered, until firm, at least 4 hours. If desired, serve with additional whipped topping and cherries.
1 PIECE: 299 cal., 14g fat (7g sat. fat), 5mg chol., 168mg sod., 41g carb. (36g sugars, 1g fiber), 2g pro.

TIP

CAN PINA COLADA PIES BE MADE AHEAD OF TIME?
Yes! In fact, it's a necessary step in the recipe. Pina colada pie needs several hours to chill. Feel free to make it several hours, if not a whole day, in advance.

EASY PUMPKIN PIE

Pumpkin pie does not have to be difficult to make. This one has a wonderful flavor and will be a hit at your holiday meal.
—*Marty Rummel, Trout Lake, WA*

PREP: 10 min. • **BAKE:** 50 min. + cooling • **MAKES:** 8 servings

- 3 large eggs
- 1 cup canned pumpkin
- 1 cup evaporated milk
- ½ cup sugar
- ¼ cup maple syrup
- 1 tsp. ground cinnamon
- ½ tsp. salt
- ½ tsp. ground nutmeg
- ½ tsp. maple flavoring
- ½ tsp. vanilla extract
- 1 frozen deep-dish pie crust (9 in.)
- 1 sheet refrigerated pie crust, optional
  Whipped cream, optional

1. In a large bowl, beat the first 10 ingredients until smooth; pour into pie crust. Cover edge loosely with foil.
2. Bake at 400° for 10 minutes. Reduce the heat to 350°; bake for 40-45 minutes longer or until a knife inserted in the center comes out clean. Remove foil. Cool on a wire rack.
3. If decorative cutouts are desired, roll the pie crust to ⅛-in. thickness; cut out with 1-in. to 1½-in. leaf-shaped cookie cutters. With a sharp knife, score leaf veins on cutouts.
4. Place pie on an ungreased baking sheet. Bake at 400° for 6-8 minutes or until golden brown. Remove to a wire rack to cool. Arrange around edge of pie. Garnish with whipped cream if desired.
1 PIECE: 275 cal., 11g fat (5g sat. fat), 94mg chol., 306mg sod., 38g carb. (24g sugars, 1g fiber), 6g pro.

🕐🍎🌹 AIR-FRYER MOCHA PUDDING CAKES

These mouthwatering mini cakes make the perfect treat for two. My mom used to make these when I was a little girl. Now I whip them up and pop them in my air fryer for a speedy dessert.
—*Debora Simmons, Eglon, WV*

- -

TAKES: 30 min. • **MAKES:** 2 servings

¼ cup all-purpose flour
3 Tbsp. sugar
1½ tsp. baking cocoa
½ tsp. baking powder
⅛ tsp. salt
3 Tbsp. 2% milk
1½ tsp. butter, melted
¼ tsp. vanilla extract
TOPPING
2 Tbsp. brown sugar
1½ tsp. baking cocoa
3 Tbsp. hot brewed coffee
1 Tbsp. hot water
Whipped topping, optional

1. Preheat air fryer to 350°. In a small bowl, combine the flour, sugar, cocoa, baking powder and salt. Stir in the milk, butter and vanilla until smooth. Spoon into 2 lightly greased 4-oz. ramekins. Combine brown sugar and cocoa; sprinkle over batter. Combine coffee and water; pour over topping.
2. Place ramekins on tray in air-fryer basket. Cook until a knife inserted in the center comes out clean, 15-20 minutes. Serve warm or at room temperature, with whipped topping if desired.
1 PUDDING CAKE: 229 cal., 4g fat (2g sat. fat), 9mg chol., 306mg sod., 47g carb. (33g sugars, 1g fiber), 3g pro.

5️⃣ NO-BAKE COOKIE BUTTER BLOSSOMS

Chewy and sweet, these easy treats mix Rice Krispies, cookie spread and chocolate in an unforgettable spin on an old favorite.
—*Jessie Sarrazin, Livingston, MT*

- -

PREP: 25 min. + standing • **MAKES:** about 2½ dozen

1 cup Biscoff creamy cookie spread
½ cup corn syrup
3 cups Rice Krispies
32 milk chocolate kisses

In a large saucepan, combine cookie spread and corn syrup. Cook and stir over low heat until blended. Remove from heat; stir in Rice Krispies until coated. Shape level tablespoonfuls of mixture into balls; place on waxed paper. Immediately press a kiss into center of each cookie. Let stand until set.
1 COOKIE: 93 cal., 4g fat (1g sat. fat), 1mg chol., 22mg sod., 14g carb. (10g sugars, 0 fiber), 1g pro.

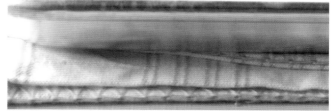

CRUNCHY APRICOT-COCONUT BALLS

My mom gave me this no-bake cookie recipe years ago when she had them on her Christmas buffet. I can't believe how simple they are to make.
—*Jane Whittaker, Pensacola, FL*

TAKES: 30 min. • **MAKES:** 2 dozen

- 1¼ cups sweetened shredded coconut
- 1 cup dried apricots, finely chopped
- ⅔ cup chopped pecans
- ½ cup fat-free sweetened condensed milk
- ½ cup confectioners' sugar

1. In a small bowl, combine coconut, apricots and pecans. Add condensed milk; mix well (mixture will be sticky).
2. Shape into 1¼-in. balls and roll in confectioners' sugar. Store in an airtight container in the refrigerator.
1 BALL: 87 cal., 4g fat (2g sat. fat), 1mg chol., 19mg sod., 12g carb. (10g sugars, 1g fiber), 1g pro.

EASY SLICE & BAKE COOKIES

These treats are larger than most slice-and-bake cookies, which I find to be ideal. The other great thing about these cookies is that you can slice however many you want to bake at a time and then enjoy them warm from the oven.
—*Heather Chambers, Largo, FL*

PREP: 30 min. + freezing • **BAKE:** 10 min./batch + cooling
MAKES: about 4 dozen

- 1 cup unsalted butter, softened
- ⅓ cup Nutella
- ¾ cup sugar
- ¾ cup packed brown sugar
- 2 large eggs, room temperature
- 1 Tbsp. vanilla extract
- 2¾ cups all-purpose flour
- 1 tsp. baking soda
- 1 tsp. salt
- 1¼ cups white baking chips

1. In a bowl, cream butter, Nutella and sugars until light and fluffy, 5-7 minutes. Beat in eggs and vanilla. In another bowl, whisk flour, baking soda and salt; gradually beat into the creamed mixture. Stir in chips.
2. Divide dough in half. Roughly shape each portion into a 12-in. roll along the edge of a 12x12-in. sheet of waxed paper. Tightly roll waxed paper over dough, using it to mold the dough into a smooth roll. Place wrapped rolls in airtight containers. Freeze until firm, about 1 hour.
3. Preheat oven to 375°. Unwrap and cut dough crosswise into ½-in. slices. Place 2 in. apart on ungreased baking sheets. Bake until lightly browned, 10-12 minutes. Remove from pans to wire racks to cool.
1 COOKIE: 123 cal., 6g fat (3g sat. fat), 19mg chol., 85mg sod., 16g carb. (10g sugars, 0 fiber), 1g pro.

PECAN BROWNIES

It's hard to eat just one of these nutty treats...good thing a batch can bake up in a matter of minutes.
—*Karen Batchelor, Bellevue, NE*

- -

TAKES: 30 min. • **MAKES:** 16 brownies

½ cup butter, cubed
2 oz. unsweetened chocolate
1 cup sugar
2 large eggs, room temperature, lightly beaten
1 tsp. vanilla extract
¾ cup all-purpose flour
½ to 1 cup chopped pecans

1. In a saucepan over low heat, melt butter and chocolate. Stir in sugar; cool slightly. Add eggs and vanilla; mix well. Stir in flour and pecans.
2. Spread into a greased 8-in. square baking pan. Bake at 350° for 15-20 minutes or until a toothpick inserted in the center comes out clean. Cool on a wire rack.
1 PIECE: 165 cal., 10g fat (5g sat. fat), 42mg chol., 66mg sod., 18g carb. (12g sugars, 1g fiber), 2g pro.

TIP

Store brownies in an airtight container for up to 2 days. In the refrigerator, they'll last up to 5 days, and in the freezer, up to 3 months.

QUICK & EASY TIRAMISU

No one can resist this classic cool and creamy dessert. It's quick to prepare but can be made ahead for added mealtime convenience.
—Taste of Home *Test Kitchen*

- -

PREP: 20 min. + chilling • **MAKES:** 6 servings

2 cups cold 2% milk
1 pkg. (3.4 oz.) instant vanilla pudding mix
1 cup heavy whipping cream
3 Tbsp. confectioners' sugar
28 soft ladyfingers, split
2½ tsp. instant coffee granules
½ cup boiling water
1 Tbsp. baking cocoa

1. In a large bowl, whisk milk and pudding mix for 2 minutes. Let stand until soft-set, about 2 minutes. In a small bowl, beat cream until it begins to thicken. Add confectioners' sugar; beat until soft peaks form. Fold into pudding; cover and refrigerate.
2. Arrange half the ladyfingers cut side up in an 11x7-in. dish. Dissolve coffee granules in the boiling water; drizzle half over the ladyfingers. Spread with half the pudding mixture. Repeat layers. Sprinkle with cocoa. Refrigerate until serving.
1 PIECE: 384 cal., 19g fat (11g sat. fat), 123mg chol., 379mg sod., 47g carb. (33g sugars, 1g fiber), 7g pro.

BANANA CREAM PIE WITH CAKE MIX CRUST

I added something special to the classic banana cream pie by topping it off with a crunchy, peanut-buttery streusel.
—*Matthew Hass, Ellison Bay, WI*

- -

PREP: 15 min. • **BAKE:** 30 min. + chilling
MAKES: 10 servings

- 1   pkg. yellow cake mix (regular size), divided
- 1   large egg, room temperature, lightly beaten
- 3   Tbsp. butter, softened and divided
- 1   cup cold 2% milk
- 1   pkg. (3.4 oz.) instant banana cream pudding mix
- 1   medium banana, sliced
- 1   carton (8 oz.) frozen whipped topping, thawed and divided
- ⅓   cup creamy peanut butter
     Additional sliced ripe banana

1. Preheat oven to 350°. Grease a 9-in. pie plate. Stir together 1¾ cups cake mix, egg and 1 Tbsp. butter until combined. Turn onto a floured surface; knead until a smooth dough forms. Roll dough to fit prepared pie plate. Flute edge. Prick bottom several times with a fork. Bake until golden brown, 12-15 minutes. Cool crust in pie plate on a wire rack.
2. Whisk milk and pudding mix 2 minutes. Fold in banana and 1 cup whipped topping. Transfer mixture to cooled crust. Top with remaining whipped topping. Refrigerate at least 3 hours.
3. Meanwhile, mix remaining cake mix, peanut butter and remaining 2 Tbsp. butter until crumbly. Transfer to a parchment-lined rimmed baking pan. Bake at 350° until golden brown, 14-18 minutes, stirring once.
4. Allow pie to cool completely. Top with additional sliced banana and some of the crumb topping (save additional crumb topping for another use).
1 PIECE: 394 cal., 16g fat (8g sat. fat), 30mg chol., 526mg sod., 55g carb. (35g sugars, 1g fiber), 6g pro.

TIP When you're rolling out and fluting crust, work quickly so the dough doesn't get too soft and sticky.

EASY APPLE CRISP

Here's an easy apple crisp. It's a delicious dessert perfect for young cooks to prepare. It's super simple to make, as there is no crust—just a crumbly topping. Plus, with apples and oats, it's a wholesome treat.
—*Sheri Hatten, Devil's Lake, ND*

- -

PREP: 20 min. • **BAKE:** 50 min.
MAKES: 16 servings

- 10   to 11 cups sliced peeled tart apples
- ½   cup sugar
- 1   tsp. ground cinnamon, divided
- 1   cup all-purpose flour
- 1   cup packed brown sugar
- ½   cup quick-cooking oats
- 1   tsp. baking powder
- ¼   tsp. ground nutmeg
- ½   cup cold butter, cubed
     Vanilla ice cream, optional

Preheat oven to 375°. Place apples in a large bowl. Combine sugar and ½ tsp. cinnamon; sprinkle over apples and toss to coat. Transfer to a greased 13x9-in. baking dish. Combine flour, brown sugar, oats, baking powder, nutmeg and the remaining ½ tsp. cinnamon; cut in butter until mixture resembles coarse crumbs. Sprinkle over apples. Bake until the apples are tender, 50-60 minutes. Serve warm with vanilla ice cream if desired.
1 SERVING: 199 cal., 6g fat (4g sat. fat), 15mg chol., 80mg sod., 36g carb. (27g sugars, 1g fiber), 1g pro.

FLORIDA ORANGE CAKE

With juice in the cake and marmalade in the frosting, this recipe is a perfect showcase for our Florida oranges. Everyone comments on how luscious the cake tastes.
—*Terry Bray, Auburndale, FL*

PREP: 10 min. • **BAKE:** 30 min. + cooling • **MAKES:** 16 servings

1 pkg. yellow cake mix (regular size)
1 cup orange juice
3 large eggs, room temperature
⅓ cup water
⅓ cup canola oil
FROSTING
1 pkg. (8 oz.) cream cheese, softened
¼ cup butter, softened
1 Tbsp. orange marmalade
3 cups confectioners' sugar

1. Preheat oven to 350°. In a large bowl, combine the cake mix, orange juice, eggs, water and oil; beat on low speed for 30 seconds. Beat on medium speed for 2 minutes.
2. Pour into a greased 9x9-in. baking pan. Bake until a toothpick inserted in the center comes out clean, 30-35 minutes. Cool on a wire rack.
3. For frosting, in a small bowl, beat cream cheese and butter until smooth. Beat in orange marmalade and confectioners' sugar. Spread over cake. If desired, swirl with additional orange marmalade. Store in the refrigerator.
1 PIECE: 347 cal., 14g fat (6g sat. fat), 57mg chol., 315mg sod., 53g carb. (39g sugars, 0 fiber), 3g pro.

PM 🍎

BLACKBERRY DAIQUIRI SHERBET

The summer I decided to make sherbet, which is one of my favorite desserts, blackberries were in season in my mom's garden. I love the flavor of daiquiris, and the two blend together beautifully!
—*Shelly Bevington, Hermiston, OR*

PREP: 15 min. • **PROCESS:** 30 min./batch + freezing
MAKES: 1¼ qt.

3 cups fresh or frozen blackberries, thawed
1 cup sugar
¼ tsp. salt
1 can (12 oz.) evaporated milk
2 Tbsp. lime juice
1 tsp. rum extract
½ tsp. citric acid

1. Place blackberries, sugar and salt in a food processor; puree until smooth. Press through a fine-mesh strainer into a bowl; discard seeds and pulp. Stir remaining ingredients into puree.
2. Fill cylinder of ice cream maker no more than two-thirds full; freeze according to the manufacturer's directions. Transfer the sherbet to freezer containers, allowing headspace for expansion. Freeze until firm, 8 hours or overnight.
½ CUP: 147 cal., 3g fat (2g sat. fat), 12mg chol., 96mg sod., 28g carb. (26g sugars, 2g fiber), 3g pro.

TIP
Don't use actual rum in place of the rum extract. The alcohol will keep the sherbet from freezing solid.

WATERMELON FRUIT PIZZA

Fruit pizza is an easy and refreshing way to end a summer meal. Top it with any fruit you may have on hand and add other toppings like fresh mint, toasted shredded coconut or chopped nuts.
—Taste of Home *Test Kitchen*

PREP/COOK TIME: 10 min. • **MAKES:** 8 servings

- 4 oz. cream cheese, softened
- 4 oz. frozen whipped topping, thawed
- ½ tsp. vanilla extract
- 3 Tbsp. confectioners' sugar
- 1 round slice of whole seedless watermelon, about 1 in. thick
  Assorted fresh fruit
  Fresh mint leaves, optional

1. In a small bowl, beat cream cheese until smooth. Gently fold in the whipped topping, then the vanilla and confectioners' sugar until combined.

2. To serve, spread watermelon slice with cream cheese mixture. Cut into 8 wedges and top with your fruit of choice. If desired, garnish with fresh mint.

1 PIECE: 140 cal., 7g fat (5g sat. fat), 14mg chol., 45mg sod., 17g carb. (16g sugars, 0 fiber), 1g pro. **DIABETIC EXCHANGES:** 1½ fat, 1 fruit.

PINA COLADA FLUFF

Here's a recipe from one of my grandma's vintage cookbooks. This light and refreshing island-inspired dessert will transport you to a tropical paradise with each bite.
—Crystal Jo Bruns, Iliff, CO

PREP/COOK TIME: 15 min. + chilling • **MAKES:** 7 servings

- 1 can (20 oz.) crushed pineapple, undrained
- 1 pkg. (3.4 oz.) instant vanilla pudding mix
- 1 tsp. coconut rum or rum extract
- 2 cups miniature marshmallows
- 1 cup sweetened shredded coconut, toasted
- ½ cup finely chopped pistachios, toasted
- 1 carton (8 oz.) frozen whipped topping, thawed

In a large bowl, combine pineapple, pudding mix and rum. Add marshmallows, coconut and pistachios. Fold in whipped topping. Chill until serving.

1 CUP: 369 cal., 14g fat (10g sat. fat), 0 chol., 172mg sod., 57g carb. (46g sugars, 2g fiber), 3g pro.

TIP

If you don't have rum extract on hand, try coconut, pineapple or citrus extract with equally good results. Find these extracts in the baking aisle of your local grocery or specialty food store.

TRIPLE FRUIT FREEZE

These pops won't turn your tongue blue or neon green like many store-bought pops because they're made with fresh fruit—grapes, blueberries and kiwifruit. What could be better?

—*Colleen Ludovice, Wauwatosa, WI*

PREP: 20 min. + freezing • **MAKES:** 10 pops

- 1   cup sliced peeled kiwifruit (about 3 medium)
- 1   cup water, divided
- 2   Tbsp. sugar, divided
- 10 wooden pop sticks and 10 freezer pop molds or 10 paper cups (3 oz. each)
- 1   cup fresh blueberries or frozen unsweetened blueberries
- ½   cup seedless red grapes
- ½   cup red grape juice

1. Place kiwi, ½ cup water and 1 Tbsp. sugar in a food processor; pulse until combined. Pour into molds or paper cups. Top the molds or paper cups with foil and insert sticks through foil. Freeze until firm, about 2 hours.

2. Place the blueberries and remaining ½ cup water and 1 Tbsp. sugar in food processor; pulse until combined. Spoon over the kiwi layer. Freeze, covered, until firm, about 2 hours.

3. Wipe food processor clean. Repeat with the grapes and grape juice. Spoon over the blueberry layer. Freeze the pops, covered, until firm.

1 POP: 50 cal., 0 fat (0 sat. fat), 0 chol., 3mg sod., 12g carb. (10g sugars, 1g fiber), 0 pro.
DIABETIC EXCHANGES: 1 starch.

EASY BOURBON PECAN PIE

This pie has a mellow bourbon flavor that's not too strong and not too sweet. And it is easy, crunchy and chewy—just what you want in a pecan pie.

—*Nick Iverson, Denver, CO*

PREP: 10 min. + freezing • **BAKE:** 1¼ hours
MAKES: 10 servings

- 12 oz. toasted pecan halves, divided
- 4   large eggs, room temperature
- ½   cup packed dark brown sugar
- ¼   cup sugar
- 1   cup dark corn syrup
- 8   Tbsp. unsalted butter, melted
- ¼   cup bourbon
- 2   tsp. vanilla extract
- ¼   tsp. salt
- 1   sheet refrigerated pie crust
     Vanilla ice cream, optional

1. In a food processor, pulse half the pecans until coarsely chopped; reserve remaining pecans. Combine eggs and sugars until well mixed. Add the next 5 ingredients and chopped pecans.

2. Unroll crust into a 9-in. metal pie plate; flute edge. Pour filling into crust. Arrange reserved pecan halves over filling. Place filled pie in freezer for 30 minutes.

3. Preheat oven to 425°. Bake until crust is set, about 15 minutes. Reduce the oven setting to 350°; continue baking until pie is puffed and set in the middle, about 1 hour (tent loosely with foil if needed to prevent overbrowning). Cool. If desired, serve with vanilla ice cream.

NOTE: To toast nuts, bake in a shallow pan in a 350° oven for 5-10 minutes or cook in a skillet over low heat until lightly browned, stirring occasionally.

1 PIECE: 600 cal., 41g fat (11g sat. fat), 103mg chol., 221mg sod., 56g carb. (43g sugars, 3g fiber), 7g pro.

TIP
Dark brown sugar adds a nice caramel flavor to this pecan pie. Don't worry if you only have light brown sugar; you'll get less caramel flavor but more intense bourbon flavor.

FROZEN CHOCOLATE MONKEY TREATS

Everyone needs a fun, friendly way for kids to play with food. These rich bites are nutty and yummy. Just coat bananas in chocolate and dip them into peanuts, sprinkles or coconut.
—*Susan Hein, Burlington, WI*

- -

PREP: 20 min. + freezing • **MAKES:** 1½ dozen

- 3 **medium bananas**
- 1 **cup dark chocolate chips**
- 2 **tsp. shortening**
   Optional toppings: Chopped peanuts, toasted sweetened shredded coconut and colored jimmies

1. Cut each banana crosswise into 6 pieces (about 1 in. thick). Insert a toothpick into each piece; transfer to a waxed paper-lined baking sheet. Freeze until completely firm, about 1 hour.
2. In a microwave, melt chocolate and shortening; stir until smooth. Dip banana pieces in chocolate mixture; allow excess to drip off. Dip pieces in toppings as desired; return to baking sheet. Freeze at least 30 minutes before serving.
NOTE: To toast coconut, bake in a shallow pan in a 350° oven for 5-10 minutes or cook in a skillet over low heat until golden brown, stirring occasionally.
1 TREAT: 72 cal., 4g fat (2g sat. fat), 0 chol., 0 sod., 10g carb. (7g sugars, 1g fiber), 1g pro. **DIABETIC EXCHANGES:** 1 fat, ½ starch.

BLUEBERRY DUMP CAKE

When I need a quick dessert, this is the recipe I reach for most of the time. I usually have the ingredients on hand so I can whip it together in just a few minutes.
—*Rashanda Cobbins, Milwaukee, WI*

- -

PREP TIME: 10 min. **Cook TIME:** 35 min. • **MAKES:** 12 servings

- 1 **can (21 oz.) blueberry pie filling**
- ½ **tsp. almond extract**
- 2 **cups fresh or frozen blueberries**
- ⅓ **cup packed brown sugar**
- 1 **pkg. (16½ oz.) yellow cake mix**
- ¾ **cup butter, melted**
   Whipped cream, optional

1. Preheat oven to 350°. Mix pie filling and almond extract; spread into a greased 11x7-in. baking dish. Stir together blueberries and brown sugar; place over pie filling. Sprinkle with cake mix; drizzle with butter.
2. Bake until golden brown, 30-35 minutes. Cool on a wire rack. If desired, serve with whipped cream and additional blueberries.
½ CUP: 374 cal., 13g fat (8g sat. fat), 31mg chol., 380mg sod., 64g carb. (44g sugars, 2g fiber), 1g pro.

RHUBARB CRISP

I found this recipe on a box of Quaker Oats about 20 years ago. It's quicker and easier to make than pie. It's versatile, too, because you can add strawberries in spring or apples in fall. I usually pop it into the oven shortly before we sit down to eat so we can enjoy it warm for dessert.

—C.E. Adams, Charlestown, NH

- -

PREP: 15 min. • **BAKE:** 45 min. • **MAKES:** 8 servings

- ¾ **cup sugar**
- 3 **Tbsp. cornstarch**
- 3 **cups sliced fresh rhubarb or frozen rhubarb, thawed**
- 2 **cups sliced peeled apples or sliced strawberries**
- 1 **cup quick-cooking or old-fashioned oats**
- ½ **cup packed brown sugar**
- ½ **cup butter, melted**
- ⅓ **cup all-purpose flour**
- 1 **tsp. ground cinnamon**
  Vanilla ice cream, optional

1. In a large bowl, combine sugar and cornstarch. Add rhubarb and apples or strawberries; toss to coat. Spoon into an 8-in. cast-iron skillet or other ovenproof skillet.

2. In a small bowl, combine the oats, brown sugar, butter, flour and cinnamon until the mixture resembles coarse crumbs. Sprinkle over fruit. Bake at 350° until crisp is bubbly and fruit is tender, about 45 minutes. If desired, serve warm with ice cream.

1 CUP: 320 cal., 12g fat (7g sat. fat), 31mg chol., 124mg sod., 52g carb. (36g sugars, 3g fiber), 3g pro.

5i
EASY CHOCOLATE ICE CREAM

This super simple chocolate ice cream is the perfect treat at a moment's notice. It's also a bonus in that most of the ingredients are kitchen staples.

—Taste of Home *Test Kitchen*

- -

PREP: 10 min. • **PROCESS:** 20 min. + freezing • **MAKES:** 1½ qt.

- 2 **cups half-and-half cream**
- 1½ **cups sugar**
- ½ **cup baking cocoa**
- 1 **tsp. vanilla extract**
- 2 **cups heavy whipping cream**

Combine half-and-half, sugar, cocoa and vanilla in a blender; process on low until smooth. Stir in heavy cream. Freeze in an ice cream freezer according to manufacturer's directions.

½ CUP: 288 cal., 18g fat (12g sat. fat), 65mg chol., 31mg sod., 28g carb. (28g sugars, 0 fiber), 2g pro.

TIP

WHAT TYPE OF COCOA POWDER IS BEST FOR HOMEMADE CHOCOLATE ICE CREAM?

This recipe is all about the indulgent chocolate flavor, so don't be afraid to splurge on a high-quality cocoa. Choose the powder you like, whether it's regular cocoa or Dutch-processed.

QUICK MANGO SORBET

QUICK MANGO SORBET

Last summer, I decided to try my hand at making a passion fruit and mango sorbet. But fresh fruits require more prep and are difficult to find ripened at the same time. So I experimented using frozen fruit and juice, and voila! Both are readily available and inexpensive, too.
—Carol Klein, Franklin Square, NY

- -

TAKES: 5 min. • **MAKES:** 2½ cups

- 1 pkg. (16 oz.) frozen mango chunks, slightly thawed
- ½ cup passion fruit juice
- 2 Tbsp. sugar

Place all ingredients in a blender; cover and process until smooth. Serve the sorbet immediately. If a firmer texture is desired, cover and freeze at least 3 hours.
½ CUP: 91 cal., 0 fat (0 sat. fat), 0 chol., 2mg sod., 24g carb. (21g sugars, 2g fiber), 1g pro.

EASY RHUBARB SAUCE

Celebrate spring with the sweet-tart taste of rhubarb in this simple sauce. I enjoy it on toast, English muffins and pancakes, but it's equally decadent drizzled on pound cake or ice cream.
—Jackie Hutshing, Sonoma, CA

- -

TAKES: 20 min. • **MAKES:** 1¼ cups

- ⅓ cup sugar
- ¼ cup water
- 2¼ cups sliced fresh or frozen rhubarb
- 1 tsp. grated lemon zest
- ⅛ tsp. ground nutmeg
- Pound cake or vanilla ice cream

1. In a small saucepan, bring sugar and water to a boil. Add rhubarb; cook and stir until rhubarb is tender and mixture is slightly thickened, 5-10 minutes. Remove from heat; stir in lemon zest and nutmeg.
2. Serve warm or chilled over pound cake or ice cream. Refrigerate leftovers.
NOTE: If using frozen rhubarb, measure rhubarb while still frozen, then thaw completely. Drain in a colander, but do not press liquid out.
¼ CUP: 64 cal., 0 fat (0 sat. fat), 0 chol., 2mg sod., 16g carb. (14g sugars, 1g fiber), 1g pro.

CANTALOUPE A LA MODE

This special dessert is a refreshing finale to a warm-weather meal. Garnish with fresh mint or basil for an extra burst of flavor.
—*Nancy Walker, Granite City, IL*

TAKES: 15 min. • **MAKES:** 4 servings (1 cup sauce)

- ½ cup water
- ½ cup sugar
- 2 Tbsp. lemon juice
- 1 Tbsp. cornstarch
- 1 tsp. grated lemon zest
- 1 cup fresh or frozen blueberries
- 2 small cantaloupes, halved and seeded
- 2 cups vanilla ice cream
  Fresh mint, optional

In a small saucepan, combine the first 5 ingredients; bring to a boil over medium heat. Boil and stir until thickened, about 2 minutes. Add blueberries; cook until heated through. Fill cantaloupe with ice cream; top with sauce. Garnish with mint if desired.

1 SERVING: 337 cal., 8g fat (5g sat. fat), 29mg chol., 74mg sod., 67g carb. (56g sugars, 3g fiber), 5g pro.

STRAWBERRY CRUNCH ICE CREAM CAKE

Growing up, I loved treats from the ice cream truck that rolled through my neighborhood. This ice cream cake is inspired by one of those crunchy strawberry novelties.
—*Lisa Kaminski, Wauwatosa, WI*

PREP: 20 min. + freezing • **BAKE:** 25 min. + cooling
MAKES: 9 servings

- 36 Golden Oreo cookies, divided
- 4 Tbsp. butter, melted
- 3 cups vanilla ice cream, softened
- 5 cups strawberry ice cream, softened
- 1 carton (8 oz.) frozen whipped topping, thawed
- 1 pkg. (1 oz.) freeze-dried strawberries, coarsely crushed
  Fresh strawberries, optional

1. Line a 9x9-in. baking pan with parchment. Preheat oven to 350°. Finely crush 24 cookies. In a small bowl, mix the cookie crumbs and butter. Press onto the bottom of prepared pan. Bake for 25-30 minutes or until firm. Cool on a wire rack.
2. Spread vanilla ice cream onto crust; freeze, covered, until firm. Spread with strawberry ice cream and then whipped topping; freeze, covered, until firm.
3. Coarsely crush remaining cookies. Combine cookie crumbs and freeze-dried strawberries; sprinkle over whipped topping. Freeze, covered, until firm, 8 hours or overnight. Remove cake from freezer. Lifting with parchment, remove from pan. Gently peel off parchment. Let stand 10 minutes before cutting. If desired, garnish with fresh strawberries.

1 PIECE: 584 cal., 30g fat (16g sat. fat), 54mg chol., 280mg sod., 72g carb. (33g sugars, 2g fiber), 6g pro.

CARAMEL FLUFF & TOFFEE TRIFLE

The best part of this stunning dessert is you need only five ingredients to put it together.
—*Daniel Anderson, Kenosha, WI*

PREP: 15 min. + chilling • MAKES: 12 servings

- 2 cups heavy whipping cream
- ¾ cup packed brown sugar
- 1 tsp. vanilla extract
- 1 prepared angel food cake (8 to 10 oz.), cut into 1-in. cubes
- 1 cup milk chocolate English toffee bits

1. In a large bowl, beat the cream, brown sugar and vanilla just until blended. Refrigerate, covered, 20 minutes. Beat until stiff peaks form.
2. In a 4-qt. glass bowl, layer one-third of each of the following: cake cubes, whipped cream and toffee bits. Repeat layers twice. Refrigerate until serving.
1 SERVING: 347 cal., 22g fat (13g sat. fat), 61mg chol., 227mg sod., 38g carb. (27g sugars, 0 fiber), 2g pro.

POTS DE CREME

Looking for an easy dessert recipe that's still guaranteed to impress? Served in pretty stemmed glasses, this classic chocolate custard really sets the tone.
—*Connie Dreyfoos, Cincinnati, OH*

PREP: 15 min. + chilling • MAKES: 5 servings

- 1 large egg
- 2 Tbsp. sugar
  Dash salt
- ¾ cup half-and-half cream
- 1 cup semisweet chocolate chips
- 1 tsp. vanilla extract
  Optional: Whipped cream and assorted fresh fruit

1. In a small saucepan, combine the egg, sugar and salt. Whisk in cream. Cook and stir over medium heat until mixture reaches 160° and coats the back of a metal spoon.
2. Remove from the heat; whisk in chocolate chips and vanilla until smooth. Pour mixture into small dessert dishes. Cover and refrigerate, 8 hours or overnight. If desired, garnish with whipped cream and fruit.
⅓ CUP: 246 cal., 15g fat (9g sat. fat), 55mg chol., 66mg sod., 28g carb. (25g sugars, 2g fiber), 4g pro.

5i
EASY KEY LIME PIE

You need only five ingredients to create this refreshing pie. It's easy enough to make for a weeknight dessert, but special enough for weekend gatherings.
—Taste of Home *Test Kitchen*

PREP: 20 min. + chilling • **MAKES:** 8 servings

- 1   pkg. (8 oz.) cream cheese, softened
- 1   can (14 oz.) sweetened condensed milk
- ½   cup Key lime juice or lime juice
- 1   graham cracker crust (9 in.)
- 2   cups whipped topping
     Lime slices, optional

In a large bowl, beat cream cheese until smooth. Beat in milk and lime juice until blended. Transfer to crust. Refrigerate, covered, at least 4 hours. Just before serving, garnish with whipped topping and, if desired, lime slices.

1 PIECE: 417 cal., 22g fat (13g sat. fat), 46mg chol., 274mg sod., 48g carb. (42g sugars, 0 fiber), 7g pro.

TIP

If you don't have Key lime juice, regular lime juice will work with equally good results. Key limes are a bit more tart than their traditional counterparts, but a pie made with this substitution will still have plenty of zing.

5i 🍎
SONORAN SUNSET WATERMELON ICE

If you didn't think watermelon and cilantro could go together in a dessert, this recipe will give you a pleasant surprise! Sprinkle pomegranate seeds and a sprig of cilantro on top for extra flair.
—Jeanne Holt, St. Paul, MN

PREP: 15 min. + cooling • **PROCESS:** 10 min. + freezing
MAKES: 6 servings

- ½   cup sugar
- ¼   cup water
- 4   cups cubed seedless watermelon
- 3   Tbsp. lime juice
- 2   Tbsp. pomegranate juice
- 1   Tbsp. minced fresh cilantro
     Dash salt

1. In a small saucepan, bring sugar and water to a boil; cook and stir until sugar is dissolved. Cool completely.
2. Puree watermelon in a blender. Transfer to a large bowl; stir in sugar syrup and remaining ingredients. Refrigerate until cold.
3. Pour watermelon mixture into cylinder of ice cream maker; freeze according to manufacturer's directions. Transfer to freezer containers, allowing headspace for expansion. Freeze 4 hours or until firm.
½ CUP: 100 cal., 0 fat (0 sat. fat), 0 chol., 246mg sod., 26g carb. (24g sugars, 0 fiber), 1g pro. **DIABETIC EXCHANGES:** 1½ starch, ½ fruit.

CHERRY GRUNT

Back when I was cooking the hot lunch main dish for about 1,300 students a day, I needed simple recipes to make at home. This easy old-fashioned dessert was always a favorite in our house.
—Judy Meikle, Cherokee, IA

PREP: 15 min. • **COOK:** 25 min. • **MAKES:** 10 servings

- 1 can (16 oz.) pitted tart red cherries, undrained
- 1½ cups water
- ¾ cup sugar, divided
- ¼ cup butter, divided
- 1 cup all-purpose flour
- 1½ tsp. baking powder
  Pinch salt
- ⅓ cup 2% milk
- ½ tsp. vanilla extract

1. Place cherries and juice in a straight-sided skillet or Dutch oven along with water, ½ cup sugar and 2 Tbsp. butter. Simmer for 5 minutes.
2. Meanwhile, sift together the flour, baking powder, salt and remaining ¼ cup sugar; place in a bowl. Cut in remaining butter with a pastry blender. Add milk and vanilla; stir to combine.
3. Drop by tablespoonfuls over cherry mixture; cover and simmer until dumplings are cooked through, about 20 minutes.
½ CUP: 183 cal., 5g fat (3g sat. fat), 13mg chol., 128mg sod., 34g carb. (24g sugars, 1g fiber), 2g pro.

PUMPKIN CRUNCH PARFAITS

Have your little ones lend a hand with this dessert! It's a great treat for Thanksgiving or Halloween.
—Lorraine Darocha, Berkshire, MA

TAKES: 20 min. • **MAKES:** 6 servings

- ¾ cup 2% milk
- 1 pkg. (3.4 oz.) instant vanilla pudding mix
- 2 cups whipped topping
- 1 cup canned pumpkin
- ½ tsp. pumpkin pie spice
- 1 cup chopped pecans
- 32 gingersnap cookies, crushed (about 1½ cups)
  Optional: Additional whipped topping and chopped pecans

1. In a large bowl, beat milk and pudding mix on low speed 2 minutes. Stir in whipped topping, pumpkin and pie spice. Fold in pecans.
2. Spoon half of the mixture into 6 parfait glasses; top with half of the gingersnap crumbs. Repeat layers. If desired, top with additional whipped topping and chopped pecans. Refrigerate any leftovers.
1 PARFAIT: 447 cal., 23g fat (7g sat. fat), 4mg chol., 486mg sod., 55g carb. (31g sugars, 3g fiber), 5g pro.

REVIEW

"Everyone really loved this. Will make again for sure!"
—QUEENPENGUIN, TASTEOFHOME.COM

- FROZEN FRUIT WHIP -

A fast finale to any meal is as close as the freezer. Everyone has room for some of this light, refreshing dessert.

In a large bowl, combine 1 carton (8 oz.) thawed **frozen whipped topping** and 1 can (14 oz.) **sweetened condensed milk**; fold in 4 cups **frozen unsweetened blackberries** and 1 pkg. (12 oz.) **frozen unsweetened raspberries**. Serve immediately or refrigerate until serving. Freeze leftovers; remove from the freezer 30 minutes before serving.

FEEDING A CROWD

Grab a plate and get ready to dig into these tasty feed-a-crowd favorites. These recipes for big-batch mains, sides, desserts and more are sure to be a hit at your next party or potluck.

ARTICHOKE SPINACH CASSEROLE

Although he isn't a fan of spinach, my husband loves this dish. The combination of ingredients may sound unusual, but the flavors meld well. It's an excellent side vegetable dish for a formal dinner.
—Judy Johnson, Missoula, MT

PREP: 25 min. • **BAKE:** 25 min.
MAKES: 14 servings

- 1 lb. fresh mushrooms, sliced
- ⅓ cup chicken broth
- 1 Tbsp. all-purpose flour
- ½ cup evaporated milk
- 4 pkg. (10 oz. each) frozen chopped spinach, thawed and squeezed dry
- 2 cans (14½ oz. each) diced tomatoes, drained
- 2 cans (14 oz. each) water-packed artichoke hearts, rinsed, drained and thinly sliced
- 1 cup sour cream
- ½ cup mayonnaise
- 3 Tbsp. lemon juice
- ½ tsp. garlic powder
- ¼ tsp. salt
- ¼ tsp. pepper
  Paprika, optional

1. In a large skillet, cook mushrooms and broth over medium heat until tender, about 3 minutes. Remove mushrooms with a slotted spoon and set aside.
2. Whisk flour and milk until smooth; add to skillet. Bring to a boil; cook and stir for 2 minutes. Remove from the heat; stir in spinach, tomatoes and mushrooms.
3. Place half of the sliced artichoke hearts in an ungreased 13x9-in. baking dish. Top with half of the spinach mixture. Repeat layers. Combine sour cream, mayonnaise, lemon juice, garlic powder, salt and pepper; dollop over casserole. Sprinkle with paprika if desired.
4. Bake, uncovered, at 350° until bubbly, 25-30 minutes.
¾ CUP: 136 cal., 10g fat (3g sat. fat), 17mg chol., 249mg sod., 8g carb. (3g sugars, 2g fiber), 4g pro.

LEMON CHIFFON BLUEBERRY DESSERT

This cool and creamy no-bake dessert is perfect for hot summer days. I sometimes use raspberries for half of the blueberries to add a patriotic flair.
—Jodie Cederquist, Muskegon, MI

PREP: 25 min. + chilling
MAKES: 15 servings

- 1½ cups graham cracker crumbs (about 24 squares)
- 1⅓ cups sugar, divided
- ½ cup butter, melted
- 1½ cups fresh blueberries, divided
- 1 pkg. (3 oz.) lemon gelatin
- 1 cup boiling water
- 11 oz. cream cheese, softened
- 1 tsp. vanilla extract
- 1 carton (16 oz.) frozen whipped topping, thawed

1. Combine cracker crumbs, ⅓ cup sugar and butter, reserving 2 Tbsp. for topping. Press the remaining crumb mixture into a 13x9-in. dish. Sprinkle the crust with 1 cup blueberries.
2. In a small bowl, dissolve gelatin in boiling water; cool. In a large bowl, beat cream cheese and remaining 1 cup sugar. Add vanilla; mix well. Slowly add dissolved gelatin. Fold in whipped topping. Spread over blueberries. Refrigerate, covered, until set, about 3 hours. Top with reserved crumb mixture and remaining blueberries. Refrigerate leftovers.
1 PIECE: 344 cal., 19g fat (14g sat. fat), 39mg chol., 187mg sod., 39g carb. (29g sugars, 1g fiber), 3g pro.

BEEF & BLUE CHEESE CROSTINI

These little gems are ridiculously easy, impressive and delicious. They are also inexpensive to make. Seriously, you will look like a rock star when you serve these!
—*Mandy Rivers, Lexington, SC*

TAKES: 30 min. • **MAKES:** 3 dozen

1	French bread baguette (10½ oz.)
	Cooking spray
½	tsp. coarsely ground pepper
½	cup reduced-fat sour cream
2	Tbsp. minced chives
1	Tbsp. horseradish
¼	tsp. salt
1¼	lbs. shaved deli roast beef
⅓	cup crumbled blue cheese
	Additional minced chives

1. Preheat oven to 400°. Cut the baguette into 36 slices. Place on ungreased baking sheets. Spritz with cooking spray. Sprinkle with pepper. Bake until lightly browned, 4-6 minutes.

2. Meanwhile, in a small bowl, combine sour cream, chives, horseradish and salt. Top toasts with beef; dollop with sour cream mixture. Sprinkle with cheese and additional chives.

1 APPETIZER: 48 cal., 1g fat (1g sat. fat), 11mg chol., 176mg sod., 5g carb. (0 sugars, 0 fiber), 4g pro.

BUTTERSCOTCH DELIGHT

This creamy layered dessert is popular whenever I serve it.
—*Barbara Edgemon, Belleview, FL*

PREP: 15 min. + chilling • **BAKE:** 20 min. • **MAKES:** 20 servings

- ½ cup cold butter
- 1 cup all-purpose flour
- 1 cup finely chopped walnuts
- 1 pkg. (8 oz.) cream cheese, softened
- 1 cup confectioners' sugar
- 1 carton (8 oz.) frozen whipped topping, thawed, divided
- 3½ cups cold 2% milk
- 2 pkg. (3.5 oz. each) instant butterscotch pudding mix
- ½ cup coarsely chopped walnuts

1. Preheat oven to 350°. In a large bowl, cut butter into flour until mixture resembles coarse crumbs; stir in finely chopped walnuts. Press into a greased 13x9-in. baking dish. Bake until golden brown, 17-20 minutes. Cool on a wire rack.
2. In a large bowl, beat cream cheese and sugar until smooth. Fold in 1 cup whipped topping; spread over crust.
3. In another bowl, beat milk and pudding mix for 2 minutes or until thickened. Spread over cream cheese layer. Spread with the remaining whipped topping; sprinkle with coarsely chopped walnuts. Cover and refrigerate until set, about 1 hour.
1 PIECE: 272 cal., 17g fat (8g sat. fat), 27mg chol., 251mg sod., 24g carb. (18g sugars, 1g fiber), 4g pro.

SPICY CHUCK WAGON BEANS

Baked beans don't get any easier! All you have to do is open some cans, chop an onion, and add a dash (or two) of hot sauce. They'll simmer to perfection in minutes.
—*James Schend, Pleasant Prairie, WI*

TAKES: 30 min. • **MAKES:** 24 servings

- 1 Tbsp. canola oil
- 1 medium onion, chopped
- 2 cans (28 oz. each) baked beans
- 3 cans (15 oz. each) chili beans, undrained
- 2 cans (15 oz. each) black beans, rinsed and drained
- 2 pkg. (7 oz. each) frozen fully cooked breakfast sausage links, thawed and cut into ½-in. pieces
- 1 cup beer or reduced-sodium chicken broth
- 2 chipotle peppers in adobo sauce, minced
- 1 to 2 Tbsp. hot pepper sauce

In a Dutch oven, heat oil over medium-high heat; saute onion until tender, 3-5 minutes. Stir in remaining ingredients; bring to a boil. Reduce heat; simmer, uncovered, until beans are thickened and flavors are blended, about 15 minutes, stirring occasionally.
⅔ CUP: 221 cal., 8g fat (3g sat. fat), 15mg chol., 663mg sod., 30g carb. (2g sugars, 8g fiber), 10g pro.
SLOW COOKER OPTION: In a greased 6-qt. slow cooker, combine all ingredients, omitting oil. Cook, covered, on low 6-8 hours, until heated through.

POTLUCK CHICKEN VEGETABLE SOUP

I experimented with various combinations of ingredients, and this is the chicken soup I love best. It's especially good for potlucks or to share with friends..
—*Bertha Vogt, Tribune, KS*

- -

PREP: 30 min. + cooling
COOK: 2 hours 5 min.
MAKES: 16 servings (about 4 qt.)

- 1 roasting chicken (about 5 lbs.), cut up and skin removed
- 2 celery ribs, sliced
- 1 large onion, chopped
- 2½ qt. water
- 1 can (14½ oz.) stewed tomatoes
- 4 medium carrots, sliced
- 2 medium potatoes, peeled and cubed
- 1 medium turnip, peeled and cubed
- 2 Tbsp. chicken bouillon granules
- ½ tsp. minced fresh parsley
- ¾ tsp. each dried basil, oregano and tarragon
- ¾ tsp. salt
- ¾ tsp. pepper
- ½ tsp. garlic powder
- 2 cups fresh broccoli florets
- 2 cups frozen peas, optional

1. Place the chicken, celery, onion and water in a Dutch oven; bring to a boil. Skim off fat. Reduce heat; cover and simmer until chicken is tender, 1½ to 2 hours. Remove chicken; cool.
2. Remove meat from bones and cut into bite-size pieces; return to pan. Add the tomatoes, carrots, potatoes, turnip, bouillon and seasonings; bring to a boil. Reduce the heat; cover and simmer for 20 minutes. Add the broccoli and peas if desired; simmer until the vegetables are tender, 15-20 minutes longer.
1 CUP: 195 cal., 9g fat (2g sat. fat), 55mg chol., 537mg sod., 10g carb. (4g sugars, 2g fiber), 19g pro.

TIP
Try switching up the veggies and seasonings in this chicken soup to make it your own. Experiment with sauteed mushrooms, canned corn or green beans. Or add a dash of Italian seasoning and red pepper flakes for a new taste.

CAULIFLOWER PARMESAN CASSEROLE

A lighter version of a classic white sauce coats the cauliflower in this perfect potluck buffet dish. Thick and creamy with a golden brown top layer, it's a super side dish that tastes as comforting as it looks.
—*Taste of Home Test Kitchen*

- -

PREP: 30 min. • **BAKE:** 30 min.
MAKES: 12 servings

- 3 pkg. (16 oz. each) frozen cauliflower, thawed
- 1 large onion, chopped
- ⅓ cup butter, cubed
- ⅓ cup all-purpose flour
- ½ tsp. salt
- ¼ tsp. ground mustard
- ¼ tsp. pepper
- 2 cups fat-free milk
- ½ cup grated Parmesan cheese

TOPPING
- ½ cup soft whole wheat bread crumbs
- 2 Tbsp. butter, melted
- ¼ tsp. paprika

1. Preheat oven to 350°. Place 1 in. of water in a Dutch oven; add cauliflower. Bring to a boil. Reduce heat; cover and cook until crisp-tender, 4-6 minutes. Drain and pat dry.
2. Meanwhile, in a large saucepan, saute onion in butter until tender. Stir in the flour, salt, mustard and pepper until blended; gradually add milk. Bring to a boil; cook and stir until thickened, 1-2 minutes. Remove from the heat. Add cheese; stir until melted.
3. Place cauliflower in a greased 13x9-in. baking dish. Pour the sauce over the top.
4. For topping, combine the bread crumbs, butter and paprika. Sprinkle over sauce. Bake, uncovered, until casserole is bubbly, 30-35 minutes.
¾ CUP: 142 cal., 8g fat (5g sat. fat), 22mg chol., 257mg sod., 13g carb. (5g sugars, 3g fiber), 6g pro. **DIABETIC EXCHANGES:** 1½ fat, 1 vegetable, ½ starch.

POTLUCK SPARERIBS

When I want to bring home an empty pan from a potluck, I turn to this recipe. The ribs always disappear in minutes!
—*Sheri Kirkman, Lancaster, NY*

PREP: 10 min. • **BAKE:** 1¾ hours • **MAKES:** 12 servings

- 6 lbs. pork spareribs
- 1½ cups ketchup
- ¾ cup packed brown sugar
- ½ cup white vinegar
- ½ cup honey
- ⅓ cup soy sauce
- 1½ tsp. ground ginger
- 1 tsp. salt
- ¾ tsp. ground mustard
- ½ tsp. garlic powder
- ¼ tsp. pepper

1. Cut ribs into serving-sized pieces; place with the meaty side up on racks in 2 greased 13x9-in. baking pans. Cover tightly with foil. Bake at 350° for 1¼ hours or until meat is tender.
2. Remove racks; drain and return ribs to pans. Combine the remaining ingredients; pour over ribs. Bake, uncovered, for 30-40 minutes or until sauce coats ribs, basting occasionally.
NOTE: Ribs also can be grilled over medium-hot heat in place of the last 30-40 minutes of baking.
4 OZ. COOKED PORK: 551 cal., 32g fat (12g sat. fat), 128mg chol., 1065mg sod., 34g carb. (28g sugars, 0 fiber), 32g pro.

SPRING ONION PIMIENTO CHEESE GRITS

Grits were a breakfast staple when I was growing up. Even today, we still have them about three times a week. The trick with grits is the more you whisk, the creamier they'll be.
—*Melissa Pelkey Hass, Waleska, GA*

PREP: 15 min. • **COOK:** 20 min. • **MAKES:** 16 servings

- 2 cups uncooked stone-ground yellow grits
- 1 pkg. (8 oz.) cream cheese, softened
- ½ cup mayonnaise
- 3 cups shredded Monterey Jack cheese
- 1 jar (4 oz.) diced pimientos, drained
- 3 green onions, diced
- 1 tsp. sugar
  Dash cayenne pepper
- ¼ cup butter, softened
  Salt and pepper to taste

1. Prepare grits according to package directions. Keep warm.
2. Meanwhile, using a mixer, beat the cream cheese. Add mayonnaise; continue beating until creamy. Add the next 5 ingredients, mixing until well blended.
3. Stir butter and pimiento cheese mixture into the warm grits; season to taste. Mix well.
¾ CUP: 281 cal., 20g fat (10g sat. fat), 41mg chol., 231mg sod., 19g carb. (1g sugars, 1g fiber), 8g pro.

CHUNKY DROP COOKIES

I love these sweet and salty gems. The night before, I measure out the pretzels, peanuts, raisins and chocolate. Assembly goes quickly the next day.
—Kelly Ward-Hartman, Cape Coral, FL

PREP: 15 min. • **BAKE:** 10 min./batch
MAKES: 6½ dozen

- 1 cup butter, softened
- 1 cup packed brown sugar
- ½ cup sugar
- 2 large eggs, room temperature
- 3 tsp. vanilla extract
- 2½ cups all-purpose flour
- ¾ tsp. baking powder
- 2 cups halved pretzel sticks
- 1 cup coarsely chopped dry roasted peanuts
- 1 cup semisweet chocolate chunks
- 1 cup raisins

1. Preheat oven to 350°. In a large bowl, cream butter and sugars until light and fluffy, 5-7 minutes. Add eggs, 1 at a time, beating well after each addition. Beat in vanilla. Combine flour and baking powder; gradually add to creamed mixture and mix well. Stir in pretzels, peanuts, chocolate chunks and raisins.

2. Drop by tablespoonfuls 2 in. apart onto ungreased baking sheets. Bake until edges are golden brown, 10-14 minutes. Cool for 2 minutes before removing to wire racks.

1 COOKIE: 86 cal., 4g fat (2g sat. fat), 11mg chol., 44mg sod., 11g carb. (7g sugars, 1g fiber), 1g pro.

VEGETABLE BEEF SOUP

When we come in from playing in the snow, I serve this hearty vegetable beef soup.
—Nancy Soderstrom, Roseville, MN

PREP: 25 min. + cooling • **COOK:** 2¼ hours
MAKES: 20 servings (6 qt.)

- 1   boneless beef chuck roast (2½ to 3 lbs.)
- 4   qt. water
- 1   cup medium pearl barley
- 1½ cups chopped onion
- 1½ cups chopped celery
- 1   tsp. salt
- 1   tsp. pepper
- 1   can (28 oz.) diced tomatoes, undrained
- 1½ cups chopped carrots
- 1   pkg. (16 oz.) frozen mixed vegetables
- ¼   cup minced fresh parsley
- ½   tsp. dried basil
- ¼   tsp. dried thyme
- ¼   tsp. garlic salt

1. Place roast in a large Dutch oven. Add the water, barley, onion, celery, salt and pepper; bring to a boil. Reduce heat; cover and simmer for 1¼ hours or until the meat is tender.

2. Remove meat; cool. Cut into bite-sized pieces. Skim fat from broth. Add beef and remaining ingredients; bring to a boil. Reduce the heat; cover and simmer for 45 minutes or until vegetables are tender.

1¼ CUPS: 163 cal., 6g fat (2g sat. fat), 37mg chol., 235mg sod., 15g carb. (4g sugars, 4g fiber), 13g pro.

CRANBERRY-STUFFED BEEF TENDERLOIN

Fresh cranberries and cranberry juice lend a satisfying sweet-tart taste to beef tenderloin. Serving plated dishes to guests makes for a pretty presentation.
—Carolyn Cope, Allston, MD

PREP: 25 min. • **BAKE:** 50 min.
MAKES: 12 servings (1 cup sauce)

- 1   cup fresh or frozen cranberries, thawed
- ¼   cup dry red wine or beef broth
- 2   shallots, chopped
- 1   Tbsp. butter
- 1   beef tenderloin roast (4 lbs.)
- ¼   tsp. salt
- ¼   tsp. pepper

CRANBERRY WINE SAUCE

- 2   shallots, chopped
- 2   Tbsp. butter, divided
- ¾   cup cranberry juice
- ¾   cup dry red wine or beef broth
- ½   cup beef broth
- ½   tsp. minced fresh thyme

1. Preheat the oven to 425°. In a large saucepan, combine the cranberries, wine, shallots and butter. Cook over medium heat until berries pop, about 15 minutes.

2. Cut a lengthwise slit down the center of the tenderloin to within ½ in. of bottom. Open tenderloin so it lies flat. On each half, make another lengthwise slit down the center to within ½ in. of bottom; open the roast. Flatten with a meat mallet to ½-in. thickness.

3. Sprinkle beef with salt and pepper; spread cranberry mixture over meat.

Roll up jelly-roll style, starting with a long side. Tie tenderloin at 2-in. intervals with kitchen string. Place on a rack in a shallow roasting pan.

4. Bake beef tenderloin until meat reaches desired doneness (for medium-rare, a thermometer should read 135°; medium, 140°; medium-well, 145°), 40-50 minutes. Let stand for 10 minutes before slicing.

5. Meanwhile, saute shallots in 1 Tbsp. butter until tender. Add the juice, wine, broth and thyme. Bring to a boil; cook until liquid is reduced by half, about 20 minutes. Remove from the heat; stir in remaining butter. Serve the sauce with beef and, if desired, garnish beef with additional fresh thyme sprigs.

4 OZ. COOKED BEEF WITH ABOUT 1 TBSP. SAUCE: 271 cal., 12g fat (5g sat. fat), 74mg chol., 109mg sod., 5g carb. (3g sugars, 1g fiber), 33g pro.

NO-BAKE PEANUT BROWNIES

Enlist the little ones to help make these chocolaty peanut butter brownies. I like that I can whip up a fun treat while keeping my kitchen cool, especially in summer.
—Connie Ward, Mt. Pleasant, IA

PREP: 25 min. + chilling
MAKES: 16 servings

- 4 cups graham cracker crumbs
- 1 cup chopped peanuts
- ½ cup confectioners' sugar
- ¼ cup peanut butter
- 2 cups semisweet chocolate chips
- ¾ cup evaporated milk
- 1 tsp. vanilla extract

1. In a large bowl, combine the crumbs, peanuts, sugar and peanut butter until crumbly. In a small saucepan, melt the chocolate chips and milk over low heat, stirring constantly until smooth. Remove from the heat; add vanilla.

2. Pour the chocolate mixture over crumb mixture and stir until well blended. Spread evenly in a greased 9-in. square dish. Cover and refrigerate for 1 hour.

1 BROWNIE: 169 cal., 9g fat (3g sat. fat), 2mg chol., 78mg sod., 22g carb. (12g sugars, 2g fiber), 3g pro.

MAMA'S CARNITAS

My husband loves to cook Mexican dishes, while I'm more of an Italian-style cook. The joke in our house is that I should leave all the Mexican cooking to him. However, this dish of mine turned out so amazing that my husband fell in love! It's all in the meat. If you can get an all-natural pork shoulder, it makes all the difference.
—Chelsea Wickman, Painesville, OH

PREP: 25 min. • **COOK:** 9 hours
MAKES: 16 servings

- 3 garlic cloves, minced
- 1 Tbsp. minced fresh cilantro
- ½ tsp. salt
- ½ tsp. dried oregano
- ½ tsp. chili powder
- ½ tsp. ground cumin
- ½ tsp. paprika
- ½ tsp. pepper
- ¼ tsp. cayenne pepper
- 1 bone-in pork shoulder roast (5 to 7 lbs.)
- ½ cup unsweetened pineapple juice
- ½ cup reduced-sodium soy sauce
- ½ cup beef stock
- ¼ cup lime juice
- 2 Anaheim peppers, seeded and diced
- 16 flour tortillas (8 in.)
- 1 cup creme fraiche or sour cream
- 2 cups shredded Monterey Jack cheese

1. In a small bowl, combine the first 9 ingredients. Cut roast in half; rub all sides with spice mixture. Place in a 5-qt. slow cooker coated with cooking spray. Combine the pineapple juice, soy sauce, stock, lime juice and peppers; pour the mixture around meat.

2. Cover and cook on low for 9-11 hours or until the meat is tender.

3. Remove meat from slow cooker; skim fat from cooking juices. When cool enough to handle, remove the meat from the bones; discard bones. Shred meat and return to slow cooker; heat through.

4. With a slotted spoon, spoon ½ cup filling off center on each tortilla. Top each with 1 Tbsp. creme fraiche and 2 Tbsp. cheese. Fold sides and ends over filling and roll up.

FREEZE OPTION: Place shredded pork in freezer containers; top with juices. Cool and freeze. To use, partially thaw in the refrigerator overnight. Heat through in a covered saucepan, stirring occasionally; add a little broth if necessary.

NOTE: Wear disposable gloves when cutting hot peppers; the oils can burn skin. Avoid touching your face.

1 FILLED TORTILLA: 494 cal., 26g fat (12g sat. fat), 97mg chol., 758mg sod., 31g carb. (1g sugars, 2g fiber), 32g pro.

NO-BAKE CHOCOLATE HAZELNUT THUMBPRINTS

Years ago, a friend gave me a recipe for chocolate peanut treats that didn't require baking. I thought it was a quick and clever way to whip up a batch of sweet snacks without heating up the kitchen, and I started making different variations. This one includes luscious chocolate-hazelnut spread and crunchy hazelnuts. Yum!
—Lisa Speer, Palm Beach, FL

- -

PREP: 30 min. + chilling
MAKES: about 3½ dozen

1 carton (8 oz.) spreadable cream cheese
1 cup semisweet chocolate chips, melted
½ cup Nutella
2¼ cups graham cracker crumbs
1 cup finely chopped hazelnuts, toasted
1 cup whole hazelnuts, toasted

1. Beat cream cheese, melted chocolate chips and Nutella until blended. Stir in graham cracker crumbs. Refrigerate until firm enough to roll, about 30 minutes.
2. Shape mixture into 1-in. balls; roll in chopped hazelnuts. Make an indentation in the center of each with the end of a wooden spoon handle. Fill with a hazelnut. Store between layers of waxed paper in an airtight container in the refrigerator.
NOTE: To toast nuts, bake in a shallow pan in a 350° oven for 5-10 minutes or cook in a skillet over low heat until lightly browned, stirring occasionally.
1 COOKIE: 111 cal., 8g fat (2g sat. fat), 3mg chol., 46mg sod., 10g carb. (6g sugars, 1g fiber), 2g pro.

TIP
The easiest way to melt chocolate chips is in the microwave. Place in a microwave-wave safe bowl and cook at 50% power for 1 minute. Remove chips from microwave and give them a stir. Continue to microwave in 30-second increments, stirring frequently, until the chocolate has fully melted. Because each microwave behaves differently, keep a careful eye on your chocolate.

CREAMY BUFFALO CHICKEN DIP

This slightly spicy dip cleverly captures the flavor of buffalo chicken wings. Using canned chicken eases preparation.
—Allyson DiLascio, Saltsburg, PA

TAKES: 30 min. • **MAKES:** 5 cups

- 1 pkg. (8 oz.) cream cheese, softened
- 1 cup Louisiana-style hot sauce
- 1 cup ranch salad dressing
- 3 cans (4½ oz. each) chunk white chicken, drained and shredded
- 1 cup shredded cheddar cheese
   Thinly sliced green onions, optional
   Corn or tortilla chips
   Celery sticks

1. In a small bowl, combine the cream cheese, hot sauce and salad dressing. Stir in chicken.
2. Spread into an ungreased 11x7-in. baking dish. Sprinkle with cheddar cheese. Bake, uncovered, at 350° for 20-22 minutes or until heated through. If desired, sprinkle with green onions. Serve with chips and celery sticks.
2 TBSP.: 69 cal., 6g fat (2g sat. fat), 15mg chol., 156mg sod., 1g carb. (0 sugars, 0 fiber), 3g pro.

MAPLE-GINGER GLAZED CARROTS

I first made this dish for my family and friends one Thanksgiving. Not only are the seasoned carrots lovely on any table, but they taste terrific, too.
—Jeannette Sabo, Lexington Park, MD

PREP: 15 min. • **COOK:** 25 min. • **MAKES:** 16 servings

- 4 lbs. medium carrots, cut into ¼-in. slices
- ¼ cup water
- 3 Tbsp. butter, divided
- 1 Tbsp. minced fresh gingerroot
- ⅓ cup maple syrup
- 1 Tbsp. cider vinegar
- ½ tsp. salt
- ¼ tsp. pepper
   Minced fresh parsley, optional

1. In a Dutch oven, combine the carrots, water, 2 Tbsp. butter and ginger. Cover and cook for 10 minutes. Uncover and cook until carrots are crisp-tender, 6-8 minutes longer.
2. Stir in the syrup, vinegar, salt and pepper. Cook, stirring frequently, until sauce is thickened, 5-6 minutes. Stir in remaining butter. If desired, garnish with parsley.
¾ CUP: 83 cal., 2g fat (1g sat. fat), 6mg chol., 168mg sod., 15g carb. (9g sugars, 3g fiber), 1g pro. **DIABETIC EXCHANGES:** 2 vegetable, ½ fat.

BIG-BATCH JAMBALAYA

I make this dish for a big annual party because it feeds so many people. I end up craving it the rest of the year!
—Kecia McCaffrey, South Dennis, MA

PREP: 25 min. • **COOK:** 55 min.
MAKES: 13 servings (2½ qt.)

- 1 boneless skinless chicken breast, cubed
- 3 Tbsp. olive oil, divided
- ½ lb. cubed fully cooked ham
- ½ lb. smoked kielbasa or Polish sausage, cubed
- 2 medium green peppers, coarsely chopped
- 2 medium onions, coarsely chopped
- 6 garlic cloves, minced
- 2 cans (14½ oz. each) beef broth
- 1 can (28 oz.) crushed tomatoes
- 1½ cups water
- ¾ cup Dijon mustard
- ¼ cup minced fresh parsley
- 2 Tbsp. Worcestershire sauce
- 1½ to 2 tsp. cayenne pepper
- ½ tsp. dried thyme
- 1½ cups uncooked long grain rice
- 1 lb. uncooked medium shrimp, peeled and deveined

1. In a Dutch oven, cook chicken in 1 Tbsp. oil until no longer pink; remove and set aside. In the same pan, cook and stir the ham, kielbasa, peppers and onions in remaining 2 Tbsp. oil until onions are tender. Add garlic; cook 1 minute longer.
2. Stir in the broth, tomatoes, water, mustard, parsley, Worcestershire, cayenne and thyme. Bring to a boil. Reduce the heat; cover and simmer for 10 minutes.
3. Add rice and return to a boil. Reduce heat; cover and simmer for 25-30 minutes or until rice is tender. Stir in shrimp and chicken; cook 2-4 minutes longer or until shrimp turn pink.
1 CUP: 288 cal., 11g fat (3g sat. fat), 71mg chol., 1185mg sod., 30g carb. (2g sugars, 2g fiber), 18g pro.

EASY VEGETABLE LASAGNA

Bursting with fresh garden favorites, this lasagna is a vegetable lover's dream. The pasta layers are generously stuffed with roasted zucchini, mushrooms, peppers and onion in homemade tomato sauce.
—Susanne Ebersol, Bird-in-Hand, PA

PREP: 45 min. • **BAKE:** 20 min. + standing
MAKES: 12 servings

- 1 large onion, chopped
- 1 Tbsp. olive oil
- 6 garlic cloves, minced
- 1 can (28 oz.) tomato puree
- 1 can (8 oz.) tomato sauce
- 3 Tbsp. minced fresh basil
- 3 Tbsp. minced fresh oregano
- 1 tsp. sugar
- ½ tsp. crushed red pepper flakes

ROASTED VEGETABLES
- 4 cups sliced zucchini
- 3 cups sliced fresh mushrooms
- 2 medium green peppers, cut into 1-in. pieces
- 1 medium onion, cut into 1-in. pieces
- ½ tsp. salt
- ¼ tsp. pepper
- 6 lasagna noodles, cooked, rinsed and drained
- 4 cups shredded part-skim mozzarella cheese
- 1 cup shredded Parmesan cheese

1. Preheat the oven to 450°. In a large saucepan, saute onion in oil until tender over medium heat; add garlic and cook 1 minute longer. Stir in the tomato puree, sauce and seasonings. Bring to a boil. Reduce heat; simmer, uncovered, until slightly thickened, 20-25 minutes.
2. Meanwhile, in a large bowl, combine the vegetables, salt and pepper. Transfer to two 15x10x1-in. baking pans coated with cooking spray. Bake until golden brown, 15-18 minutes. Reduce oven temperature to 400°.
3. Spread ½ cup sauce into a 13x9-in. baking dish coated with cooking spray. Layer with 3 noodles, 1¾ cups sauce, and half of the roasted vegetables and cheeses. Repeat layers.
4. Cover and bake for 10 minutes. Uncover and bake until bubbly and golden brown, 10-15 minutes longer. Let stand for 10 minutes before serving. If desired, garnish with additional fresh oregano.
1 PIECE: 258 cal., 11g fat (6g sat. fat), 29mg chol., 571mg sod., 23g carb. (6g sugars, 3g fiber), 16g pro. **DIABETIC EXCHANGES:** 2 medium-fat meat, 2 vegetable, ½ starch.

GINGER-CREAM BARS

I rediscovered this old-fashioned recipe recently and now it's everyone's new favorite. Even little ones have asked for these frosted bars as treats.
—Carol Nagelkirk, Holland, MI

PREP: 20 min. • **BAKE:** 20 min. • **MAKES:** 5 dozen

- 1 cup butter, softened
- 1 cup sugar
- 2 cups all-purpose flour
- 1 tsp. salt
- 2 tsp. baking soda
- 1 Tbsp. ground cinnamon
- 1 Tbsp. ground cloves
- 1 Tbsp. ground ginger
- 2 large eggs, room temperature
- ½ cup molasses
- 1 cup hot brewed coffee

FROSTING
- ½ cup butter, softened
- 3 oz. cream cheese, softened
- 2 cups confectioners' sugar
- 2 tsp. vanilla extract
   Chopped nuts, optional

1. Preheat oven to 350°. Cream butter and sugar. Sift together flour, salt, baking soda and spices; add to creamed mixture. Add eggs, 1 at a time, beating well after each addition, and molasses. Blend in coffee. Spread in a 15x10x1-in. baking pan.
2. Bake 20-25 minutes. Cool. For frosting, cream the butter and cream cheese; add confectioners' sugar and vanilla. Spread over bars. If desired, top with nuts.
1 BAR: 101 cal., 5g fat (3g sat. fat), 20mg chol., 126mg sod., 13g carb. (9g sugars, 0 fiber), 1g pro.

PIEROGI CASSEROLE

Mashed potatoes and shredded cheddar cheese take center stage in this delicious take on lasagna. The layered entree comes together without much fuss, and people line up for seconds.
—Margaret Popou, Kaslo, BC

PREP: 20 min. • **BAKE:** 25 min. + standing • **MAKES:** 12 servings

- 1 cup finely chopped onion
- ¼ cup butter, cubed
- 2 cups 4% cottage cheese, drained
- 1 large egg
- ¼ tsp. onion salt
- 2 cups mashed potatoes (with added milk and butter)
- 1 cup shredded cheddar cheese, divided
- ¼ tsp. salt
- ⅛ tsp. pepper
- 9 lasagna noodles, cooked and drained
   Optional: sour cream and chopped chives

In a skillet, saute onion in butter until tender. In a bowl, combine the cottage cheese, egg and onion salt. In another bowl, combine the potatoes, ⅔ cup cheddar cheese, salt and pepper. Place 3 noodles in a greased 13x9-in. baking dish. Top with the cottage cheese mixture and 3 more noodles. Top with potato mixture, remaining noodles and sauteed onion. Top with the remaining ⅓ cup cheese. Cover and bake at 350° until heated through, 25-30 minutes. Let stand 10 minutes before serving. If desired, top with chopped chives and serve with sour cream.
1 PIECE: 223 cal., 10g fat (7g sat. fat), 50mg chol., 425mg sod., 23g carb. (3g sugars, 2g fiber), 10g pro.

SAVORY ZUCCHINI BREAD PUDDING

I've been serving this dish for years and always receive compliments on it. If you don't have day-old bread in your pantry, simply slice fresh bread and bake it at 300° for 10 minutes before cubing it.
—*Mary Ann Dell, Phoenixville, PA*

PREP: 25 min. • **BAKE:** 40 min.
MAKES: 12 servings

1	small onion, chopped
1	celery rib, chopped
3	Tbsp. butter
1	cup all-purpose flour
2	Tbsp. sugar
1	tsp. baking powder
1	tsp. salt
1	tsp. ground cinnamon
1	tsp. poultry seasoning
½	cup canned pumpkin
2	large eggs
⅓	cup 2% milk
¼	cup butter, melted
4	cups cubed day-old bread
3	medium zucchini, chopped
½	cup shredded cheddar cheese

1. In a small skillet, saute onion and celery in butter until tender.

2. In a large bowl, combine the flour, sugar, baking powder, salt, cinnamon and poultry seasoning. In a bowl, whisk pumpkin, eggs, milk and butter; stir into the dry ingredients just until moistened. Fold in the bread cubes, zucchini, cheese and onion mixture.

3. Transfer mixture to a greased 13x9-in. baking dish. Cover and bake at 325° for 30 minutes. Uncover; bake 10-15 minutes longer or until lightly browned.

¾ CUP: 182 cal., 10g fat (6g sat. fat), 58mg chol., 408mg sod., 20g carb. (5g sugars, 2g fiber), 5g pro.

REVIEW

"This dish was delicious! Sort of like a stuffed zucchini boat, except all mixed together in a convenient casserole. I was skeptical about the pumpkin but really liked the flavor combination in the end."

—MARGARETJOY, TASTEOFHOME.COM

SAUSAGE BACON BITES

These tasty morsels are perfect with almost any egg dish or as finger foods that party guests can just pop into their mouths.
—*Pat Waymire, Yellow Springs, OH*

PREP: 20 min. + chilling • **BAKE:** 35 min.
MAKES: about 3½ dozen

- ¾ lb. sliced bacon
- 2 pkg. (8 oz. each) frozen fully cooked breakfast sausage links, thawed
- ½ cup plus 2 Tbsp. packed brown sugar, divided

1. Cut bacon strips widthwise in half; cut sausage links in half. Wrap a piece of bacon around each piece of sausage. Place ½ cup brown sugar in a shallow bowl; roll sausages in sugar. Secure each with a toothpick. Place in a foil-lined 15x10x1-in. baking pan. Cover and refrigerate 4 hours or overnight.
2. Preheat oven to 350°. Sprinkle wrapped sausages with 1 Tbsp. brown sugar. Bake until the bacon is crisp, 35-40 minutes, turning once. Sprinkle with remaining brown sugar.
1 PIECE: 51 cal., 4g fat (1g sat. fat), 6mg chol., 100mg sod., 4g carb. (4g sugars, 0 fiber), 2g pro.

> **REVIEW**
>
> *"This made a great last-minute after-school snack for a house unexpectedly filled with tween boys! Obviously I didn't wait 4 hours. But I was voted best mom that afternoon!"*
> —MAMAKNOWSBEST, TASTEOFHOME.COM

PINA COLADA LUSH

This is such a fantastic warm-weather dessert—it's so light and refreshing, and a breeze to make! I love how the tart pineapple pairs with the sweet coconut.
—*Jennifer Stowell, Deep River, IA*

PREP/• BAKE: 20 min. + chilling
MAKES: 15 servings

- 2 cups graham cracker crumbs
- ½ cup butter, melted
- ½ cup packed brown sugar
- 1 pkg. (8 oz.) cream cheese, softened
- 1 can (8 oz.) crushed pineapple, drained
- ½ cup confectioners' sugar
- 1 tsp. vanilla extract
- 2 cups whole milk
- 1 pkg. (3.4 oz.) instant coconut cream pudding mix
- 1 carton (8 oz.) frozen whipped topping, thawed, divided
- ½ cup sweetened shredded coconut, toasted
  Maraschino cherries, optional

1. Combine the graham cracker crumbs, butter and brown sugar in a large bowl. Press onto the bottom and up sides of a greased 13x9-in. baking dish.
2. In a second bowl, beat together cream cheese, pineapple and confectioners' sugar. Stir in the vanilla extract; spread into crust.
3. In same bowl, whisk together milk and pudding mix until thickened, about 2 minutes. Fold in 1 cup whipped topping; spread pudding mixture over the cream cheese mixture. Top with the remaining whipped topping.
4. Sprinkle with the toasted coconut. Refrigerate, covered, until set, about 3 hours. If desired, garnish with cherries.
1 PIECE: 324 cal., 18g fat (12g sat. fat), 35mg chol., 251mg sod., 37g carb. (28g sugars, 1g fiber), 3g pro.

LAYERED STRAWBERRY POUND CAKE DESSERT

My mother's cousin shared this recipe more than 50 years ago. Our family has enjoyed it ever since, especially on hot days.
—*Vickie Britton, Hobbs, NM*

PREP: 20 min. + chilling • **MAKES:** 24 servings

- 1   loaf (10¾ oz.) frozen lb. cake, thawed
- 1   pkg. (8 oz.) cream cheese, softened
- 1   can (14 oz.) sweetened condensed milk
- ⅓ cup lemon juice
- 1   carton (12 oz.) frozen whipped topping, thawed
- 1   container (16 oz.) frozen sweetened sliced strawberries, thawed

1. Cut pound cake into ½-in. slices; place in bottom of a 13x9-in. baking dish. In a large bowl, beat cream cheese until smooth. Beat in milk and lemon juice until blended. Fold in 2⅔ cups whipped topping and 1½ cups strawberries with juice.
2. Spread mixture over pound cake. Top with remaining whipped topping. Refrigerate, covered, at least 4 hours or overnight. Top with the remaining ½ cup strawberries in juice before serving.
1 PIECE: 195 cal., 10g fat (7g sat. fat), 34mg chol., 88mg sod., 24g carb. (20g sugars, 0 fiber), 3g pro.

SESAME OMELET SPINACH SPIRALS

These pretty spirals would be perfect for a buffet of international hors d'oeuvres. They remind me of sushi. The dipping sauce is an exotic accompaniment to this fun finger food.
—*Roxanne Chan, Albany, CA*

PREP: 25 min. • **COOK:** 10 min.
MAKES: about 2½ dozen (⅓ cup sauce)

- 4   Tbsp. tahini
- 4   spinach tortillas (8 in.), warmed
- 6   large eggs
- 2   Tbsp. each finely chopped green onion, sweet red pepper and canned water chestnuts
- 2   Tbsp. shredded carrot
- 1   tsp. minced fresh gingerroot
- ¼ tsp. crushed red pepper flakes
- 2   tsp. sesame oil, divided

DIPPING SAUCE
- ¼ cup reduced-sodium soy sauce
- 1   Tbsp. minced fresh cilantro
- 1   garlic clove, minced
- 1   tsp. sesame seeds, toasted
- 1   tsp. rice vinegar
- 1   tsp. sesame oil
- ¼ tsp. grated orange zest

1. Spread tahini over tortillas. In a small bowl, whisk eggs, onion, red pepper, water chestnuts, carrot, ginger and pepper flakes.
2. Heat a large nonstick skillet over medium heat; lightly brush with some of the oil. Pour ⅓ cup egg mixture into the pan; cook for 1 minute or until set. Flip egg mixture and cook 30 seconds to 1 minute longer or until lightly browned. Place omelet on a tortilla; roll up. Repeat 3 times, brushing skillet as needed with remaining oil. Cut wraps into 1-in. slices.
3. Combine the sauce ingredients; serve with spirals.
1 SPIRAL: 51 cal., 3g fat (1g sat. fat), 40mg chol., 121mg sod., 4g carb. (0 sugars, 0 fiber), 2g pro.

- BLT TURKEY SALAD -

This salad variation of the classic BLT sandwich is great with garlic bread or garlic toast. It will satisfy even the heartiest of appetites.

In a large salad bowl, whisk ½ cup **plain yogurt**, ½ cup **mayonnaise**, 2 Tbsp. **sugar**, 2 Tbsp. **red wine vinegar** and ½ tsp. **garlic powder**. Add 6 cups torn **romaine lettuce**, 4 cups **cubed cooked turkey**, 1½ cups **chopped tomatoes**, 1½ cups shredded **part-skim mozzarella cheese**, 1½ cups shredded **cheddar cheese**, 10 **cooked and crumbled bacon strips**, ½ cup **chopped green pepper**, ½ cup **chopped red onion** and ½ cup **chopped cucumber**. Toss to coat.

RECIPE INDEX

ICON INDEX

🍽 5 INGREDIENT

🍎 EAT SMART

ⓟ OVERNIGHT